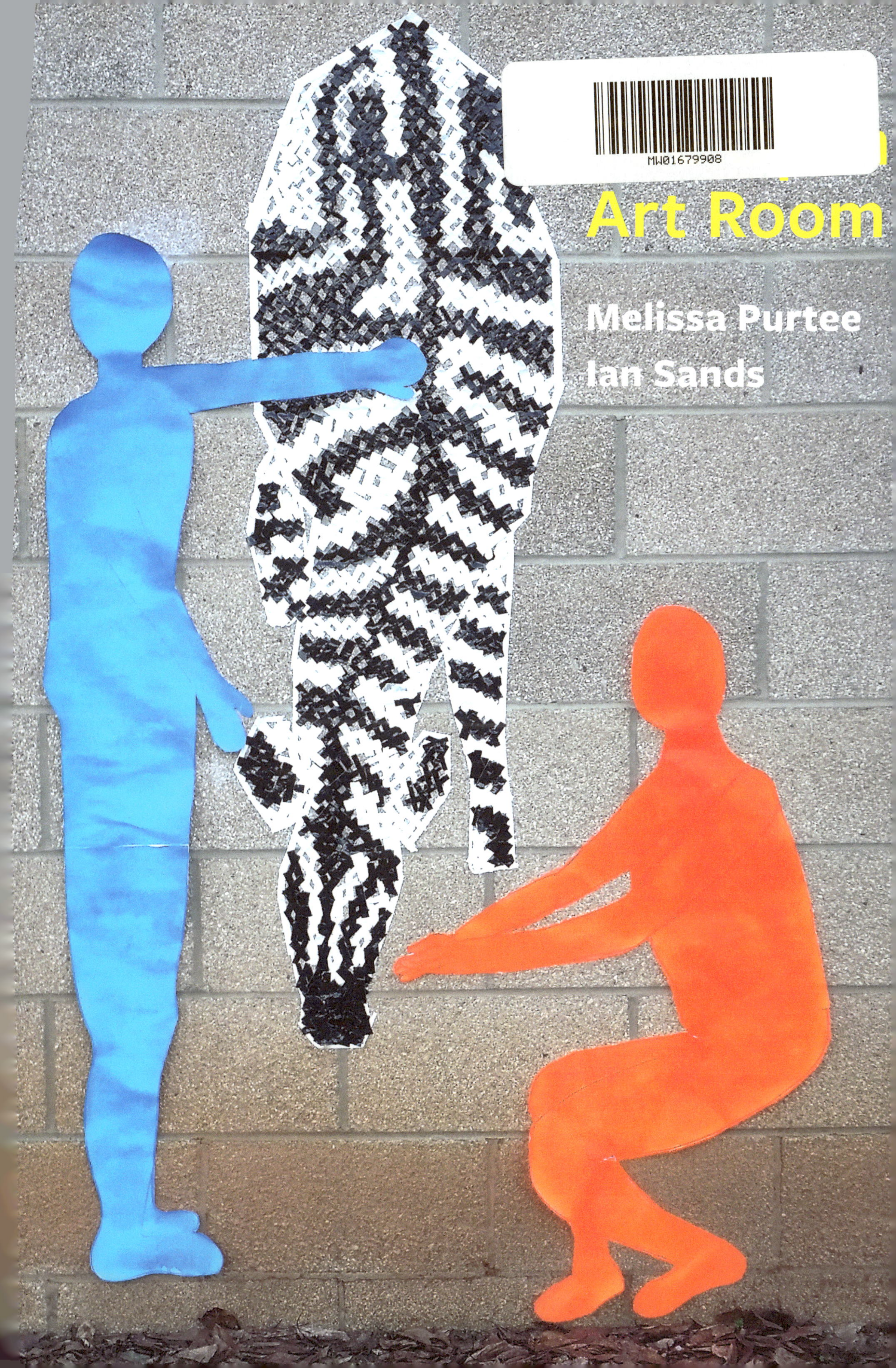

Art Room

Melissa Purtee
Ian Sands

ISBN: 978-1-61528-677-5

Library of Congress: 2017941105

5 4 3 2

Cover Design: Alissandra Seelaus, 2017.

All photographs courtesy of Melissa Purtee and Ian Sands

Publisher: Julian Wade
Editor: Robb Sandagata
Development Editor: Margaret Manos
Production Assistance: Tom Fiorelli
Design: Tina Henderson

About the Authors

Ian Sands has been teaching for more than twenty years. He currently teaches art at South Brunswick High School in Southport, North Carolina. He is also a faculty member of the Teaching for Artistic Behavior Summer Institute at the Massachusetts College of Art and Design. He is a frequent presenter at National Art Education Association annual conferences, and has been a keynote speaker for multiple state conferences. He has written multiple articles for *SchoolArts* magazine and *The Art of Education.*

Melissa Purtee has been teaching for twelve years. She currently teaches art at Apex High School in Apex, North Carolina. She frequently presents at state and national art education conferences and was the co-keynote speaker at the TAB Colorado Choice Based Art Education Conference in 2017. She is the author of the blog *Thoughts on Arting* and a contributing writer for *SchoolArts* magazine and *The Art of Education.*

Contents

Foreword

Katherine Douglas

In *The Open Art Room,* Melissa Purtee and Ian Sands have written a book that is both philosophical inspiration and a practical do-it-now resource. Joining a positive trend in art education, they describe what they are doing every day as practicing high school art teachers. In recent years, they have transformed their teaching methods to encourage and support students finding personal expression in their art-making through independent work.

Readers of *The Open Art Room* will find focused descriptions of the wide range of student skills and experiences that confront art teachers of students in grades 7–12 , often within a single class. The framework that Purtee and Sands have developed allows for all students to be supported regardless of skill or experience. Students learn via teacher whole group instruction, small group meetings, one-on-one teacher to student, peer teaching, and personal student research. The book contains thorough explanations of units, bootcamps, and media explorations adaptable to beginner, intermediate, and advanced levels. Engaging stories of student struggles and successes offer a closer look at student thought processes as they try to find their creative path.

The authors write about the influence of Studio Habits, Art 21 and Teaching for Artistic Behavior (TAB) on their practice. Taking what works best from these sources, and mixing it with their own skills and preferences, Purtee and Sands create an eclectic practice that can be customized each year to meet the needs of diverse groups of students. This innovative approach, with its invitation to teachers to create *their* own practice, offers exciting possibilities for secondary art educators to transform their classrooms into hubs of student-centered creativity.

Dedications

Melissa Purtee

For my parents, who made me believe that I could do anything.

For Katherine Douglas, who has inspired generations of artists and teachers with her ideas and willingness to teach others. Your work made this book possible.

And for my students, who amaze and inspire me. My life has been so much richer for having you in it.

Ian Sands

This book is dedicated to Brenda Brooke, art department chair at Apex High School (retired). Her forward-thinking incorporation of technology in the art room was not only innovative, it opened the door, allowing me to re-enter the teaching profession.

To Matt Wight, former principal at Apex High School, who was always supportive of the students, the arts, and the teachers (including me), even when the students and I gave him several opportunities not to be.

To Patricia Sands who encouraged a certain ninth grader to take Art One in high school even when he didn't want to . . . but how could he say no to his mom?

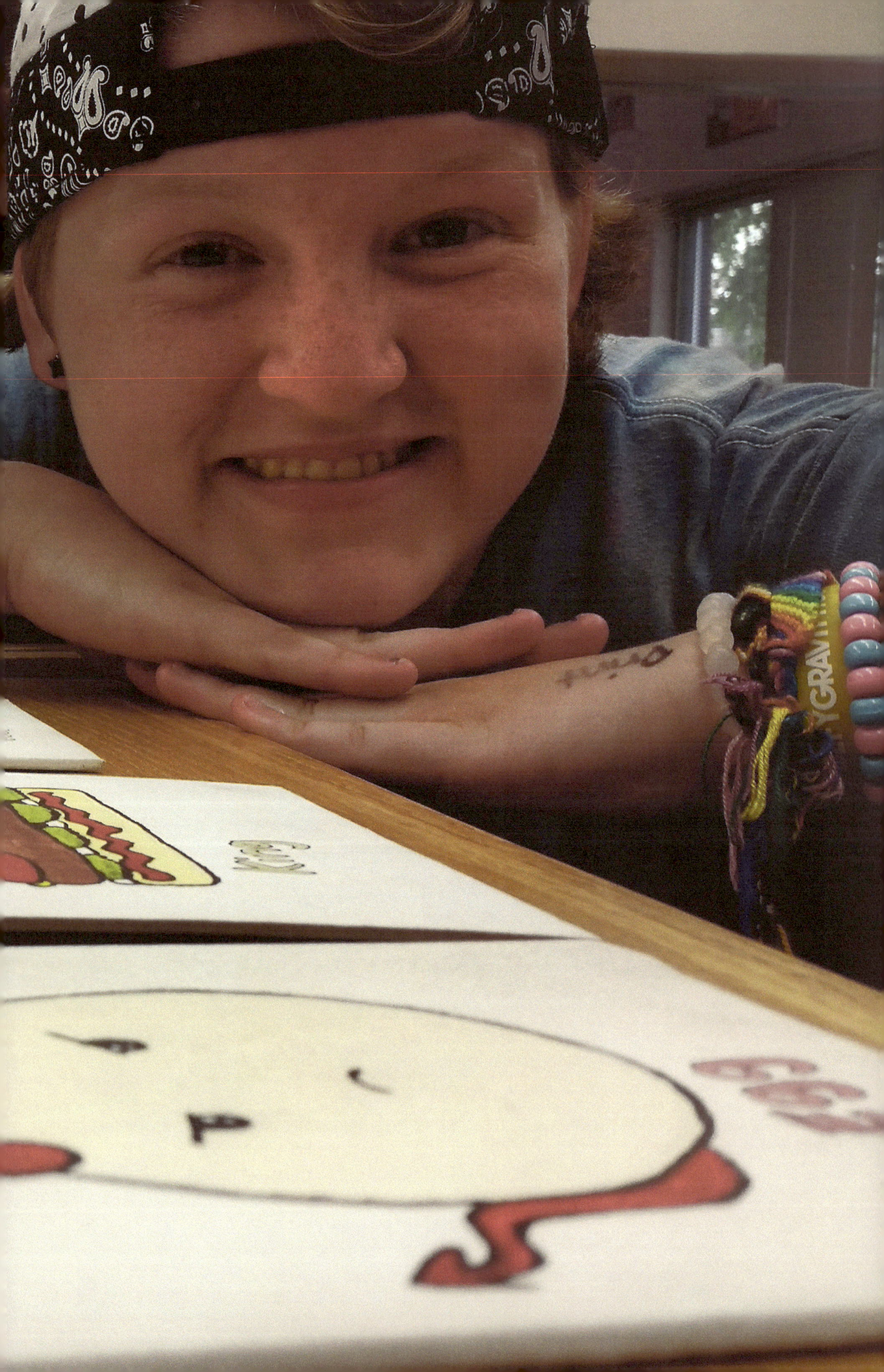

Introduction

Once, while reflecting on his invention of the original Apple computer, Steve Jobs approvingly quoted the artist Pablo Picasso as having said, "Good artists borrow; great artists steal." (Jobs himself had gotten several of his best ideas from visits to PARC Xerox, the copier manufacturer's research center in Palo Alto.) As it is hard to find where Picasso actually said this originally, some believe the idea might be better attributed to the writer T.S. Eliot, who wrote, "Immature poets imitate; mature poets steal." Whatever the case may be, we all necessarily build upon previously created works. And by the same token, while the content of this book is original, it is indebted to works that have come before, and we wish to acknowledge those who laid the foundation for the work we do today. The following are only a few of the many influences that have inspired our thinking and shaped the approach to teaching and learning that we call the Open Art Room.

Teaching for Artistic Behavior (TAB)

Teaching for Artistic Behavior, known as TAB, is an instructional approach that was developed in the 1970s by Katherine Douglas, Pauling Joseph, and John Crowe. The term "Teaching for Artistic Behavior" was established in the late 1990s when Diane Jaquith joined the group. Pioneered in elementary classrooms, this method involves setting up a variety of classroom centers, often based around types of art media. Instead of the teacher planning what artwork each student in the class will make, students choose what center to work at and what to create while they are there. A key element of this philosophy is the idea that students are artists and should be allowed to use their own ideas in personalized art-making.

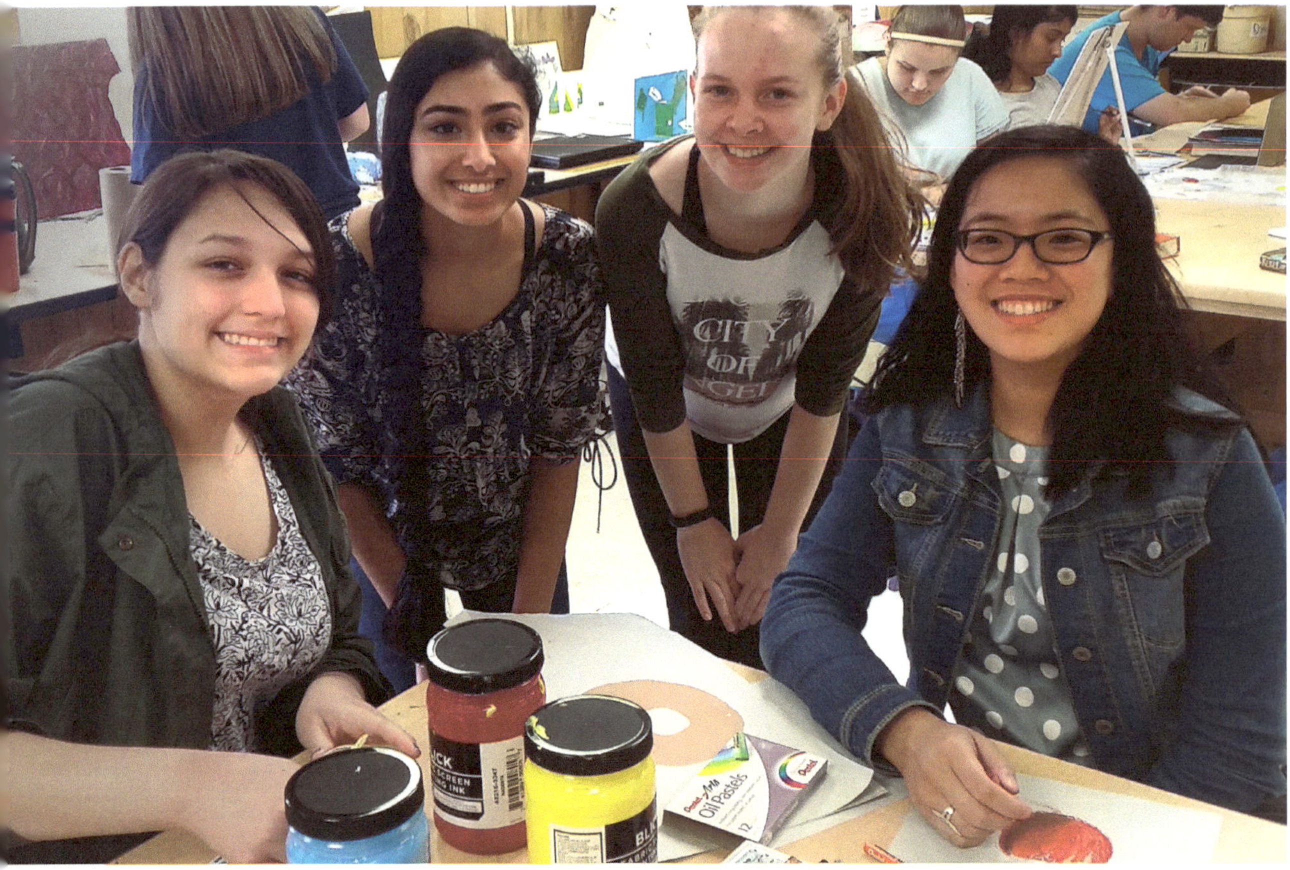

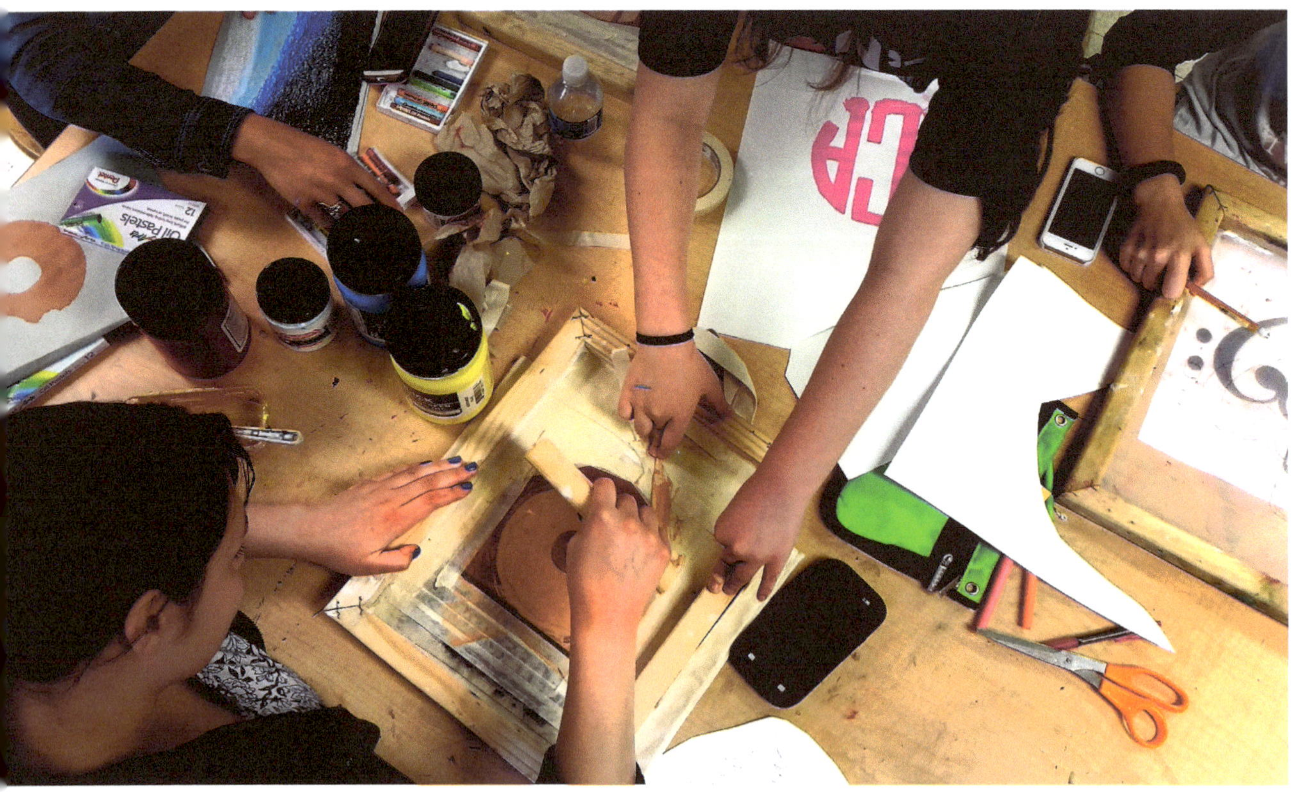

ogether to screenprint.

Three components of TAB were especially influential in the development of our philosophy: student-directed learning, teaching for creative thinking, and nonlinear pacing.

Studio Habits of Mind

Another important strand of thought that influenced the development of our approach derives from the book *Studio Thinking: The Real Benefits of Visual Arts Education* by Lois Hetland, Ellen Winner, Shirley Veenema, and Kimberly M. Sheridan.

Studio Habits of Mind are a set of eight characteristics to be incorporated by the artist/student. These eight habits can be utilized as an entry point for choice-based teaching. The habits include learning to properly use and care for tools, embracing problems, envisioning possibilities, creating art that expresses meaning, observing, reflecting, learning through experimentation, and interacting as an artist with other artists and with society in general.

These habits were the starting point for our list of artistic behaviors, which we created to be used specifically at the high school level.

Art21

A third important resource has been ART21, a nonprofit organization dedicated to presenting contemporary art and artists through research, publications, digital programs, and films. Its flagship documentary television series "Art in the Twenty-First Century" (also viewable online) features contemporary artists discussing their work in their own words. ART21 provides free resources to teachers and students, as well as teacher education programs. The two most influential concepts we stole from ART21 are using the work of contemporary artists in the classroom and basing learning around themes.

Beginnings, or How We Got Here

Melissa

I started down this path while trying to implement behavior incentives in the classroom. In my elementary art room, I offered rewards my classes could earn. If behavior expectations were met, over time, students could earn the reward of voting on a lesson—clay, painting, or any other activity they wanted. Students loved this, and it worked really well, except for one little hang-up: not everyone wanted to do the same thing. When we voted, there were always students who were disappointed. Once, when this exact scenario occurred in a fifth grade class at the end of the year, the looks on the faces of the kids who were losing the vote made me throw up my hands and declare, "All right, we'll just do it all!"

So, the next week I set up three centers, somewhat expecting chaos to ensue. You see, my school was composed of a challenging population—over 90% free and reduced lunch, low test scores, lots of behavior issues—that kind of school. The children were awesome, but I had learned over the years that I needed to keep tight control over everything. I thought it would never work for my students because of assumptions I made. I couldn't have been more wrong.

The day of reckoning arrived. One center was for paper and found-object sculpture, one for painting, and one for collage. I fought back the feeling of impending doom and invited the class into the room.

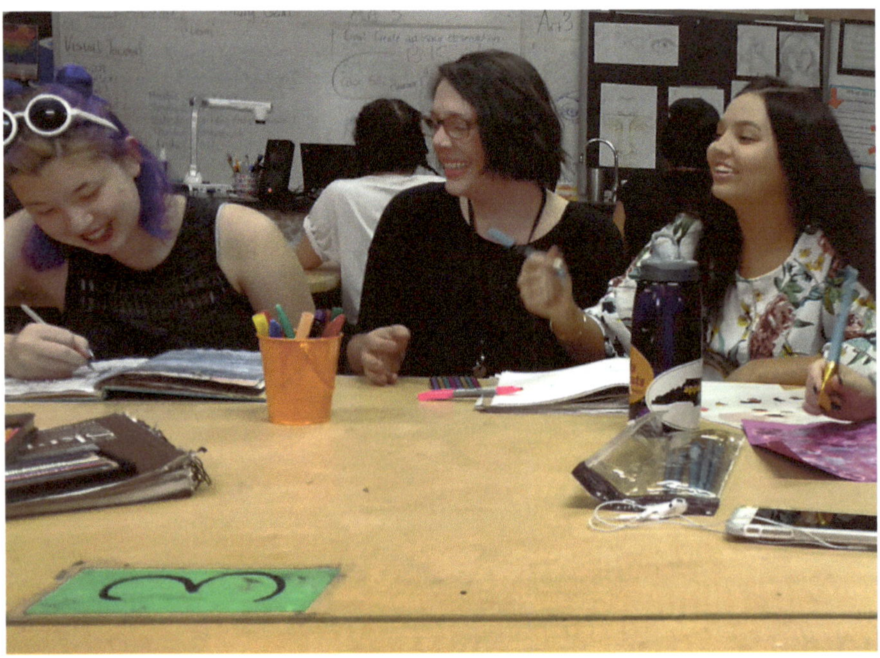

Melissa with her students.

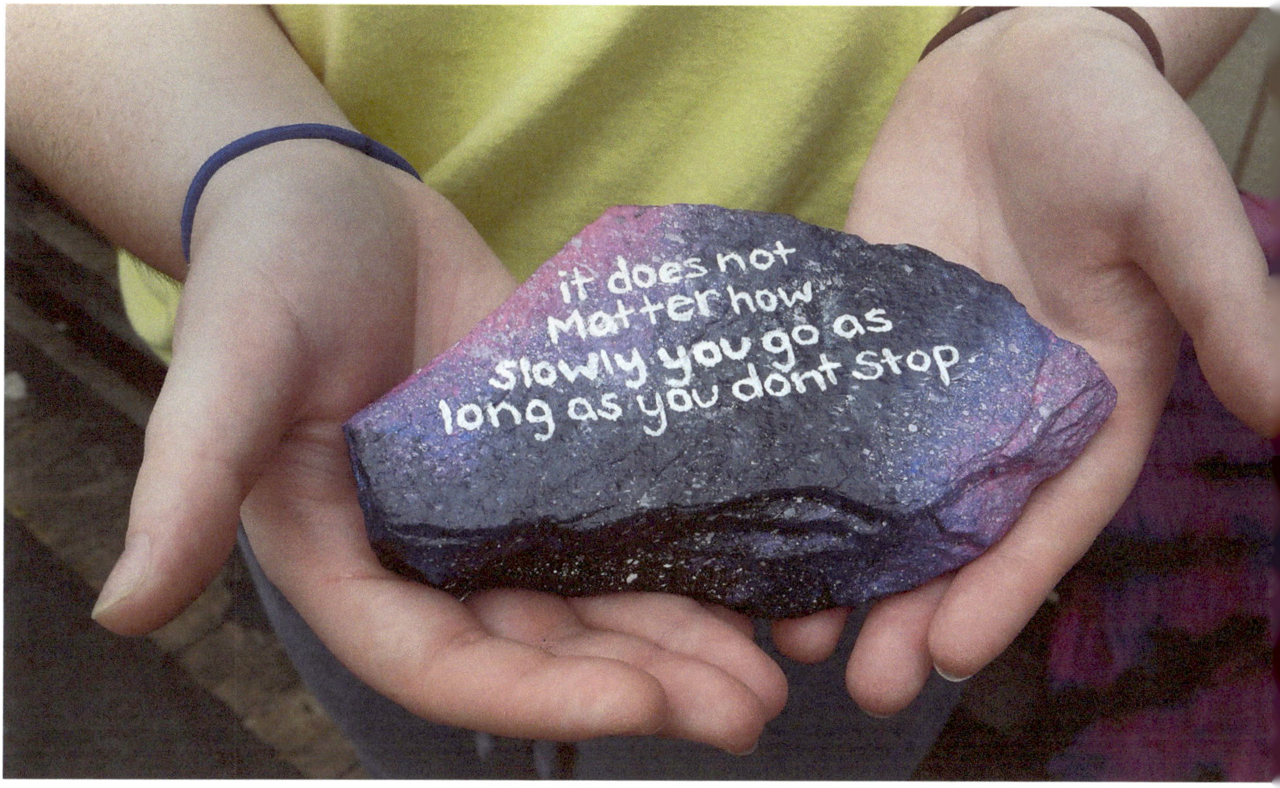

Katie shows off part of her collection for Portfolio Day.

They loved it.

They were the most focused I had ever seen them and were successfully making art without my step-by-step directions. I walked around the room like Dorothy seeing Oz in color for the first time, amazed at the level of authentic engagement I was witnessing. Then I spotted Darius. He had been my student since first grade and was the sort of child who was never a behavior problem but obviously wished to be elsewhere. He followed directions but did the minimum and normally threw his work away on the way out the door. When I observed him silently folding paper to build an intricate model plane, I was awestruck.

"Darius, this is beautiful!"

"Oh," he said as my words broke his concentration. "I build these all the time at home." What came next changed how I viewed my role as teacher forever.

"Ms. Purtee," he said. "This is better than P.E. Thank you."

Then he resumed his building, and when class was over, he carried his sculpture carefully out of the classroom, beaming with pride. In that moment my paradigm forever shifted. I knew I was going to change everything. Something that could make this boy love art had to be worth it.

Ian

I got started on this path after looking over my students' art and noticing that all the work looked the same. Their artworks were more than similar; they were indistinguishable. When I placed my students' art on the table, I couldn't tell which work belonged to which student, and it wasn't until I turned the papers over to look for their names written on the back that I knew for sure. On more than one occasion, a student would forget to sign a work, and in order to discover who created the piece, I would need to present the unsigned artwork to the class and ask.

Another realization was that all their work looked like it was created by high school students. Of course they *were* high school students, but it wasn't their skill level that gave the artwork this look. It was the way they handled the elements of art and the principles of design. Their work looked more like exercises in line variation and color theory than it did authentic art.

I started to question what was causing their work to possess these two qualities. Eventually, I realized that it had nothing to do with the students at all. It was my lessons that were causing their work to conform to these attributes. I wanted to correct these issues, but I wasn't sure where to begin.

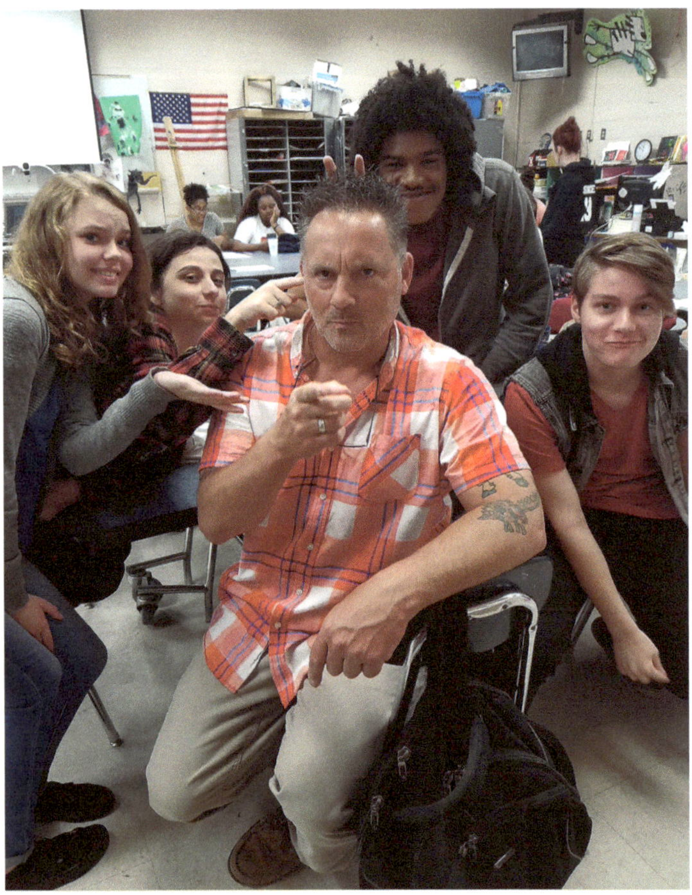

Ian with his students.

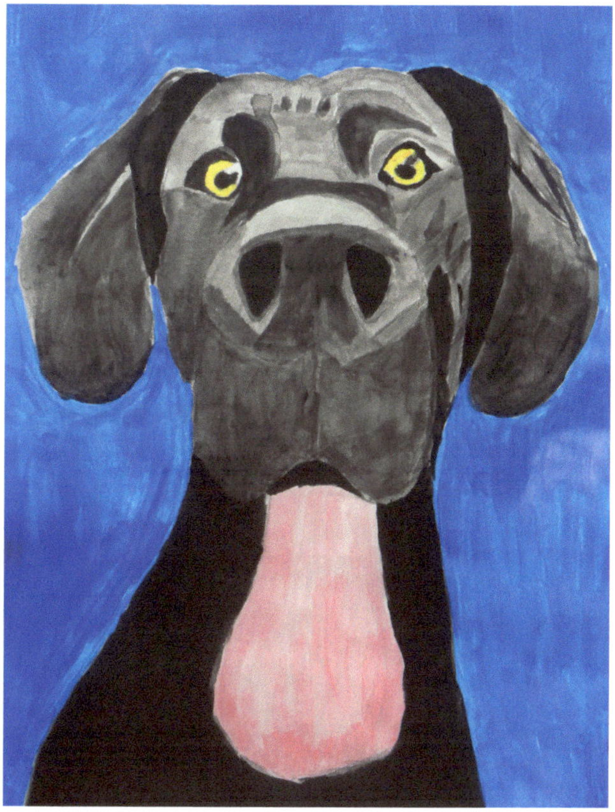

Pet portrait of the family dog painted in watercolor.

Not long after I had come to this realization, I saw a tweet that read, "If you get 25 of the same thing from students, it's not a project, it's a recipe." Ouch.

At first I let my ego get the best of me. I didn't like the thought of my projects being recipes. However, the more I thought about it, the more I realized the statement was true. I was giving my students the same project, asking them to use the same materials, on the same size paper, and with the same desired outcome. It should have been little wonder that their works all looked similar. By my doings, they weren't making art, they were following my recipe.

I began to rethink my entire teaching philosophy. I started by giving my students theme-based assignments and allowing them to decide what materials they would select to create their art. I replaced the step-by-step instructions with open-ended questions that challenged them to respond with creative solutions.

The results were outstanding. Before, I couldn't tell two works apart; now each project was created in a style that was unique to each student. Their work no longer resembled exercises in the elements and principles of art, but rather authentic works that were personal and meaningful to them. Now, I'm no longer interested in teaching art but rather in making artists.

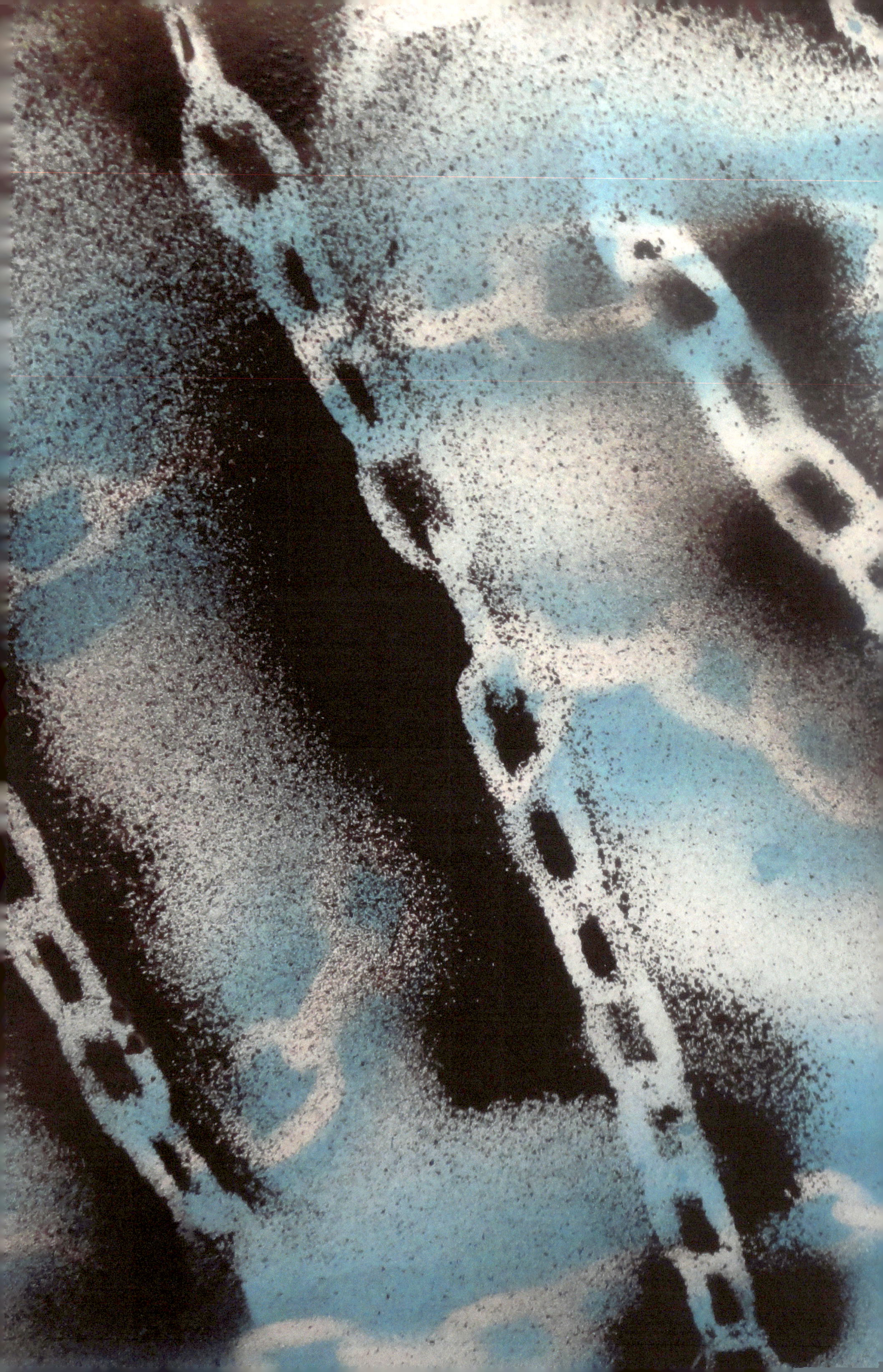

PART ONE | Getting Started

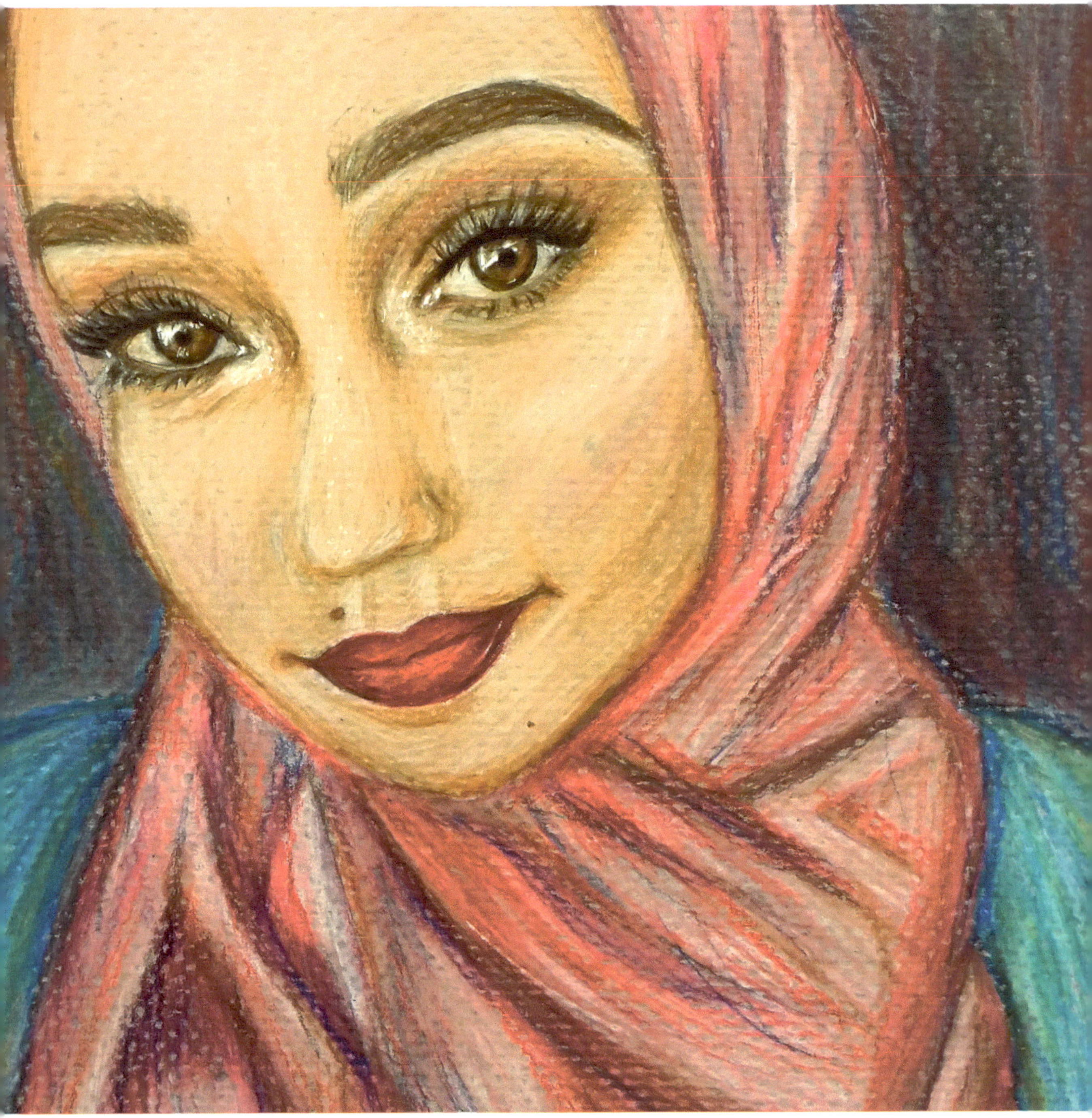

1 | What Is Choice?

We love art. Art urges us to think and feel. It shows us what it is to be human. Art provides a record of our shared history and offers a way to process the beauty and chaos of the cosmos and come to grips with the world as it is today. Combining the cultural and the natural with the personal, art empowers and enlarges our experiences of living, of understanding, of communicating, of caring, and of fully realizing ourselves and our potentialities. These are reasons why quality arts education should be in our schools.

Because art is a necessary component of a comprehensive education, we must think critically about what makes quality arts programing.

Currently, one school of thought suggests we judge instruction by the product, by the work created by students in art classrooms. The world we live in overwhelmingly tells us that appearance gives art value, that art should be "pretty," beautifying the hallways at school and winning contests. For teachers, this means: If the work coming out of your classroom doesn't look good, you are not doing your job. This mindset is remarkably pervasive, and it trickles down from the society at large to the school leadership, the art teacher, and eventually to the student.

We feel quite the opposite. We believe this view of the value of art and the nature of quality can cause enormous damage. The pressure to produce visually stunning work compels teachers to plan lessons that will consistently produce a "good" outcome. Art teachers are experts at this. They formulate each step with the final product in mind and guide students through the creative process like a mother holding her toddler by the hand. The work looks good, but the problem with this kind of spoon-feeding is that the students don't really get the chance to *create*. They miss the opportunity to experience the power and significance of true self-expression. They may even be left with a misconception of what art-making is all about. To teach authentic art-making we have to take a fully holistic view.

Art is so much more than the final product—it is a process. The planning, designing, revising, and reflecting that art-making requires, skills that we call "artistic behaviors," are activities that have enormous value in the art classroom and in the real world. If we want our students to learn how to engage with their own creativity and make art in a way that is authentic, it is essential that we offer them pathways to independence and help them practice artistic behaviors as foundational skills.

The facilitation of self-expression has to be a pervasive goal, not merely something that students will be exposed to later, when they are deemed "skilled" enough. These artistic behaviors can be directly taught as learnable skills, as part of every project, K-12. We ought to take the expectation for "pretty" out of art education and instead instill expectations for meaning and for creative thinking. The intent of this book is to help teachers accomplish these goals by providing a framework for teaching students to think like artists.

What Makes the Open Art Room Different?

The Open Art Room looks and operates in a unique way, incorporating different levels of choice to match the content being taught. There are three main levels of student choice used in the Open Art Room:

Teacher Directed: The teacher makes the decision or sets specific limitations.

Modified Choice: Students are given a limited range of options from which to choose.

Full Choice: Limitations are minimal. The student is responsible for making all important choices.

To explain the difference between traditional art instruction and full or modified choice in practice, we'll use as an example a skills-based painting lesson that might be taught in a high school introductory art course.

Teacher-Directed

A painting lesson might be centered around specific skills, like mixing colors and understanding tints and shades. The teacher explains these terms, then leads the class in guided practice, possibly mixing value scales with acrylic. Next, each student further practices new learning by completing a similar work grouped around a central subject, such as a monochromatic

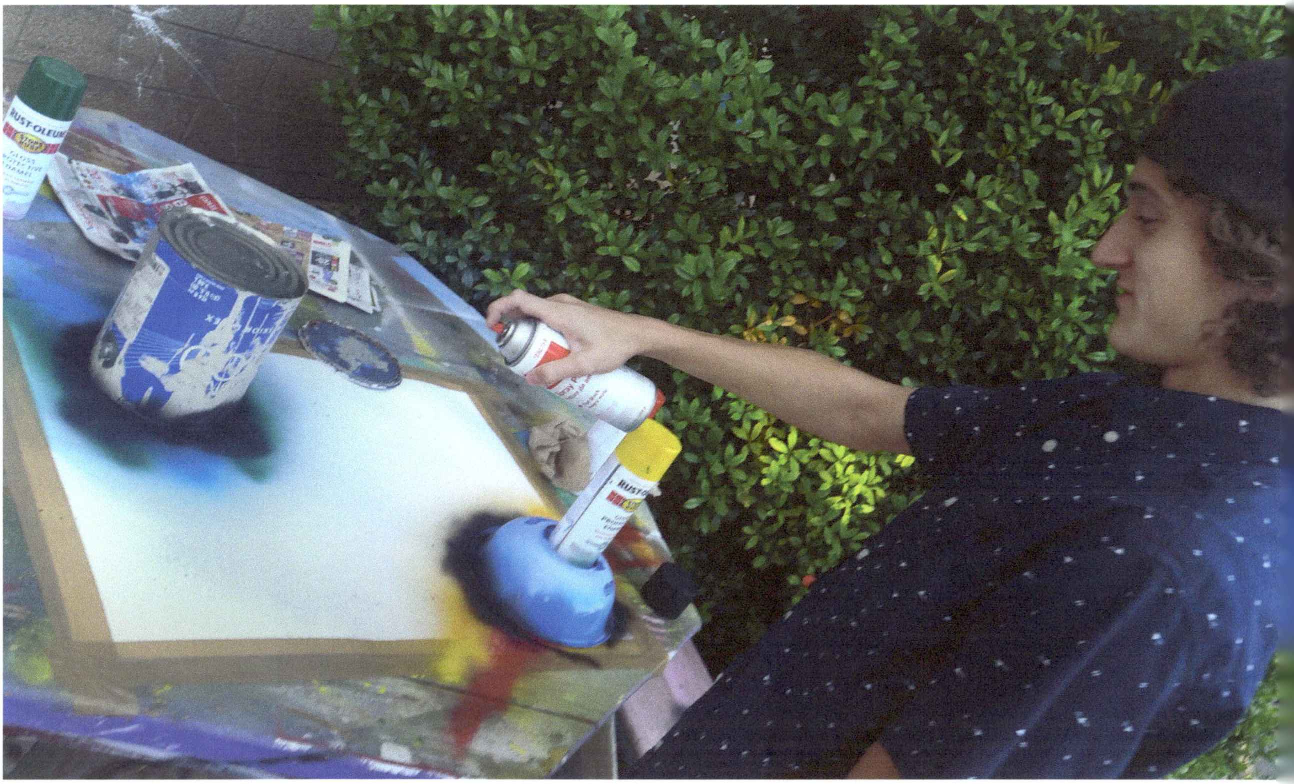

Timmy experiments with spray paint on the art patio.

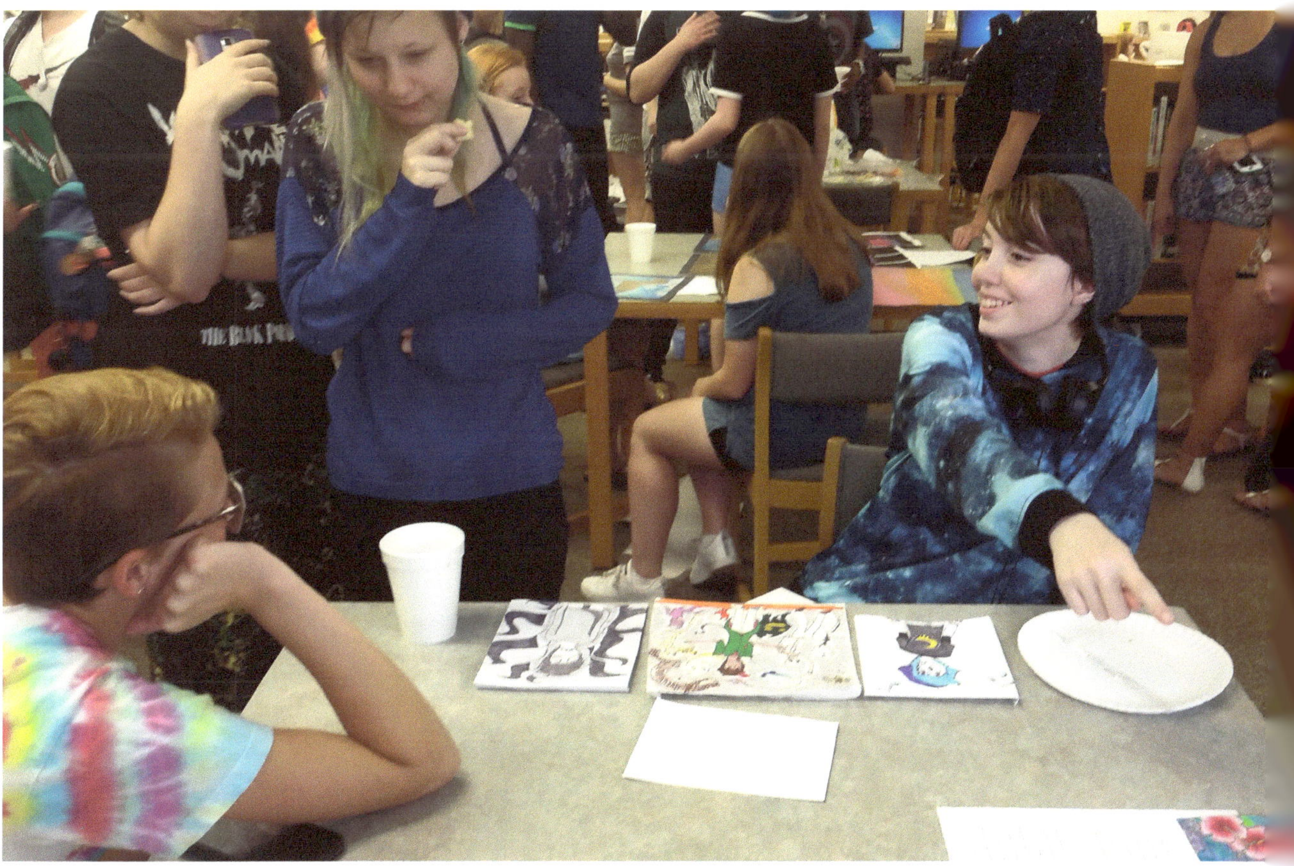

Students show off their hard work on Portfolio Day.

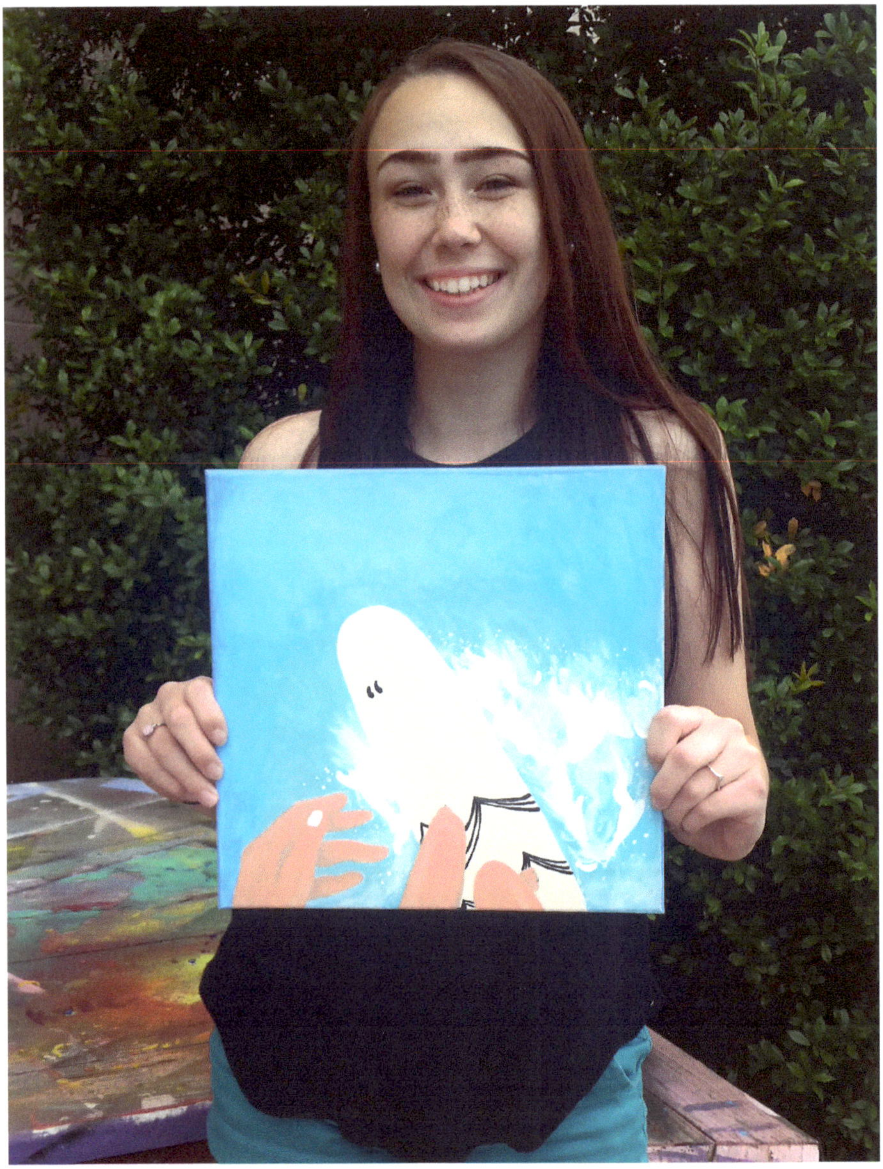

Tori with part of her Portfolio Day collection.

portrait or work in a specific artist's style. The teacher selects the process from planning to completion, including the subject matter, the media, and often the dimensions of the final artwork. The student's task is to mix paint correctly and make limited choices about color or subject matter within closely set parameters.

Modified Choice

A painting lesson might include similar elements, like value scales, but cover more material to provide a range of choices. One way to accomplish this is to take students through a painting "Bootcamp," a short and focused period of skill development. In the Bootcamp, tints and shades are covered in watercolor and acrylic, as are basic color theory, color mixing, and various paint application techniques. New learning is supported by reference materials found in the room and online. This intense period of learning is followed by an open-ended project in which students create paintings of their choice, further exploring the medium of paint in ways that speak to them. For this project students are responsible for choosing the type of paint, the subject, the style, and the size of the work. Asking students to make these decisions requires them to apply new learning and creates an authentic assessment of skill development.

Full Choice

The lesson begins with an assigned theme or the student's own ideas. It is up to the individual student to decide how to respond to the prompt through use of media and the content. New learning varies on a student-by-student basis and based on what information the student needs in order to realize his or her vision. In this context, teacher input related to paint might range from reviewing the basics to the demonstration of an advanced technique—it depends on the specific needs of the students at that point in time.

Who's Responsible?

Another way to think about the differences between traditional teaching methods and full or modified choice is through the lens of responsibility. In a traditional setting the teacher is responsible for almost every component of the lesson, from selecting the materials to the subject of the work. The decisions left to students often are few in number and small in importance. The student is asked to reproduce, emulate, or copy.

Choice-based instruction shifts responsibility from teacher to student. In a modified choice instructional model, responsibility is more equally shared. The teacher takes responsibility for providing a limited range of choices, resource material, and thematic guidelines. Students are responsible for applying new learning by selecting materials and deciding how best to use them. In the Open Art Room, the teacher operates as a guide or sounding board for the students' ideas and vision. The student takes on the majority of responsibility and decision making. The student is asked to create, not to copy or reproduce the teacher's example.

Each approach to instruction has strengths and weaknesses. Art teachers are often judged on the visual appeal of student artwork. Traditional methods give the instructor the most control over the aesthetics of the final product. An experienced art teacher is a master at orchestrating artwork that has consistent visual appeal. However, such control comes at a cost. The planning and problem solving of an artwork involves valuable conceptual learning experiences. When students don't have a chance to take on this responsibility, the learning experience is less than what it could be. Conversely, giving the role of planning to students extends the potential for learning. Ultimately, teaching creativity means letting students make decisions.

Goals of the Open Art Room

When implementing a new program, whether it's as simple as adding a new unit or as complex as changing an entire curriculum, setting the intended goals is a necessary step. The goals become the outline for implementation. Everything that goes into the program should lead to achieving one or more of the goals. Anything that does not point toward the goals is extraneous and should be removed.

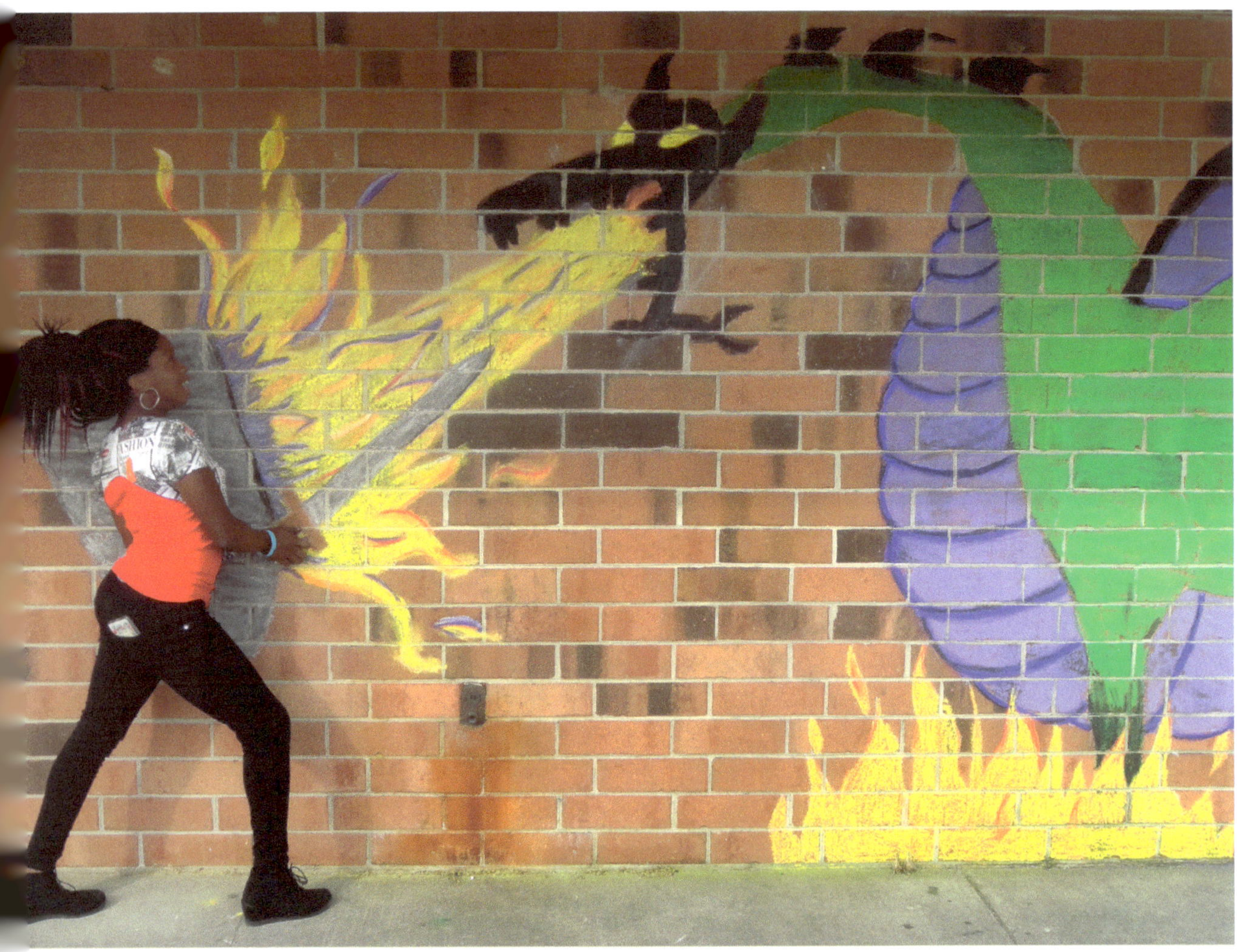

chalk mural.

There are four main goals of the Open Art Room. Each of these goals is designed to increase student self-sufficiency in all aspects of the art-making process, from ideation through design, to creation and reflection. These goals include: Making Artists, Teaching for Artistic Behavior, Focusing on Conceptual and Creative Thinking, and Creating an Inclusive Art-Making Experience.

Making Artists

Art teachers have long embraced the "Make Art" mantra. It is emblazoned on bumper stickers, T-shirts, posters, and even coffee mugs. There is good reason for the wide-ranging popularity of this slogan. Making art is what art teachers want their students to do. It's what art teachers do. The responsibility of the art teacher is to teach students to make art. However, for the Open Art Room model to be truly successful, a paradigm shift in thinking is required. The Open Art Room teacher stops focusing on "making art" and concentrates on "making artists."

This difference in thinking can be understood by comparing the product versus the process. Art teachers who are focused on making art incorporate a product-based mentality into their teaching. Inherent in this way of thinking is the desire for a predetermined outcome, for what the student's project will look like when it is completed.

By contrast, the Open Art Room teacher is interested in making artists. The teacher's focus is on the knowledge and attitude that the students acquire by creating art. While the product may be an outcome, the focus of the teacher's lessons is on what takes place during the process of making.

Our phrase "making artists" should not be misunderstood. It should not be interpreted that we expect our students to become artists in the future, or that we wish to lead all students into art careers. Rather, it should be understood that we consider the students in our classrooms to be artists whose ideas deserve respect. In response to fostering their autonomy, our students develop the composure to solve problems on their own terms, and thereby experience insights applicable not only in the art room, but also in their everyday lives.

Teaching for Artistic Behavior

There are several different ways in which art education is delivered to students. Many teachers begin with a media-based curriculum, teaching units based on paint, clay, printing, and textiles. Another method involves presenting units based on skills such as drawing, shading, painting, or throwing techniques. Yet another way is to develop units around the elements and principles of art, teaching lessons on color theory, composition, and perspective. The Open Art Room refrains from these methods and instead replaces them with the goal of acquiring artistic behaviors.

As we will discuss later in the book, many units can be created by starting with the question, "What do artists do?" For example, artists often observe the world around them. This concept of observation could be fashioned into a unit titled "Artists Observe." This unit might be dedicated to helping students understand the various ways in which artists observe the world around them.

However, the art teacher does not necessarily need to develop units in this way when building a curriculum around the concept of teaching artistic behaviors. Still, a necessary objective of the Open Art Room is to cultivate and expand the student's understanding of artistic practices. This works in tandem with the first goal of Making Artists.

Focusing on Conceptual and Creative Thinking

When reviewing the first two goals, Making Artists and Teaching for Artistic Behavior, it becomes clear that the focus of the Open Art Room is on the process of creating art. While teaching skills and techniques necessary to design and produce an art product are still part of the curriculum, these elements are gained by moving through the process. The foundation of this process is conceptual and creative thinking.

Whether the level of choice is beginner, intermediate, or advanced, the objective of each lesson starts with a conceptual idea. These ideas may come from straightforward models such as prompts or themes, or they may be derived from more complex methods, challenging students to explore procedures artists use when creating art. In all cases, students are asked to think critically about the topic and to use a systematic approach to idea generation in order to formulate a visual response. Once a response has been designed, students need to consider the media, skills, and techniques required to accomplish their chosen solution. The emphasis throughout, however, remains clearly on conceptual and critical thinking.

Creating an Inclusive Art-Making Experience

The strength of using student choice in teaching is that it gives the teacher the power to facilitate a successful experience for every student. This is important in any class, but especially important in introductory classes that are made up of students with a wide variety of skills. This approach is inclusive and based on the idea that art is for everyone, not just the talented few. Creating an environment where every student experiences success involves a shift in mindset from art as skill-based to concept-based. When instruction starts with the goal of developing students' abilities to

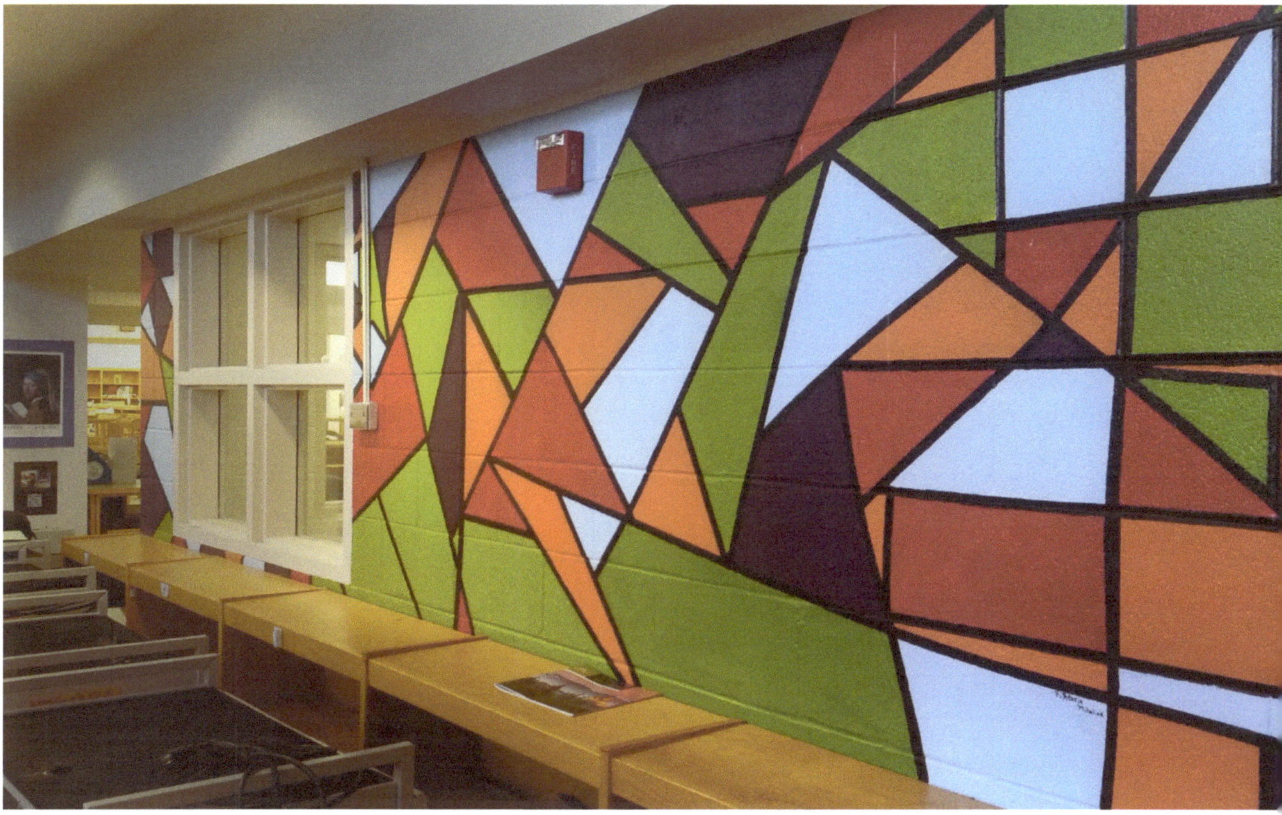

Students designed and painted this mural in the Apex High School Library after creating several smaller ones on canvas.

communicate their own concepts, the tasks of selecting the processes and materials that will work best for their individual skills, preferences, and experiences are also best placed in the hands of the students. Theme-based projects work well for concept-based teaching because they allow room for the development of individual ideas.

Another major key to making art class inclusive is getting rid of any teacher examples that students are asked to replicate with minimal changes and replacing such assignments with challenges that allow a free range of responses. When the one right answer that the teacher example creates is removed, more than one path to "good" work emerges.

This is not to say that teachers shouldn't show examples of artwork. When introducing a project, try to show a range of responses from master artists. Use examples from current working artists, who students tend to find easier to relate to, as well as work from artists of the past. It's important to consider diversity when selecting work to show students. Showing work created by artists of different genders and ethnicities makes your classroom welcoming to all of your students and exposes them to different points of view.

Making a truly inclusive classroom means creating a variety of pathways to success. Teaching a variety of skills around a central concept provides alternatives and choices for students, who can then pick what will work best

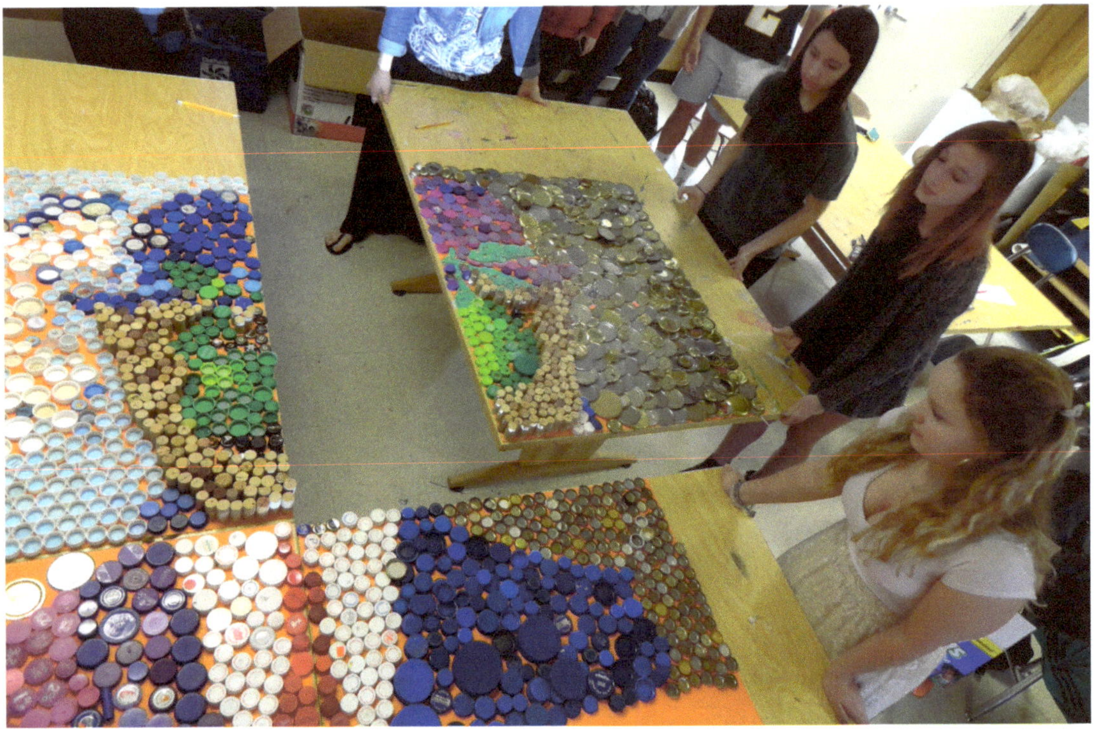

Students combining their sections of a bottlecap mural inspired by Magritte's *The Son of Man*.

for them from what they've learned. One way to teach a variety of new skills and techniques is through a short, intensive new learning period at the beginning of a lesson. For more information, see Bootcamps on page 50 and Chapter 7: Introduction to Art Bootcamp.

How the Open Art Room Benefits the Student

Before embracing any pedagogy, a teacher needs to first understand the benefits that philosophy will offer students. Naturally this goes for the Open Art Room as well. Why should this method of teaching be considered a good alternative to media or skills-based teaching? After all, curricula based on techniques or the elements and principles of art have been successfully implemented throughout the art education community. What advantages does the Open Art Room offer over other methods, and in particular, how will it benefit the students?

The primary difference between a teacher-based curriculum and the Open Art Room is in the ability of the latter to match the media and technique goals of the former, and then surpass it in five other categories. These categories include students engaging in the process, engaging in the work, going beyond the expectations of the teacher, exceeding the expectations of the rubrics, and learning to think for themselves. Let's examine these one by one.

Engaging in the Process

When we review the recurring issues that need to be addressed in education today, student engagement is always high on the list. The art room is no exception to this issue. There always seem to be one or more students who aren't engaged in what the art teacher is presenting, who do not want to work. A student-led art program does not eliminate this problem, but it does help alleviate it in certain circumstances. When students are empowered to design their own outcomes, they are more likely to take ownership of the process.

When students have ownership of their art-making process, they are likely to be more engaged in the class. They are making decisions, and these decisions will affect the outcome of their projects. It is easy for a student to dismiss a teacher-led assignment. Since they have no stake in the game, they don't see a reason to pursue any results, especially if these results appear predetermined by the teacher. When the student is in control, the stakes are higher. Their success is literally in their own hands.

Engaging in Work

Once students have taken ownership of the process, they are more likely to become invested in the project. Evidence of such investments can manifest in both physical and monetary ways. To define this evidence, we must once again compare the Open Art Room to the teacher-directed model.

Though students can become invested in a teacher-directed project, students naturally play a more passive role, waiting for materials to be distributed and directions to be given. In the Open Art Room, we find students will actively seek out desired materials. If the exact material isn't available, they will inquire about alternatives. When alternative materials do not suit their needs, it is not uncommon for students to literally invest in their project. They will spend their own money, time, and energy to shop, either in stores or online, to purchase the materials they deem necessary to create their artwork.

Going Beyond Teacher Expectations

Another benefit of student-led projects is that students will often set higher expectations than the teacher. When a teacher prescribes a project, it must necessarily be formulated to be achievable by all students in the entire class. In some ways, teachers must root their expectations to the lowest common denominator in order for their assignments to be accomplished by all students in the class, regardless of the individual students' prior experiences, skills, or passions.

Students who design their own projects naturally take into consideration their previous experiences as well as their passions. They set expectations for themselves that are often higher than those of their classmates or their teacher.

Going Beyond the Rubrics

We find in the Open Art Room that students will often advance learning objectives, surpassing even the teacher's expectations.

The rubric is a common measurement wielded by art teachers for assessments and grading. It allows the teacher to categorize educational attainments so that they can be systematically evaluated. In order to mea-

---

Robbie's Interest in Perspective

Robbie was interested in creating a linear perspective drawing as one of his projects. Robbie had had some experience with one- and two-point linear perspective in Art One, and now he wanted to expand his knowledge. We sat down to discuss the project and he asked me what the next level of perspective would be. I explained three-point linear perspective and drew a quick example. He was impressed. "What about four-point perspective?" he blurted. Before I could explain that, although it did exist, I wasn't very familiar with it, he added, "Or five-point perspective!" I stopped him before he could go any further and explained, "I'm no expert in five-point perspective, but you should look it up."

He took my advice and found a YouTube video that explained the process in detail. Robbie was soon on his way, creating the first five-point perspective drawing to ever come out of my classroom.

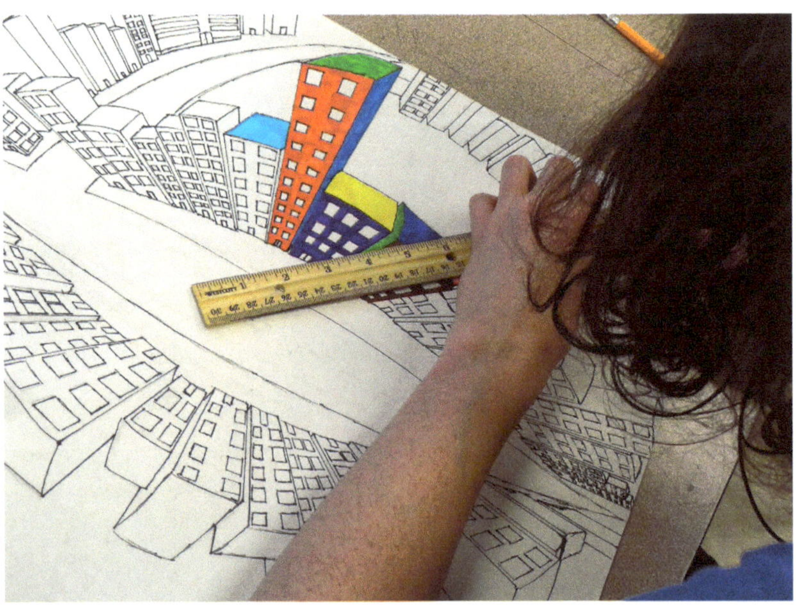

Robbie creating a five-point perspective image.

---

sure the level of success, the teacher must first determine the highest outcome a student will complete. Though rubrics are a commonly used method in assessing, they can sometimes limit the student's ability to make further progress than the teacher expects. In the Open Art Room, we often see a keen student's engagement exceed the rubric we might have reasonably set for a given assignment. For an example, read Ian's account of Robbie's interest in perspective.

Learning to Think Independently

Critical thinking has everything to do with making decisions, and one of the core principles of the Open Art Room is allowing for student choice. When students are in charge of the design process, they make decisions about all aspects of their project. They become active learners, discovering links between ideas, identifying errors, solving problems, and justifying their responses.

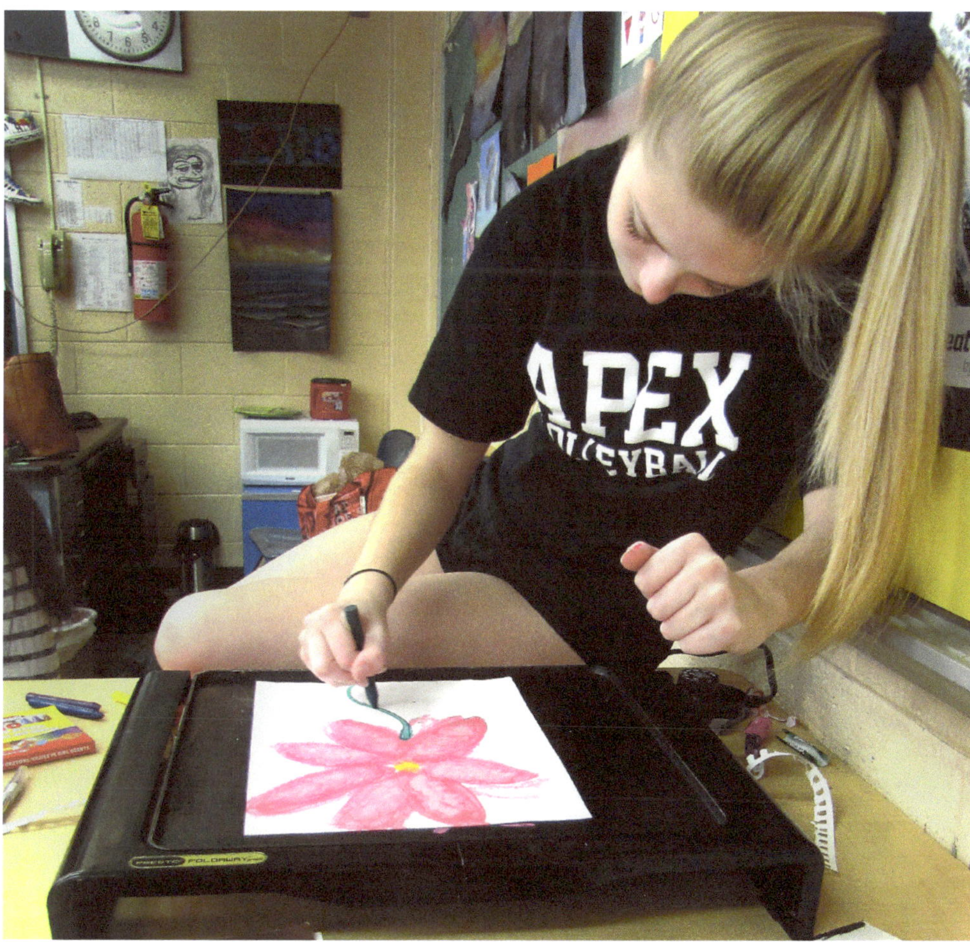

Experimenting with melted crayons on a hot plate.

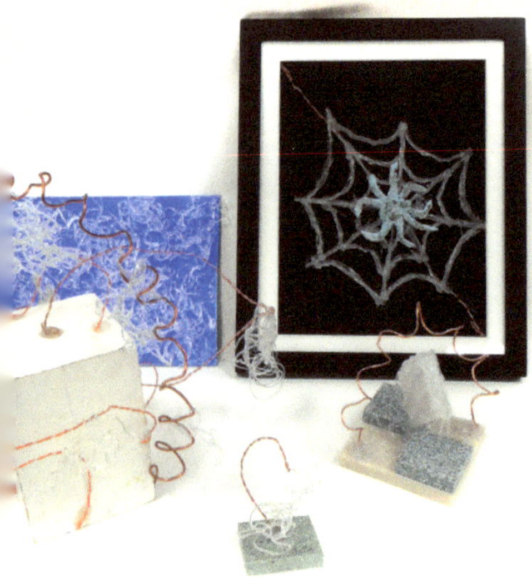

ys to create with hot glue and wire.

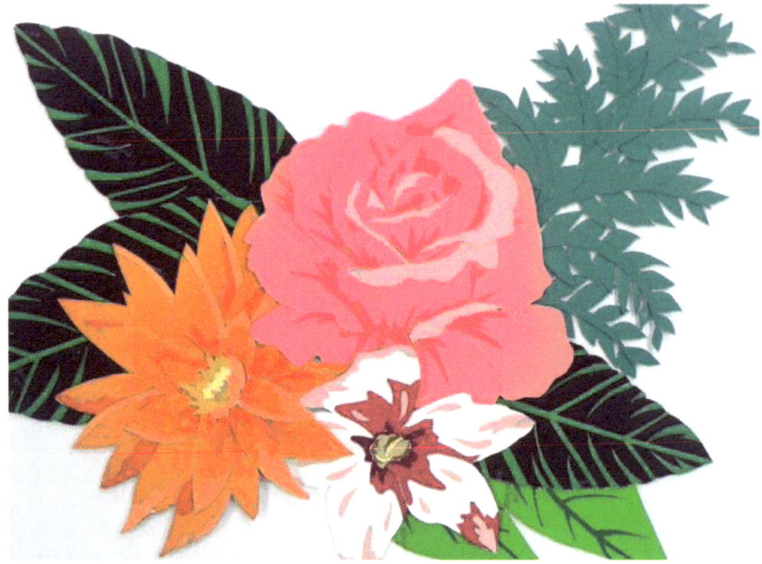

Still life created using cut paint color samples.

When students are developing ideas, they are making connections between themes and concepts. When they are considering which media would work best with their solution, they are recognizing strengths and weaknesses of different materials. When they are identifying techniques that they need to improve in order to produce their desired outcome, they are determining each technique's importance and relevance.

Growth in the ability to think for oneself is the hallmark of true education, and fostering such growth is the preeminent practical value of art education in the Open Art Room.

The Open Art Room: Choice and Individual Voice

When it comes to making authentic art, choice and individual voice are synonymous. Each decision a student makes adds another layer of individuality to his or her work. The more layers of decisions that are selected when creating a work of art, the more the piece will express the student's style, emotion, or opinion.

What Is Voice?

Taken together, a student's style, emotion, and opinion form that student's voice.

Consequently, when students are stripped of their ability to make decisions, the art they create will lose personality and tend to look similar to the art created by other students working on the same project. When this is taken to extremes, classroom projects can look so similar that it is difficult, if not impossible, to tell which student created which work of art.

The issue of diminished voice is magnified when teachers have predetermined the outcomes they expect the students to produce. Teachers often display an example of what the upcoming project will look like when completed. This sample, either designed by the teacher or created by a student in a previous class, is presented to the students before they begin the project. These samples represent the voice of the teacher, not the student.

On the other hand, when students are free from predetermined outcomes, their voices become unlocked. Their voices will be expressed as personal statements, apparent in individual works. These might be expressions of emotion, or opinion, or reaction for or against the assignment. In the history of art, many an art movement arose in direct reaction to its predecessor. In the same way, a student may elect to express support or disappointment in an assignment's topic through the choices he or she makes when creating the work.

A student's voice can also manifest gradually through a selection of creative decisions made over the course of several projects. In this manner, the student may develop a visual voice by repeating a set of unique steps that culminate in recognizable similarities, or a personal style. When we think of the artist Piet Mondrian, images of black lines and primary color shapes come to mind. When we consider Edgar Degas, we visualize ballerinas standing in snapshot-like compositions drawn in chalk pastel. Each of these artists' bodies of work are instantly recognizable because of their unique style, their artistic voice. When students are allowed the freedom to make decisions about the art-making process, their artistic voices will, naturally and of necessity, begin to emerge.

How Do We Develop Student Voice?

Developing student voice can be achieved by empowering our students to make their own decisions, allowing them to realize the value of their own ideas, and encouraging them to express their own ideas and opinions through the subject matter of their art. The student who is given this level of choice will almost inevitably produce art in his or her own voice. Their visual style will be reflected in the decisions they make regarding techniques and media. Their stories will be expressed through their ideas and the solutions they find to artistic problems. It may begin with small steps, but the more the student is provided opportunities to choose, the more the student voice will emerge and develop. In the Open Art Room, we begin the journey of voice discovery with three key areas of choice: choice in projects, choice in media, and choice in technique selection.

Students Make Decisions about Projects.

Artists who create for the sake of making art, naturally make all the decisions about the projects they have chosen to complete. They impose limitations on themselves, decide what they wish to communicate, and determine in what manner to proceed. The choice-based classroom encourages students to work like artists. In this regard, the expectation for students in a choice program is that they will at least select their own assignment, if not design one entirely.

To promote project ideation, the teacher may provide students with suggestions, such as themes, big ideas, or artistic behaviors. Some of these prompts are more restrictive and perhaps more appropriate for the student who has either not been introduced to a choice-based program or simply needs more structure. Other prompts are less restrictive, leaving more leeway for student interpretation and initiative. In either case, the goal is to move the student toward less and less restrictive project prompts until the student is confident working independently.

Students Make Decisions about Media.

In a choice-based classroom, students make decisions about the media they will use when creating a work of art. The range of choices students may select from can vary depending on the experience or the level of choice the teacher has made available, but ultimately the direction of the work is determined by the student.

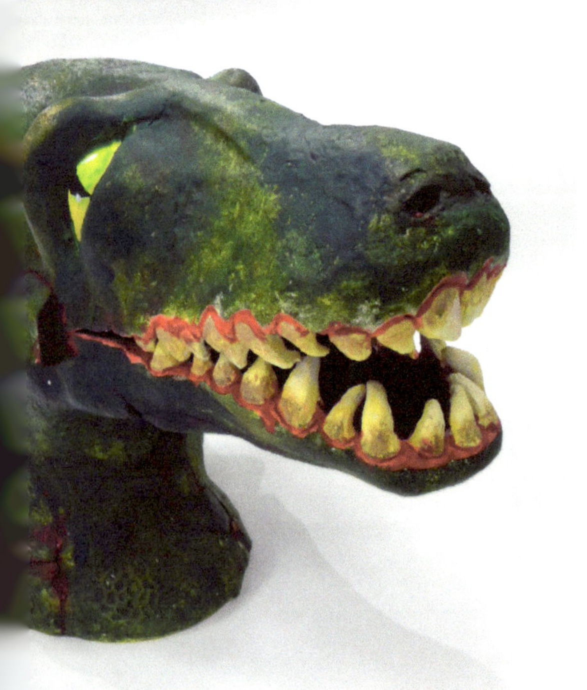

ɹre was damaged in the kiln and reassembled by

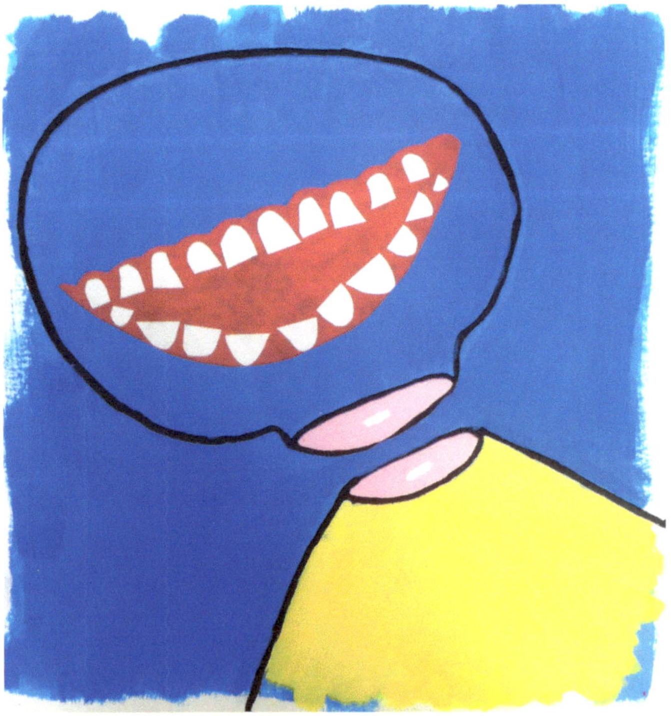

Acrylic painting inspired by an African basket.

Students have several different reasons for determining which medium they will use. They may select a medium after an assignment has been introduced because they believe it will best express the idea or concept they are exploring. Other times, a student might make a selection before responding to an assignment because he or she is simply inclined to explore that particular medium. Whatever the reasoning may be, the student who makes the decisions about medium, color, shape, and size is working as a true artist.

Students Make Decisions about Techniques.

In the Open Art Room, technique is not the main objective of units, though it might be the focus of short lessons. The objectives of units are based on artistic behaviors. Since the technique is not the objective, students are free to decide if they wish to pursue a technique or not, based on the desired outcome they envision for their project.

In choice-based teaching, the need for a particular technique is often realized on the back end of the project. For example, a student chooses a project that demonstrates scale. Her idea is to illustrate a scene in which miniature construction workers are applying cosmetics to a billboard-sized portrait. In order to obtain the results she desires, she needs to understand figure proportions to make the miniature men look realistic, and facial proportions in order to draw the portrait realistically. Rather than responding to a teacher directive to study proportion, she had decided what she wanted to create and how she wanted the outcome to look. It wasn't until she began rendering her artwork that the need to learn a new technique became apparent.

Voice Evolves Over Time

The process of creating art is evolutionary. Early Jackson Pollock paintings, though abstract, were still filled with recognizable imagery. It took years of experimentation for him to develop those familiar paint splats and drips—his signature voice and style. In the same way, our students are taking part in an artistic evolution. Each time they make and apply a personal decision, their art develops stylistically and their voice evolves.

When choices are not offered, as is often the case in the teacher-directed classroom, the student's voice goes missing. The end product might have aesthetic appeal, but the student's artistic evolution is stifled. Our goal should be for students to become independent artists. To accomplish this, they need to experiment with new and unfamiliar methods, techniques, and materials. We must recognize that students are at the beginning of their artistic evolution. We can think of them as little artist tadpoles. Rather than seeking preconceived outcomes, our units and assignments should make room for unexpected growth and the evolution of new abilities and powers.

Developing Style

Cara wasn't at all satisfied with how the portrait she had started earlier in the period was coming along. As the end of the day approached, she took her palette knife and swept paint across the image. Something about the color and the texture of that swipe caught her attention. Again, she dabbed the palette knife into the paint and swept it across the canvas from the opposite direction. A pattern emerged. With consideration, Cara repeated the process. It wasn't long before the small canvas was entirely covered with small, horizontal marks. It was at this point that I addressed Cara's work.

"I'm just messing around," was her response, but it was clear to me that she was fully engaged in the process.

"I think the pattern and texture is interesting," I said. With those words she immediately lit up. This indicated to me that she did value the work but didn't want to admit it. It wasn't a serious image like the originally intended portrait work. It was just play. However, play has value, and in this case it was producing results. I asked, "Why don't you make nine or ten more just like it?"

The next day, Cara brought in three small canvases she purchased after she left school the previous day. She started working right away, dabbing paint with her palette knife and systematically applying it to her canvas. When she finished one, she immediately started another. At the end of the day, we talked about her work, what she found satisfying about it, and where she might go from here. I gave her another piece of advice: "You need a bigger canvas."

The third day, Cara and I worked together to stretch canvas on a large frame, approximately three by four feet. Once it was stretched, Cara placed it on the floor and immediately started painting. She worked diligently and soon had an original abstract work that was all her own. She was extremely satisfied with the final results.

She had developed a technique which was becoming her style. In the following weeks she produced several more abstract works, each with a unique style that had become easily recognizable as Cara's.

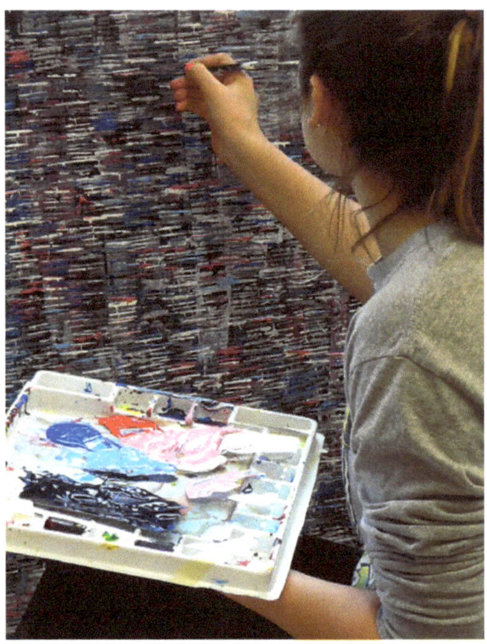

Cara working on her large, abstract painting.

Speaking Visually

As students evolve, they begin to develop a visual vocabulary. This vocabulary is unique to each student. Each choice a student makes assists in this development, and the more decisions students make, the more sophisticated their language becomes.

Early on, students might make random choices or selections based on simple criteria such as personal preferences. As students continue to grow, the explanations for their choices may become mature in nature. They will also repeat certain preferences. The combination of this repetition with the growing sophistication of their vocabulary leads to a sophisticated and authentic artistic voice.

Students who are given freedom to make choices in their art use their developing voices and vocabularies to tell their stories; they become more

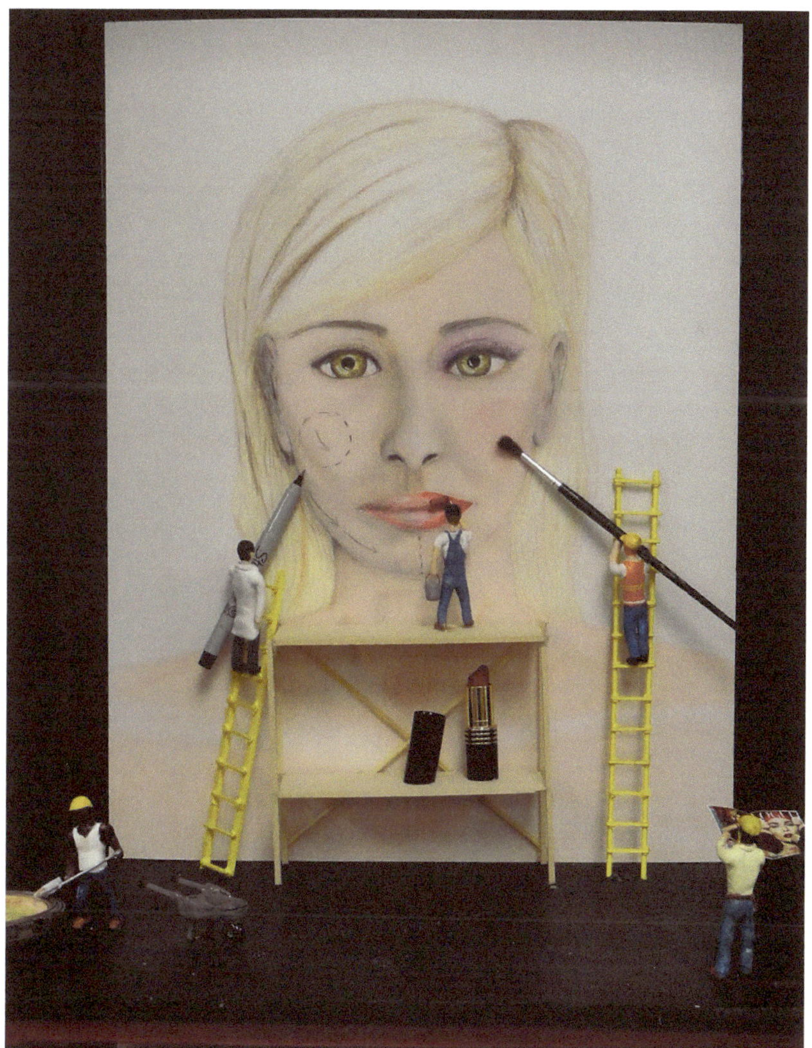

Studying proportion became important as the student worked on this project.

expressive. Many popular lesson plans found online today encourage students to learn techniques or experience a medium but leave out the personal connection. Though the technique being taught might be solid, the focus is on learning the "how to." Simplistic themes that might produce aesthetically pleasing results given the technique or medium run the risk of being shallow in meaning. Lesson plans that deny students the opportunity to present or represent a deeper, personal connection—to tell their own story—miss out on the richness and depth that a student can reveal in a work of art.

Morgan and the Butterfly

Artists often create art in order to express how they feel, explore thoughts they are having, or relate experiences they are going through. High school students are at a time in their lives when they could benefit from the opportunity to express their emotions, concerns, and even fears, through art. When given the chance, students will create works of art with remarkably deep personal meaning. Often, the stories released through their art have not been otherwise shared with classmates, let alone the teacher. One such story was revealed in an artwork titled Morgan and the Butterfly.

As Morgan relayed it to me, the face and use of color in her work reminded her of how she felt when she was diagnosed with Graves' disease the previous summer. This was news that she hadn't yet shared with the class or with me. Through her art, Morgan revealed that she felt awful and constantly sick. Morgan's plan for this picture was to have a faceless portrait in black and white with a blue butterfly on its neck. The butterfly represented the thyroid gland, which is called a butterfly because of its shape. Her use of light blue related to the support ribbon for Graves' disease. Morgan's artwork opened a dialogue about her disease within the class. Her ability to express herself through her work allowed her to finally feel comfortable sharing the challenges she was facing with other people.

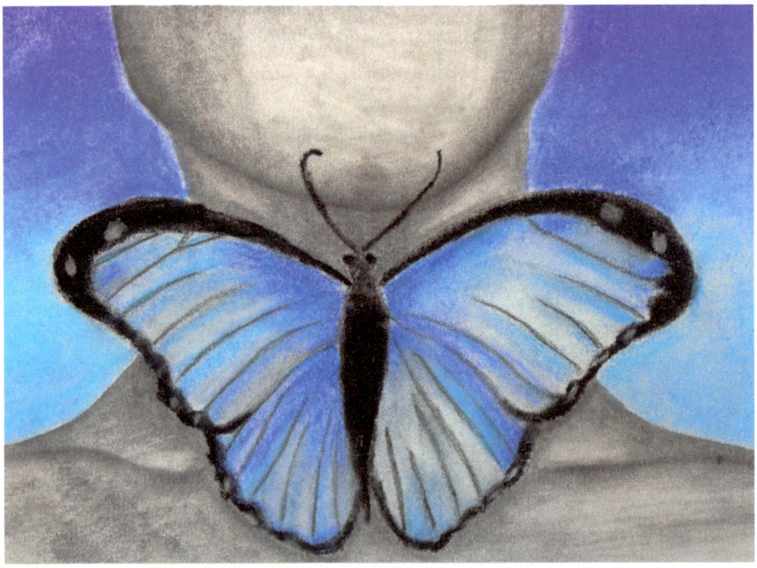

The Open Art Room and Authentic Assessment

Assessment can take place in every art room and for every art project. However, in the Open Art Room assessment may look and work differently than in a traditional teacher-directed class. This is because the criteria for creating the art and design process are much different.

What Is Authentic Assessment?

To begin with, student work designed in the Open Art Room doesn't come with an exemplar. In a teacher-directed class, completed teacher examples replace most of the ideation phase of the design process. Although students can make low-level decisions, for the most part, both teacher and student understand what the finished product is expected to be. In the Open Art Room, assessment is mandatory during the design phase of the Artistic Thinking Process. Decisions about the what, how, and why of the student project must be thoroughly worked out and communicated so that the student and teacher share an understanding of the goals and expectations before the creation phase begins.

The development phase also relies heavily on assessment. Within the teacher-directed model, most of the assessment that occurs during production is intended to keep the student on track. If the student's work is not meeting the expectations of the predetermined outcome, the teacher can assist the student by pointing out ways to accomplish the task. Assessment during production in the Open Art Room is necessary for any number of different reasons, including helping students realize what techniques or skills would be beneficial to the creation of their work, assisting students with problem solving, and recommending a potential medium.

Authentic Assessment vs. Predetermined Reflection

The last phase of the Artistic Thinking Process, reflection, also works differently in the Open Art Room. In a teacher-directed lesson, the student's work will usually be assessed based on a rubric containing specific criteria that further enforce the predetermined goals and outcomes of the lesson. Rubrics allow the teacher and student to measure which objectives were met and which were not. In the Open Art Room, where each project is as individual as the student, we do not use a rubric that is specific to each project. We will dig deeper into assessment and reflection in more detail in Chapter Four, but here are two kinds of rubrics that can be used: a high-level rubric that covers the unit topics and goals but is not based on predetermined criteria for student work; and a rubric that assesses students' application of the Artistic Thinking Process.

The Open Art Room and the National Core Art Standards

The Open Art Room connects to the 2014 National Core Visual Arts Standards in many ways. Both value student voice and the creation of personal meaning. Olivia Gude, a member of the standards writing panel, explains the standards this way: "The Next Generation Visual Arts standards are focused on student choice and on students making personally meaningful works of art and design. The standards set up scaffolding that builds students' capacities to make meaningful choices throughout the creative process." (NAEA *Art Education Journal*, January 2014).

The value hierarchy of these new national standards is shared by TAB philosophy and represents a shift in the nature of art education. It's no longer just about the product. In fact, Gude states, "It's not our job as art teachers to assess student artwork. That sounds shocking, I know, but if you reflect on it for a moment, you'll see that this statement is quite obviously true. It is our job as art teachers to assess student learning."

The basic setup and teaching structure of the Open Art Room meet many standards, since they tend to be ingrained in the teaching and learning process and are frequently present in daily instruction. Students generally meet these standards as they work through the process of making art. Moreover, we can further their learning by gearing formative and summative assessments toward these standards. For example, when thinking about *HS Proficient, VA:Cr1.1.Ia,* which asks students to start the creative process in different ways, we can assess what students know and are able to do by observing their work process and by asking questions like: What are some ways that you've found inspiration? What are some methods of planning that you have found are effective for you?

Generally speaking, all the standards can be readily met by including mini-lessons, Bootcamps, and critiques, or by incorporating them into unit topics.

For example, *HS Accomplished VA:Cr2.2.IIa,* which asks students to exhibit awareness of the ethics involved in creating art, could be addressed by teaching a short lesson on copyright, plagiarism, and fair use, then asking students to create artwork that adds meaning to another artist's work. See the lesson plan section for more examples.

National Standards in Practice

Standards	In Practice
HS Proficient, VA:Cr1.1.Ia	As part of every lesson, students learn and practice Artistic Thinking Process, applying a variety of processes for finding inspiration and designing artwork.
HS Proficient, VA:Cr1.2.Ia	Students select topics for art-making and follow the Artistic Thinking Process to work through their ideas.
HS Accomplished VA:Cr1.2.IIa	Students select materials and methods as well as plan artwork in every lesson.
HS Advanced, VA:Cr1.2.IIIa	Students select materials and methods as well as plan artwork in every lesson. Creating artwork with deeper meaning and working in series are frequent occurrences.
HS Proficient, VA:Cr2.1.Ia	Students learn and practice exploration of media when they work using key concepts of Artistic Thinking Process.
HS Accomplished, VA:Cr2.1.IIa	Students exemplify this standard as part of Open Art Room instruction.
HS Advanced, VA:Cr2.1.IIIa	All Open Art Room units include experimentation and planning. Students select personally meaningful content in every unit.
HS Advanced, VA:Cr3.1.IIIa	Students do this in every lesson as part of the Artistic Thinking Process.
HS Proficient, VA:Cn10.1.Ia	Students document the creative process through blogs, conferences, presentations, or portfolios.
HS Accomplished, VA:Cn10.1.IIa	Students engage in this work process as part of every unit.

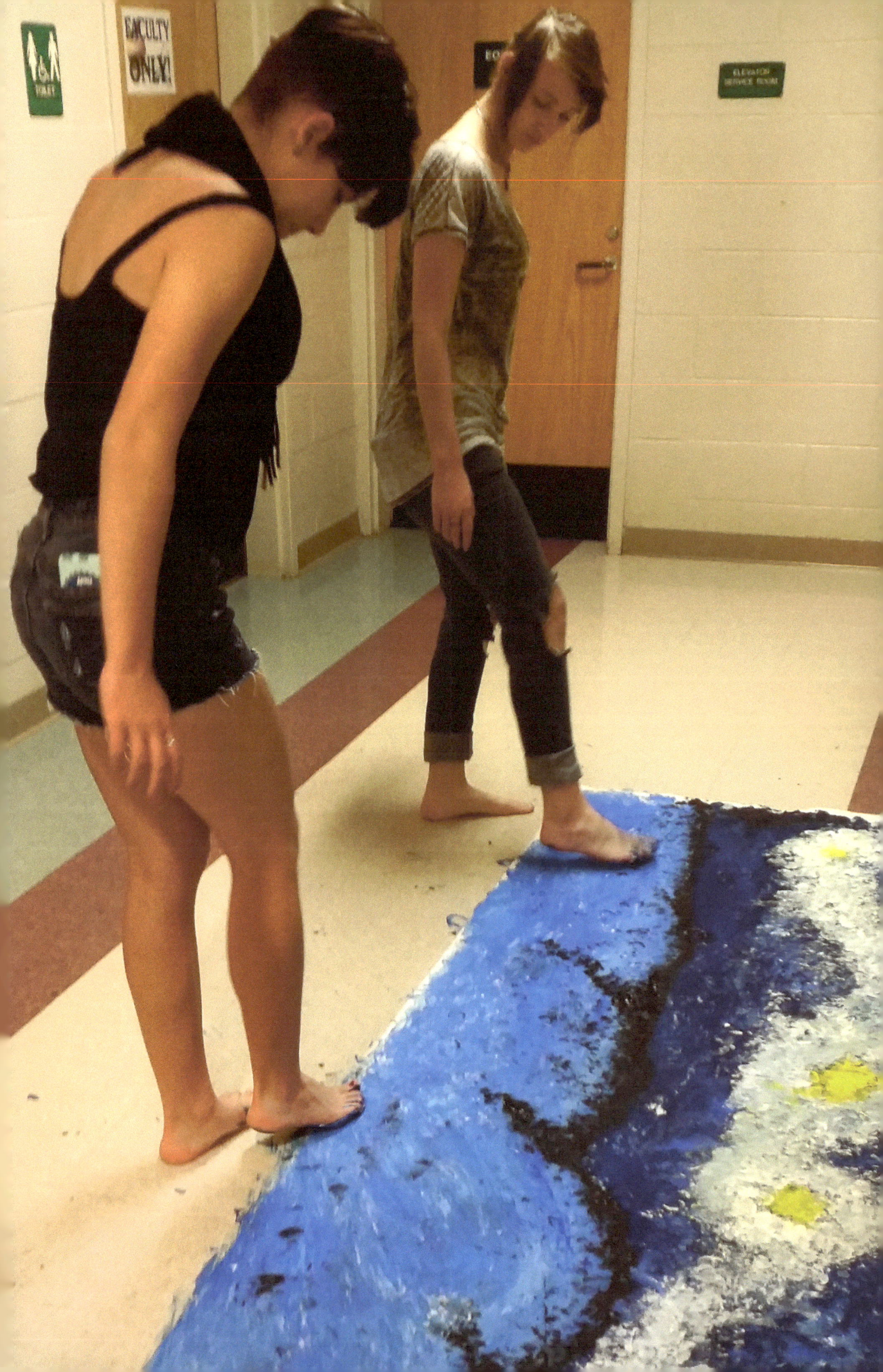
FACULTY ONLY!
ELEVATOR SERVICE ROOM

2 | Building the Framework

Implementing a new pedagogy can seem daunting, but it is quite feasible if you have the right structure in place. This chapter introduces the framework that makes the Open Art Room function, and discusses how to set up your classroom and how to build a collaborative culture that will make your classroom a productive learning environment.

The Three Pillars

The activities that students take part in during a typical visual arts class are often far removed from the making of actual art. In classrooms where the teacher determines the media, the subject matter, and the process of creating the work, the primary role of the student is to follow the steps set by the teacher, making only low-impact decisions that have little effect on the overall content or meaning of the work. Work produced this way is art-related, but fundamentally removed from actual art. The real artist in this scenario is the teacher. The Open Art Room seeks to shift the role of artist from the teacher to the student, taking the focus of instruction from producing art to empowering authentic art-making. We do this by shifting our priorities from a focus on skills that serve our own aesthetic goals to empowering students' individual art-making needs by teaching them to do the work of artists.

Teaching creative thinking has two parts: (1) organizing your curriculum to teach students to think and work like artists through the teaching of Artistic Behaviors, and (2) building student aptitudes to take ideas from conception to fruition through the Artistic Thinking Process. In this chapter, you will learn what Artistic Behaviors and Artistic Thinking Process are and how they fit together in day-to-day teaching. Next you will learn flexible instruction options for teaching technical art-making skills. Together, these three pillars—Artistic Behaviors, the Artistic Thinking Process, and Flexible Instruction—form the foundation of the Open Art Room.

Artistic Behaviors

The goal of making artists starts with requiring students to do the work that artists do, with the core belief that all individuals have something valuable to say. The role of the teacher in the Open Art Room is to create the situation in which art can be made and to coach and encourage students to think the way artists think. How do artists think? Well, they solve problems, communicate thoughts and feelings, and take stands on important issues. Artists manipulate ideas as they experiment with materials and explore the inner workings of their own creative powers and technical skills. The list, of course, is endless and it continues to grow as contemporary art evolves. Although the full range of Artistic Behaviors is a living thing that grows and changes, one thing is always consistent: the artistic concept. Always start instructional planning with the concepts that you want students to take away from the instruction. This is a common practice in the educational world and should be in art education as well, but too often we focus our teaching on how we want the artwork created during the lesson to look. The Open Art Room shifts the goal instruction from following steps to produce a set product to applying concepts to create personally meaningful art.

Artistic Behaviors are the Open Art Room's answer to the essential question: What do you want your students to know and be able to do? They provide the direction and content for our units of study, with the end goal of building students who are self-directed artists. Units of study are organized around specific artistic behaviors and use scaffolded learning experiences to help students understand complex and challenging concepts. Introduc-

Examples of Artistic Behaviors

- Artists Develop Skills
- Artists Reflect
- Artists Solve Problems
- Artists Take Risks
- Artists Create Original Art
- Artists Communicate
- Artists Advocate
- Artists Curate
- Artists Take a Stand

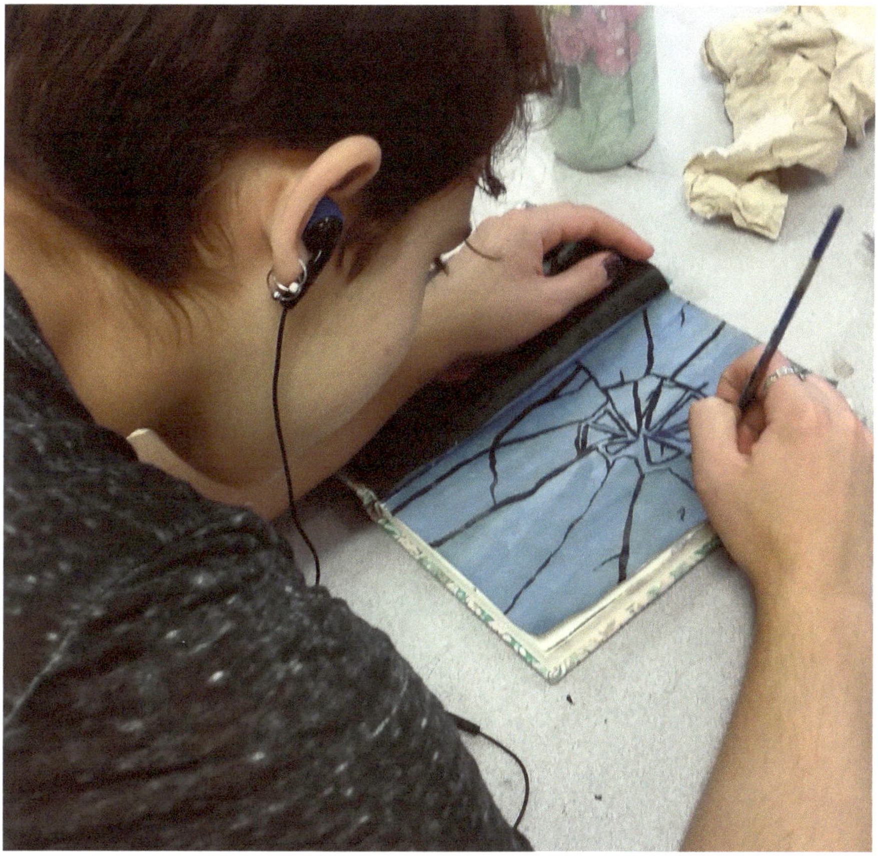

Using a sketchbook to work through ideas.

tory experiences, in the form of short projects or mini-lessons, scaffold student understanding of concepts and may also introduce related media or techniques. Art-making skills and the Artistic Thinking Process—our framework for creative decision making—are taught simultaneously with the goal of bringing all students to a place where they can make choices that are independent and intentional. After this base of knowledge has been established, units can end with open-ended, challenging projects where students are asked to apply new learning.

Teaching from the vantage point of Artistic Behaviors is a paradigm shift for both teachers and students. Planning instruction based on the "finished product" becomes a thing of the past, as does focusing mainly on skills and media. Instead, instruction is driven by the concepts students will learn. Artistic Behaviors exemplify the practices of thinking and working like artists, and are the backbone of the Open Art Room. These practices are mutually reinforcing throughout the curriculum, while students develop skills with media, planning, problem-solving, idea generation, and the ability to reflect.

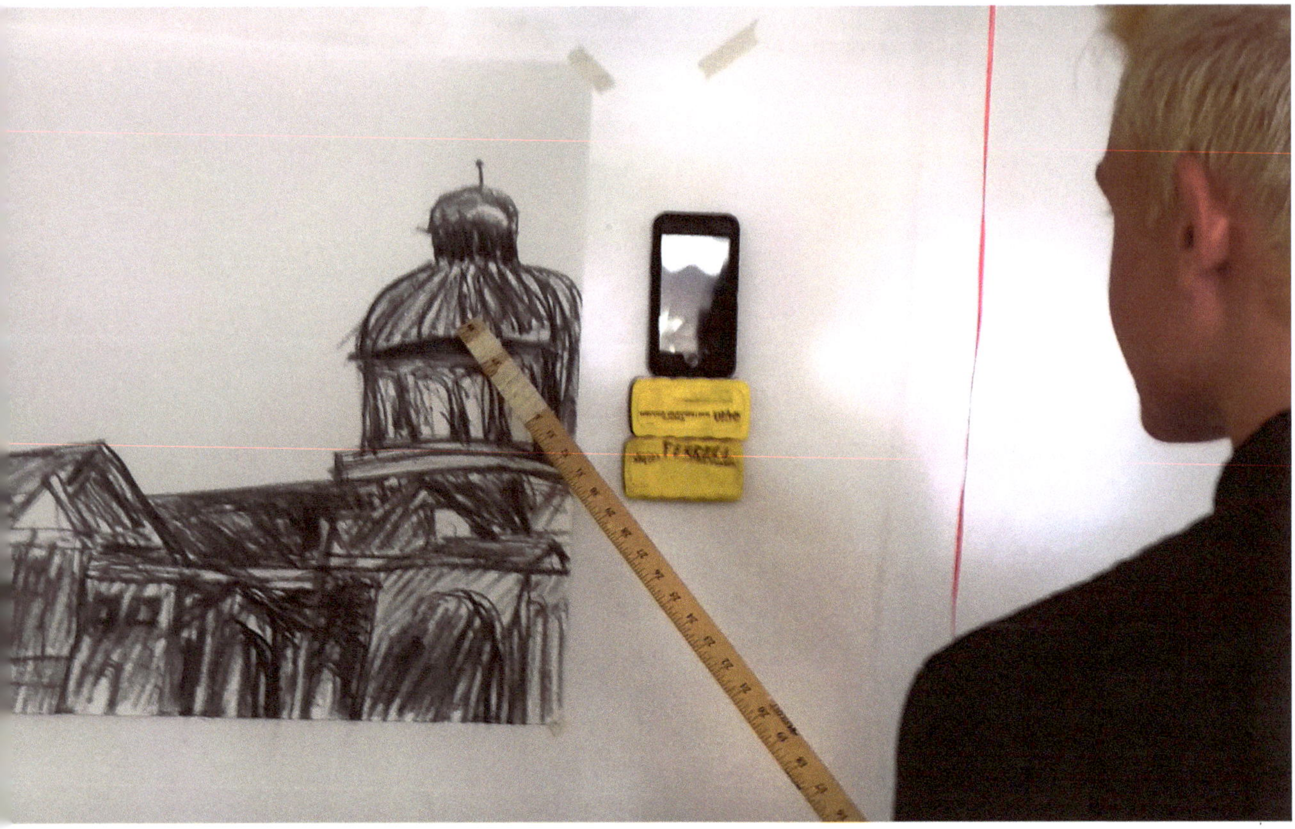

orks with a drawing tool he created as part of Artists Solve Problems (p. 185).

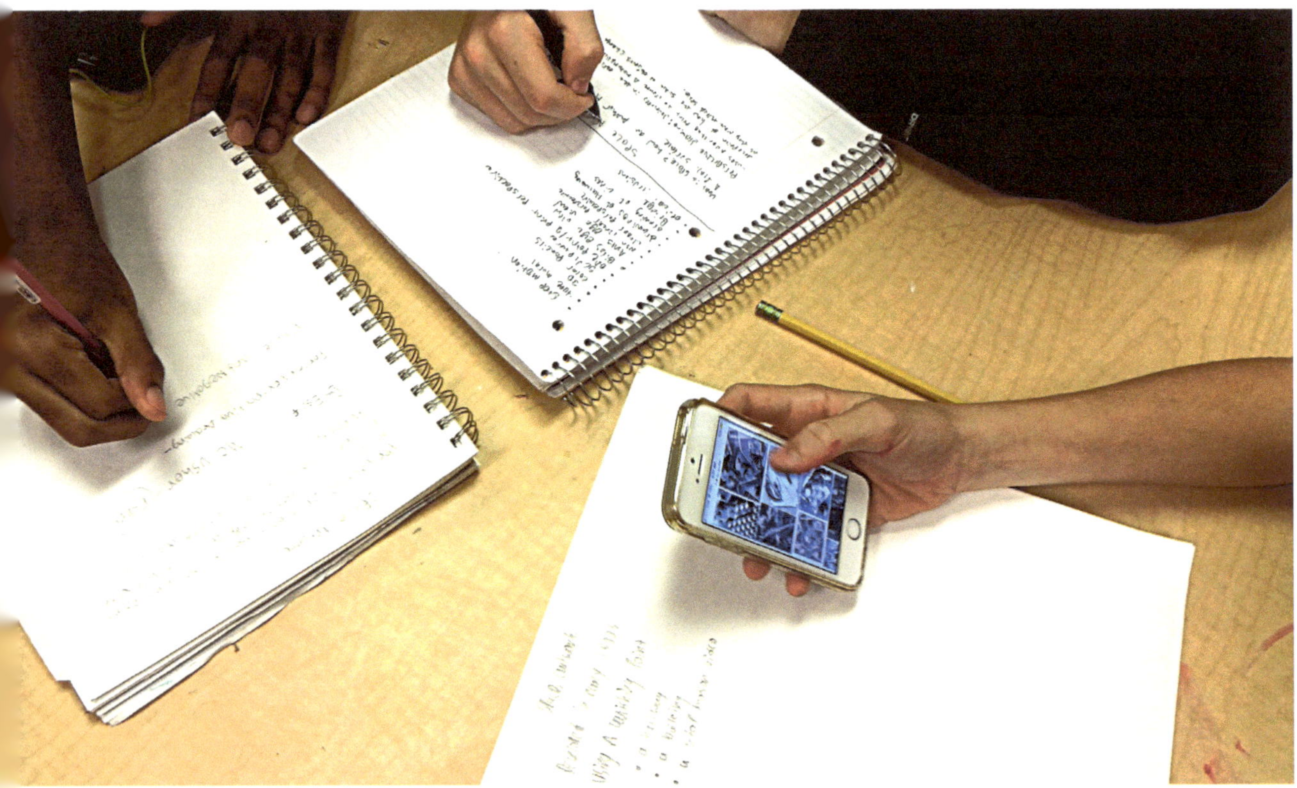

rainstorm to begin designing work.

Artistic Thinking Process

The focus of art education should be to teach students to think creativity. To facilitate this, the teacher's role is that of a guide. We provide access to the tools needed to express ideas visually, and through this develop students' skills with media, planning, problem-solving, idea generation, and the ability to reflect. We believe that creative thinking is a learned set of skills that can be taught directly and intentionally by imparting a range of strategies to use and the understanding to apply them thoughtfully. Artistic Thinking Process is the framework we use to teach these skills.

Artistic Thinking Process is both a lesson structure and a tool for students to use. It consists of four stages: inspiration, design, creation, and reflection/presentation. These stages break down the creative process in a way that is teachable and easy to follow. While students are learning the process, teachers introduce and demonstrate a variety of methods in each stage. As students become more familiar with design process options, they build creative aptitude and become increasingly able to select the methods that work best for them.

Inspiration. The stage where ideas are born is often the most challenging for students who haven't had the responsibility of deciding what to make before. Inspiration can come from many different sources: themes, media, art-making processes, personal experiences, and guiding questions. The teacher's role is to teach idea generation from multiple approaches, slowly releasing responsibility over to students as they grow in capability and comfort. In the Open Art Room, this is done in every lesson and unit through the design section of the Artistic Thinking Process. Then, when students have developed the skill set needed to find their own inspirations, the job of the teacher shifts to providing support and feedback.

Development. In this stage, ideas are thought through and refined. It is the most important section in terms of the success of the final piece, but it's also the section students typically want to skip, either because they want to dive right into an exciting idea or because they don't want to put forth the extra effort this stage requires. However, this stage is the most important for personal growth and the success of the final product because it asks kids to, in the words of Studio Habits of Mind, "Stretch and Explore." Development can involve sketching, but it's so much more: experimenting with materials or techniques, mind mapping, working ideas out in a visual journal, and making a model are all helpful design methods. The teacher's role is to teach an array of design techniques, then support students as they select which ones to use to develop their ideas.

Creation. Work is created and refined here. This stage is the most familiar to students who have taken previous art classes. In this stage, the teacher supports the student with frequent check-ins and meaningful feedback.

Reflection/Presentation. The learning experience ends with reflection and sharing work. This may include blog posts, student-teacher conferences, and presentations and critiques with small groups or the whole class. This stage also serves as a celebration of the learning that's just happened.

Artistic Thinking Process

Inspiration
Themes—Media—Process—Experience
Guiding Questions—New Skills

Development
Plan—Research—Sketch—List
Experiment—Find Resource Images
Visual Journal—Mind Map
Model—Brainstorm, Practice, Demonstration

Creation
Produce Work—Reflect—Revise —Analyze, Improve—Re-think

Reflection & Presentation
Blog—Critique—Discuss—Revise
Present—Respond

Flexible Instruction

Art is a skill-based discipline. Students need to learn and refine and apply a range of techniques and processes. A base of knowledge is a key element in providing successful choice; when we ask students to make decisions, they must have enough information to make informed choices. However, if we spend too much time on technique, we minimize our ability to offer choice. The key is to be thoughtful and concise when teaching, offer key information, and look for ways to shorten the time it takes to acquire new skills.

Bootcamps. Bootcamps are intense, focused periods of instruction that are used for teaching skills and techniques to whole classes. Bootcamps are designed to create a foundation of knowledge for beginning classes. Compared to the rest of Open Art Room instruction, they are very teacher-directed. The goal is to develop specific skills or understandings, which are directly taught, then practiced, in a short timeframe. Students are often given activities to complete that ask them to follow steps and recall knowledge, such as creating a value scale or practicing a painting technique. These tasks are never disguised as projects. Instead, they focus directly on learning and practicing new abilities. Neatness and aesthetic appeal are not the goals here. Students know up front that activities done in Bootcamps are exercises designed to teach skills. Once new learning has been acquired, students have the knowledge to make informed choices when designing artwork.

The Gradual Release of Responsibility Model, developed by Pearson and Gallagher in 1983, is an effective teaching tool that ensures that Bootcamps are short and effective learning experiences for students. It starts with a direct, whole-group lesson where the teacher shows the students a new skill or technique. Next comes guided practice, where students try the skill as it was modeled, with the teacher offering help and support. The third piece involves students applying the new knowledge in collaborative groups, which requires them to talk about the new information together as they work to apply it. Finally, students are asked to use their new skills independently. The first three steps can be done in one or two classes, with the focus on learning something new, not on making a finished image. Independent practice can be more student-directed, with students being given some choice in how they will apply what they have just learned.

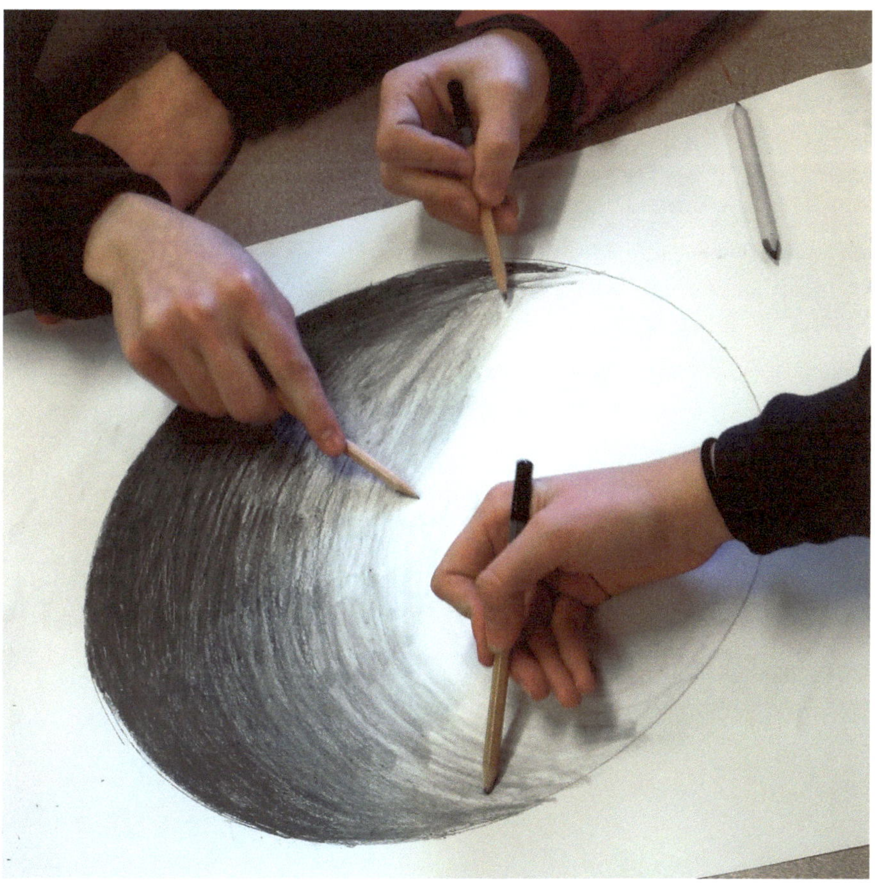

Group work learning about value during drawing bootcamp (p. 142).

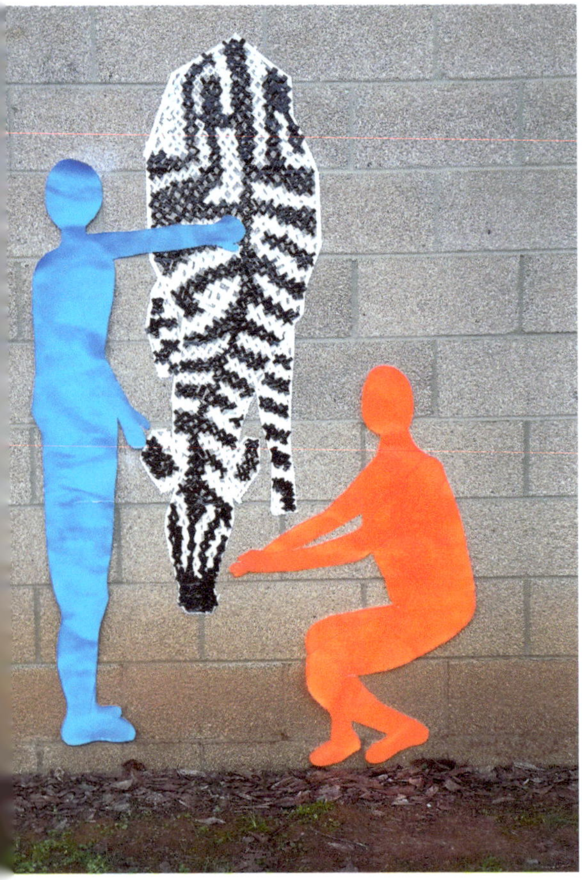

ive tape mural.

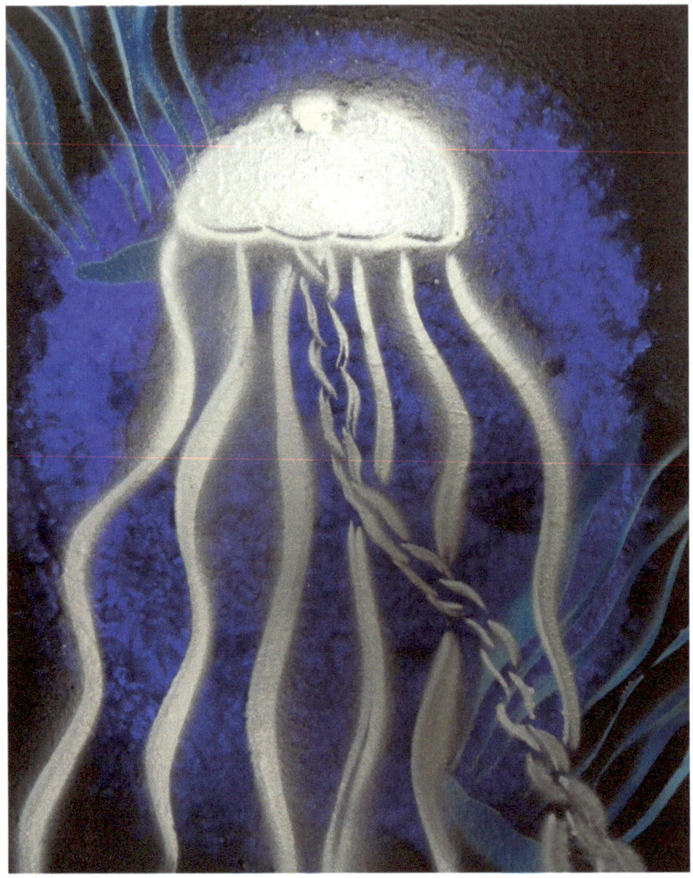

Exploring stencils and spray paint.

Mini-Lessons. Mini-lessons are short lessons that are focused on developing skills. They assume students have the foundational working knowledge of basic art-making materials and seek to build on that knowledge. They can be required or optional. For example, a short lesson on how to draw eyes with charcoal or a review of one-point perspective might be offered at the start of class.

Demonstrations. Demonstrations are requested by students or offered as a response to an observed student need. They could be offered to address skill deficits that come up during open-ended lessons or as a challenge for advanced students. For example, if one student is interested in screen printing, the teacher would demonstrate the techniques and process to all interested students. Teachers might offer a review of proportion for a student who is struggling with figure drawing.

Teaching Exploration with a Chalk Pastel Mini-Lesson

Materials: chalk pastels, construction paper, chart with examples of technique, examples of Zaria Forman's work and/or a video of her TED Talk.

Teacher Input: Start by sharing some key attributes of chalk pastels: they blend, they layer, they can be very messy. Next, quickly demonstrate a selection of techniques supported by a chart of techniques that students can use as a reference. Tell students that amazing art can be made with chalk and show examples or video of Zaria Forman's large-scale work.

Next, tell students that experimenting is a great way to figure out how to work with materials. Tell them to try some of the techniques you demonstrated. They can clean up and go to their work in progress when they finish or continue working with the pastels.

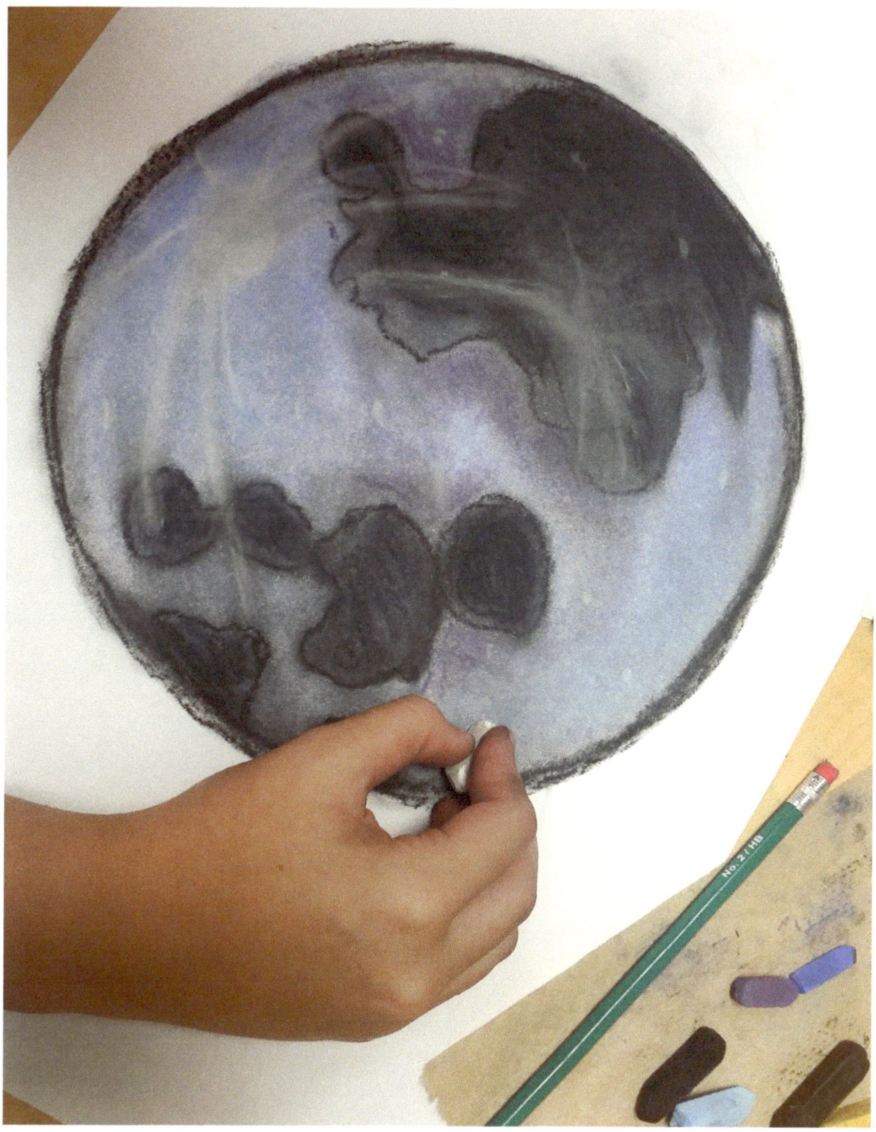

Cassie experiments with chalk pastel.

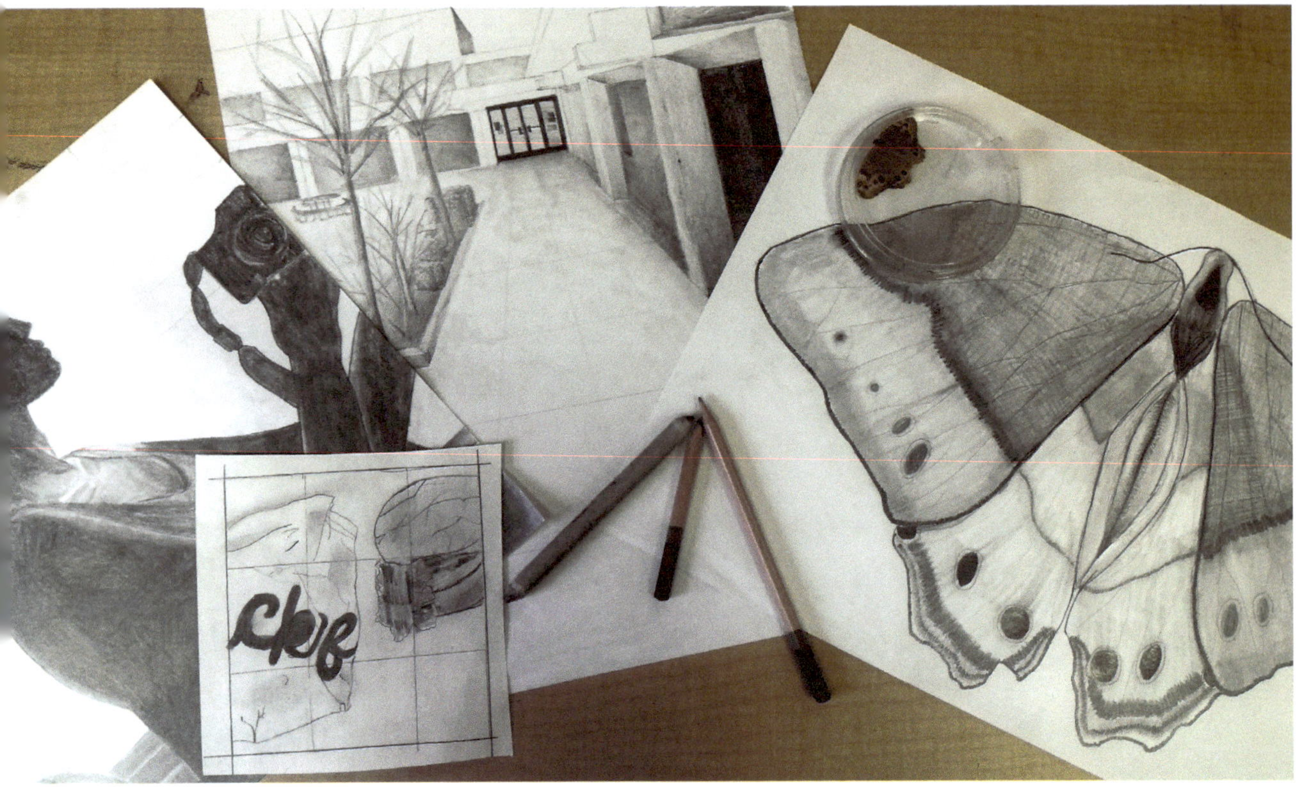

ork from drawing bootcamp (p. 142).

Teaching Skills Through Flexible Instruction

	Group Size	Participation	Goal
Bootcamp	Whole class	Required listening and application	Provide foundational knowledge
Mini-Lesson	Small group or whole class	Required listening, application optional, or optional listening	Develop skills
Demonstration	Individual or small group	Offered upon request	Meet individual learning needs

Classroom Atmosphere

Classroom atmosphere is important because it sets the stage for learning. From how students are welcomed in the door to how supplies are displayed, the classroom culture and organization of your classroom is communicating what you value as a teacher to your students, so it's essential to think about what you want them to say. The physical attributes of the space should support your instructional goals and the culture you create should support mutual respect, collaboration, and divergent thinking.

Setup and Organization

The setup and physical structure of the Open Art Room is designed to support learning by providing easy access to supplies and information. Supplies need to be easy to find and use. Ours are kept on open shelves and organized by type. All the supplies needed for painting are stored in one area, drawing supplies in another. Materials can be stored in clear bins so the content is easily visible. Each bin is labeled. Ideally, students should be able to locate any item they need independently, quickly, and easily.

When students are responsible for getting out, cleaning up, and putting away a large variety of materials on a typical day, support systems are needed to make sure the classroom stays organized. This is true even for upper-level students. Anchor charts are visuals that depict information in text and images. They are helpful for any procedure that can be difficult to remember, such as setting up a palette for acrylic paint or the supplies needed to make a monoprint. Anchor charts should reiterate procedures that have been previously taught. Using them saves valuable class time that might be wasted answering repetitive questions and helps students get to work quickly. Anchor charts don't have to be physical. QR codes that link to a YouTube video about using materials can be easily created, posted, and accessed by any student with a smartphone.

Ordering supplies for an Open Art Room can seem very daunting. You wonder how much of each material students will use. The truth is that you can't know for sure, but it doesn't matter as much as you might think. You are training your students to think creatively. If you run out of any material, challenge the students to problem solve. It's a good learning opportunity. Of course, you don't want to run out of *everything*, so here are some things to think about when ordering supplies.

It's important to keep in mind that the Open Art Room does not rely on any specific physical setup or supply list. In fact, the teaching methods described here were developed in a trailer with no sink and intermittent air conditioning. Your setup as an art teacher depends on two things: your available resources and the needs of your students. When planning seating arrangements and placing supplies, ask yourself:

- How can I best support collaboration?
- How can I arrange this space so traffic flows easily?
- How can I make it easy for students to access materials?
- What might make it easier to find supplies quickly and put them away in the correct place?
- What are common questions students have about materials, and what visuals can I create that will address those needs?

Supply Ordering and Gathering Checklist

- What Bootcamps do you plan to do? Order enough for each student to complete the exercise two to three times. They will be familiar with these materials and pick them more often.
- What materials do you plan to offer as choices? Order enough for at least half of your students to use.
- What free supplies can you access and offer? Create a bin of found objects for sculptures. Acquire cardboard to be used for 3D construction, cut into stencils, and spray-painted on. Ask your school library/media center to send you any books that they take out of circulation. Remember, you won't need an entire class set to offer a choice.
- Identify potential sources for donations or grants. Donors Choose is an excellent resource, as well as your school's PTA. Check with local businesses, such as hardware stores or frame shops, to see if they provide grants or donations to local schools.
- Ask parents for things they might want to get rid of anyway. Include a short list of materials you would love to see donated in the parent letter or course syllabus that gets sent home at the beginning of the year. If you have a class website or blog, post it there as well. Some ideas are house paint, wood scraps, old books, and used toys.

Classroom Culture

How do you want your classroom to look and feel to students? Deciding this is necessary for creating an intentional classroom culture. A key aspect of the Open Art Room is a collaborative culture. When students work together, learning is compounded as they share ideas, discuss concepts, and see multiple points of view. When students work together, it leads to more open-minded solutions. The first day of school is a powerful time to set the expectation for group work. What if, instead of going over classroom rules that, honestly, most students will tune out anyway, you played a game?

Group planning and critique (addressed in Chapter 3, Chapter 4, and Lesson Plans) are two other important elements of classroom culture in the Open Art Room. When students work together, learning time is compressed because ideas are shared and concepts are talked through, correcting misunderstandings quickly. Groups are smarter than individuals and are important learning tools, so it's important to establish that students will work together often and treat one another with respect. The type of collaborative culture this establishes will help you create a dynamic learning culture where ideas are shared and respected.

The Art Game

Goal: Introduce the structure of the Open Art Room, show where key materials are located, break the ice and have fun.

Materials: Large-scale poster or drawing paper, 2D supplies (markers, paint, crayons, colored pencil, collage materials), scissors and adhesives.

Introduction: Welcome! Tomorrow we will go over the syllabus. Today we are playing the Art Game. I've designed this game to give you a preview of how this class will work. You will be expected to develop your own ideas in this class using the Artistic Thinking Process (show visual). You will also often be expected to work in groups. Plan on working with everyone in the class at some point.

Place students into groups of four or allow students to choose their own groups.

Art Game Rules and Process:

1. Pick a theme. This will be the group's inspiration for the game. Have each group pick a theme from the following list: Freedom, Beauty, Pride, Peace, Nature, Love, Danger.
2. Next, have groups list five symbols that could represent their theme.
3. Share the rules of the game and start to play!

How It Works:

- You and your team have to illustrate the word you've chosen without using any of the five symbols you listed.
- Teams will start by planning and selecting supplies. (Show where the supplies that they can use are located.)
- Artwork needs to clearly communicate the theme you selected and be high-quality and large enough to be visible from far away.
- When time is up, your group will present your work to the class.

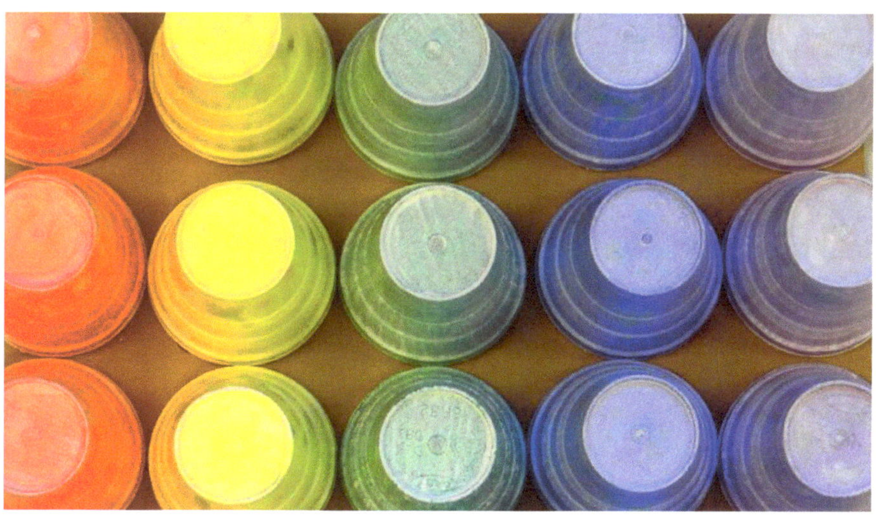

Response to the theme "pride" during the Art Game.

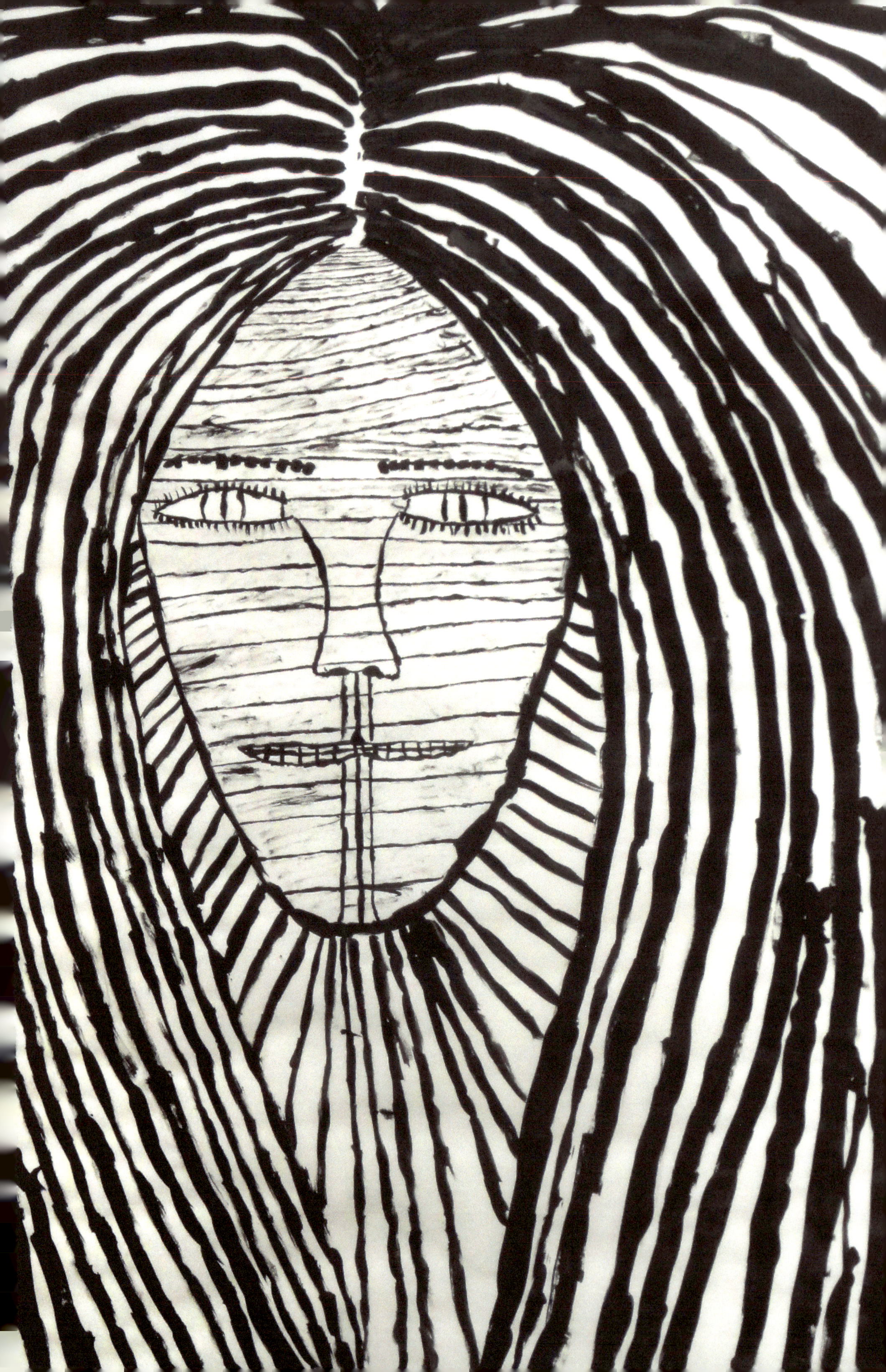

PART TWO | Implementation

This section of the book provides hands-on instructional ideas for implementing choice in secondary level (grades 6–12) art classes. It is divided into three parts: beginner, intermediate, and advanced. These categories are not based on grade level or student ability, but rather on the levels of both the teacher's and the students' prior experience with choice. The beginner level provides a model for introducing limited choices in both materials and ideation; the advanced level describes several full-choice methods; and the intermediate falls in between.

It is up to you to decide which level of choice is best for your students. However, if you are not certain where to begin, we recommend starting with the beginner level and limited choices. As students grow, become more decisive, and take ownership of their creative decisions, you can move up to the next level of choice.

The Overarching Lesson Plan Objectives

No matter which level of choice a class begins with, three overarching lesson plan objectives apply. When teaching a unit, the level of choice isn't as important as accomplishing the objectives. The objectives are what the teacher, and ultimately the student, will want to accomplish through the class. The overarching lesson plan objectives are: Students Make Decisions, Students Create in Their Voice, and Students Engage in the Process.

Students Make Decisions

Empowering students to make their own choices should be built into each unit in an Open Art Room class. Even at the beginner level, where choices are limited to only a few, it should be the student who makes the choices regarding the creation of art. Furthermore, students need to recognize the value of their own ideas. The selection process should not be simply a matter of deciding between two or three choices, but rather students should base their decisions on which choice will work best for their desired outcome.

Students Create in Their Voice

When creating art, a student should process external information, reconfigure this information in the mind, and then execute a new creation based on this process. This is how artists create art that tells a story, speak visually in their own words, and become their own artists. Units developed in the Open Art Room need to be structured to facilitate and encourage this process. There are occasions, such as exercises and mini-lessons, when students will process information without necessarily incorporating their own voices. However, summative projects should always allow for the students' individual voices to be reflected in their art.

Students Engage in the Process

Mistakes and failure are integral parts of learning. Therefore, play, experimentation, and trial and error should all be encouraged. As art teachers, our natural tendency is to instruct the student as to what will work and what will not. In an Open Art Room, students will come up with ideas they believe will address certain issues they encounter. It is in their best interest to allow them to try their ideas and discover for themselves if the results are the desired outcome or not. Many times these types of experiments result in other discoveries, even if they do not return the original desired results.

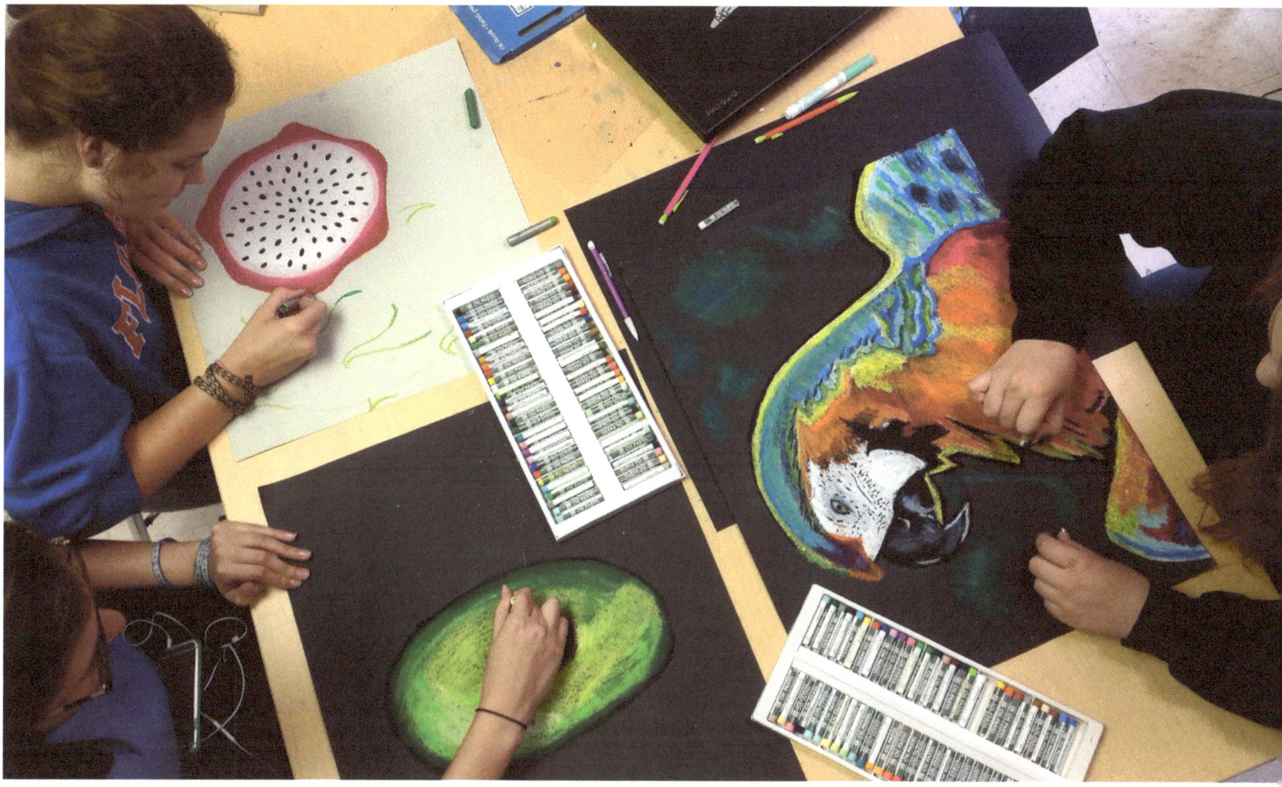

Experimenting with oil pastel.

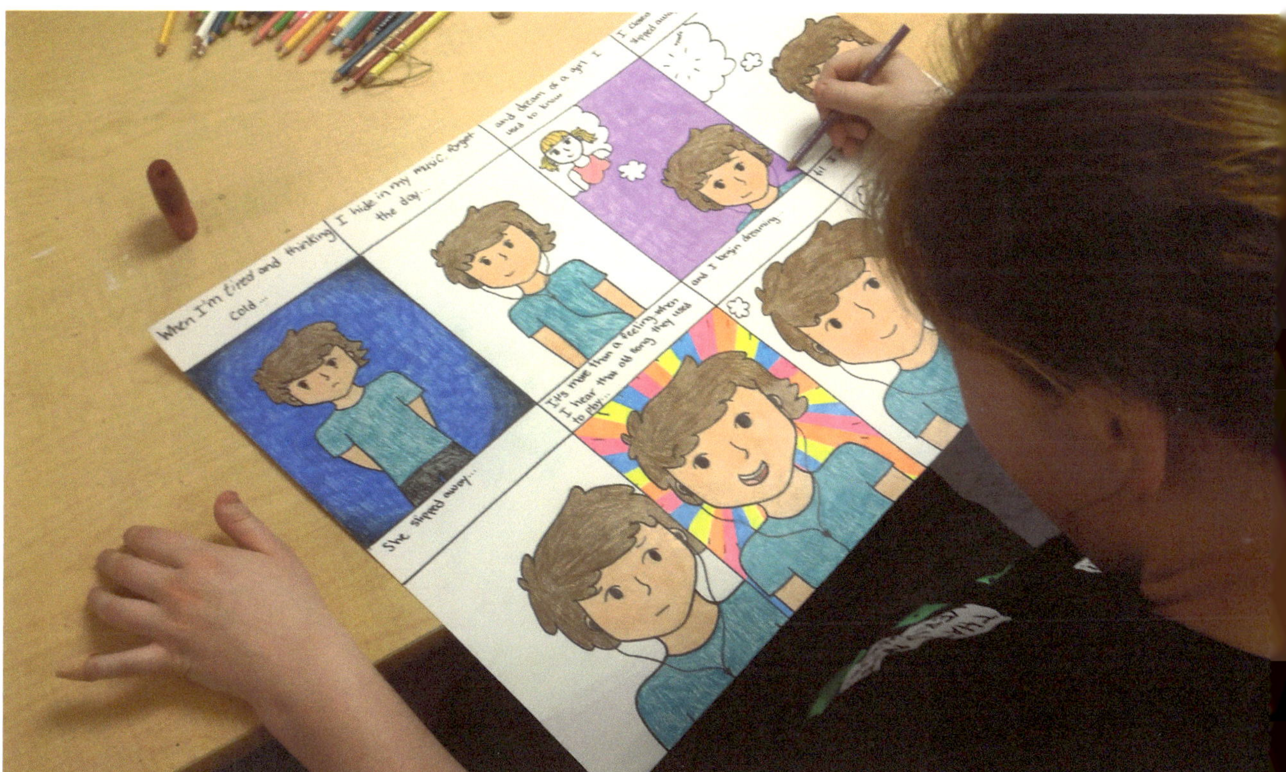

Carmel works on a cartoon as part of Artists Tell Stories.

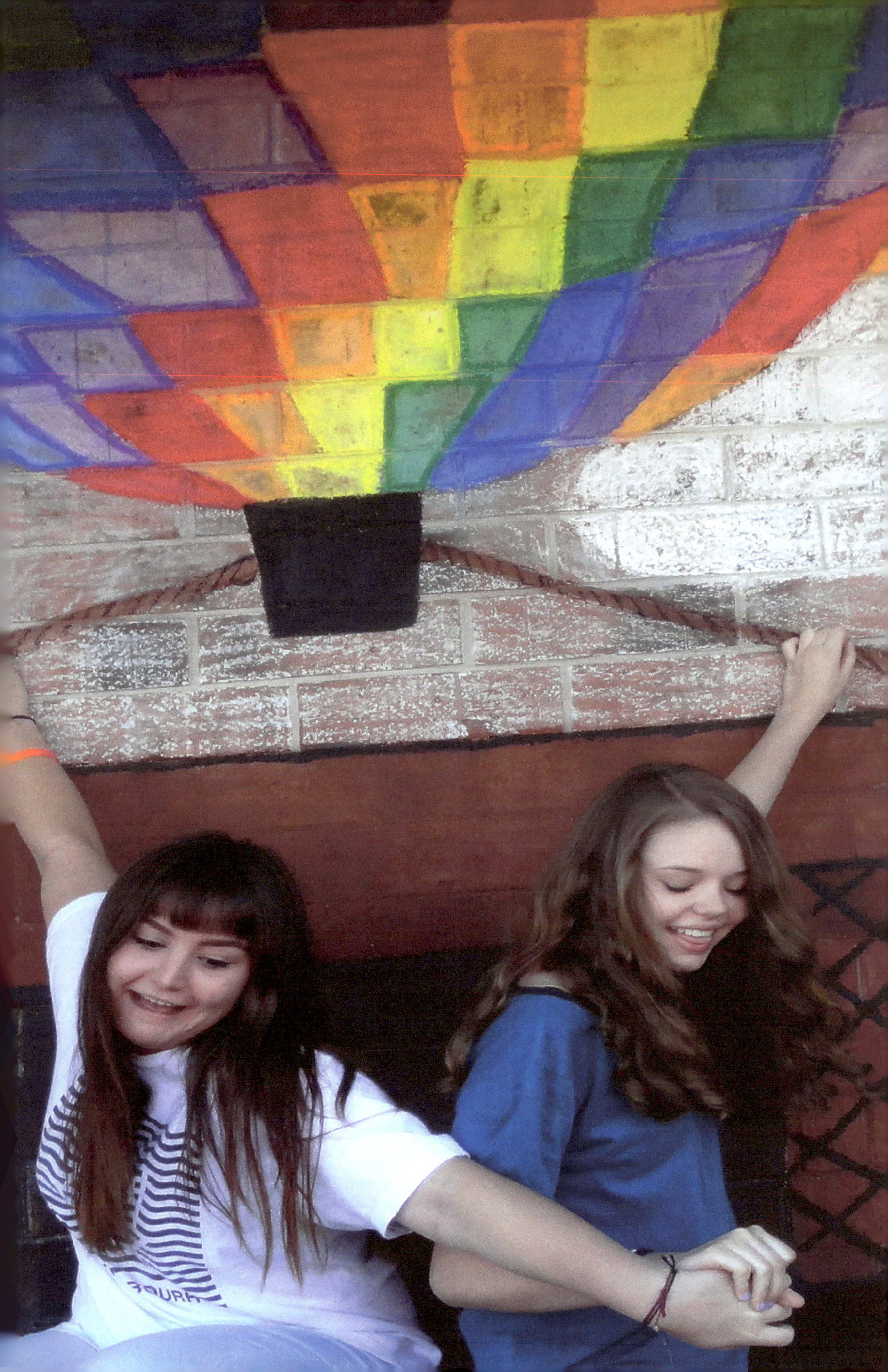

3 | Implementing Choice at the Beginning Level

Glinda, the Good Witch, in *The Wizard of Oz*, had it right when she explained to Dorothy that "It's always best to start at the beginning." This beginning is twofold. If the teacher is new to choice-based teaching, then the students will be new as well. It's important to keep in mind that this is a learning process for both teacher and the students.

Even the teacher who has spent considerable time planning a choice-based curriculum will run into issues with students if the concept is rolled out too quickly. While some students will readily adapt to choice, others will have trouble. Students who are accustomed to teacher-directed lessons may have a hard time adapting to making decisions on their own. They are expecting step-by-step instructions and will want to know what you expect them to do next. By starting slowly, by asking students to make decisions that contain limited choices, the teacher can reduce the more rigid students' frustration.

If you have ever ordered from a diner menu, you will understand the concept. There seems to be no end to the amount of different foods you can order at a diner. Diners serve breakfast, lunch, and dinner no matter the time of day. You can order scrambled eggs with a side of fries and beer at three in the morning or three in the afternoon. While such a wide variety of choices might be exciting to some people, others can easily feel overwhelmed. There is just too much to choose from.

Many restaurant owners have come to understand this and—in a move beneficial to both the restaurant and the customer—have cut back on the number of items offered on their menu. The customer is presented with a selection of items that are different enough from each other yet are of a similar culinary taste. By limiting the selection, the restaurant has actually provided a more comfortable dining experience. In order to be successful when first implementing a choice-based program, the art teacher can borrow this same menu reduction tactic.

There are several areas of a lesson plan where choices can be increased or limited depending on the needs of the class. These include limiting themes, media, and techniques, or any combination of the three.

First-round projects should involve very limited choices. Each consecutive project afterwards will have fewer and fewer limitations. Remember, the goal is to ultimately empower students to make their own choices

Limited Choice Using Themes

One method for introducing students to the concept of choice in an Open Art Room is through the use of themes. Themes can be used by presenting the student with a question or topic to inspire thought. The student considers the theme and then generates a series of possible solutions. From these possibilities, the student selects a final idea for his or her project.

Themes make an excellent starting point due to the flexibility of interpretation within a given theme. This flexibility can be modulated by either selecting concrete themes that tend to limit interpretation or by selecting abstract themes that are more open to different interpretations.

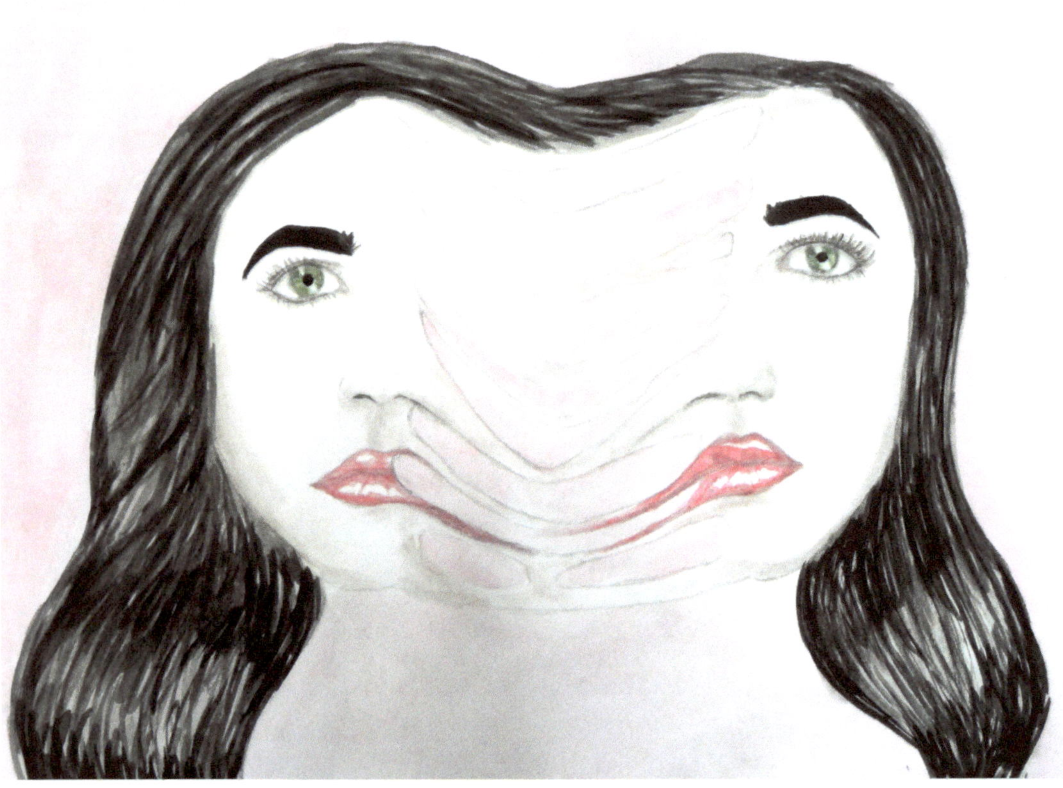

Student solution for the theme "Sticky Situation."

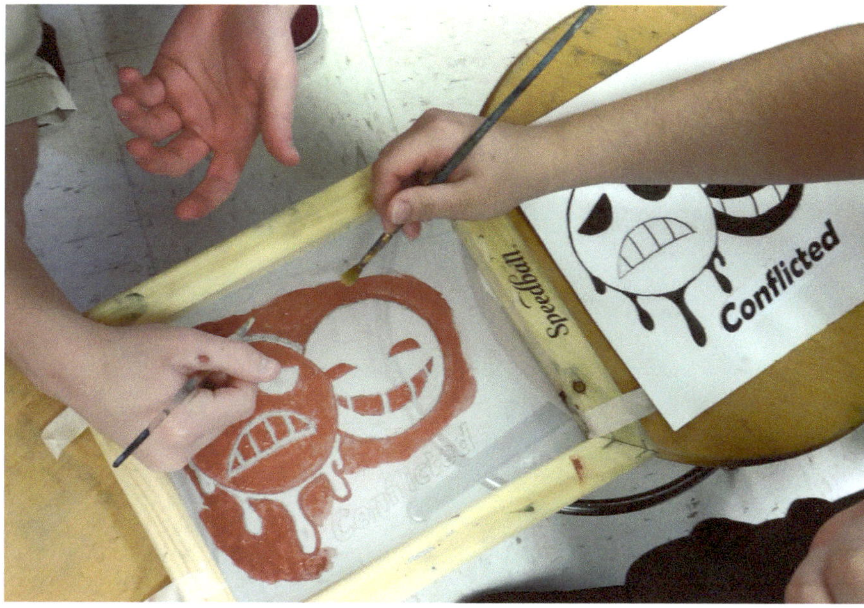

Alex's response to a portrait assignment.

Concrete themes are descriptive, which makes ideation easier for students who may be new to the concept of developing their own ideas. Concrete themes might be presented as incomplete questions that the student has to answer.

Examples include:

1. What's inside the room?
2. What happened to the garden?
3. Why did he ride the bus?

Abstract themes are less concrete and more open-ended, and are typically considered more appropriate for students who are already accustomed to word-based idea generation.

Examples include:

1. Play
2. Transformation
3. Identity

Since the purpose of themes is to introduce students to choice, it is important that the teacher move the students through the spectrum from concrete to abstract. Each theme presented should be progressively less and less restrictive with more and more possible interpretations. The next step would be to present a choice of themes. The ultimate goal is to have the students develop their own themes either through asking essential questions or exploring big ideas. (See Chapter 8 for examples.)

A Consideration When Using Themes

Themes have gained popularity with art teachers in recent years, in part due to their use by contemporary artists and by being promoted by organizations such as Art21. While it is true that contemporary artists explore themes, artists are rarely told what theme they should explore. More often, artists consider what their interests and concerns are, and decide what theme they will explore from there.

While themes do have a place in transitioning from teacher-directed to a more choice-based class, providing the theme for a class would be considered low level on the choice spectrum. When we as art teachers provide the theme, we have decided for students what they should be interested in and what they should explore. While it may be true that students will create visual responses to a provided theme, they will very likely be doing so because they are trying to satisfy an assignment, and not because they are exploring what they are interested in.

Beginning level teachers should use themes as a means of progressing towards a richer choice-based curriculum. However, as the students develop in their abilities to address choices, alternative methods of handling themes should be considered. Offering multiple themes to select from is one method for providing more options for student voice. Enabling students to consider issues and concerns that lead to the development of their own themes should be the ultimate goal.

Limited Choice Using Media

The traditional approach to presenting materials to an art class is to offer one medium at a time per project. However, this method is necessary only if the objective is to teach a particular technique using that material. In a choice-based class, where the objective is broader in scope, several different media could be offered simultaneously to cover the objective. In an advanced choice-based classroom, it is possible for every student to be working in a different medium. However, for students or teachers new to the choice-based approach, such diversity is not advisable. Limiting the amount of choices by introducing materials slowly will assure that students and teacher are not overwhelmed.

Combining or Matching Media

An effective method for offering choice in materials at a pace that can be digested in reasonable bites is by pairing media. By presenting media for an assignment in pairs, the teacher offers the student a range of choices

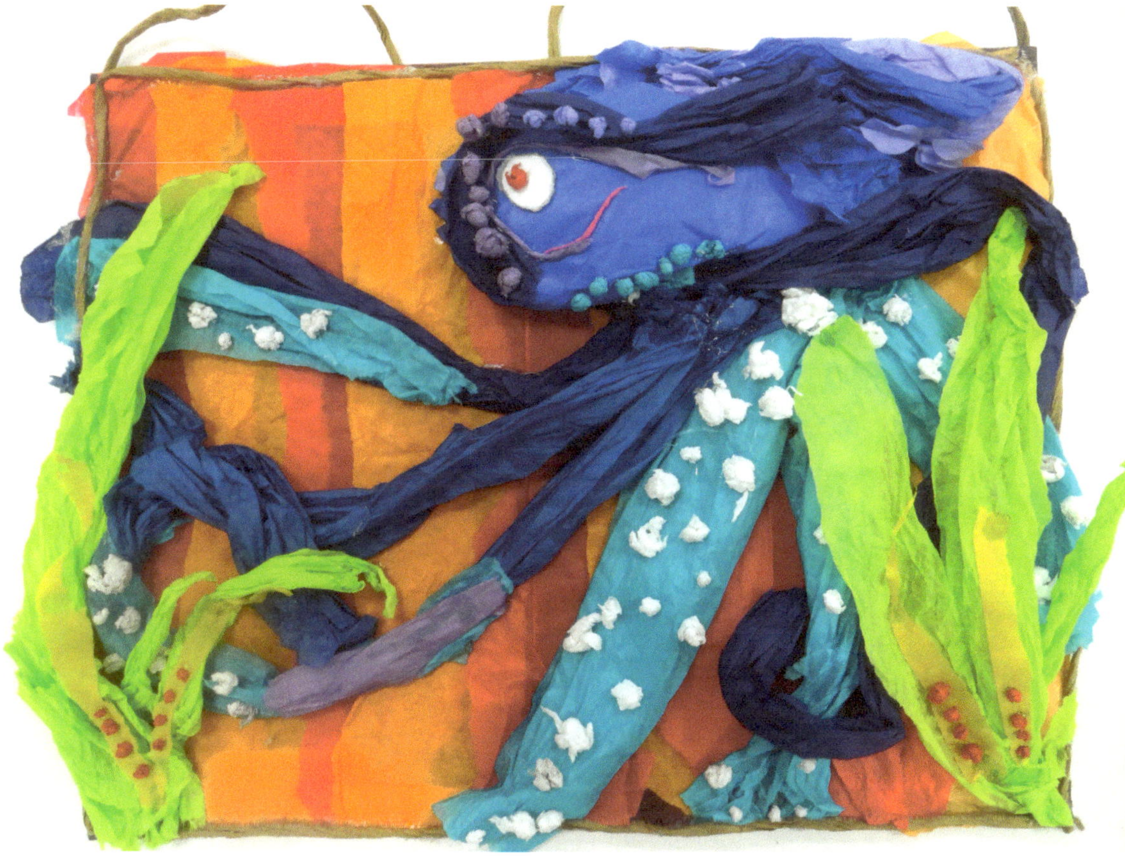

As part of the unit Artists Solve Problems, the student recreated his own painting limiting himself to tissue paper (p. 185).

of materials with properties that can readily be compared and contrasted. For example, a teacher might start the year with an assignment that is to be accomplished in black and white. The students would then be offered the choice of completing the assignment using either pencil, charcoal, or pen and ink. There are advantages to limiting the alternatives; for instance, in this example, all three implements are capable of producing high contrast in black and white, thus affording students the opportunity to evaluate their performance across a consistent range. Furthermore, these three media share techniques in common, such as blending or cross-hatching to achieve different values. Limited choice in media is a simple, practical way of introducing choice into the classroom.

Examples of Possible Media Groupings:

- Pencil, charcoal, pen and ink
- Colored pencil, marker, oil pastels
- Watercolor, acrylic paint
- Clay, plaster, other 3D sculpting materials

Teaching Techniques with Limited Choice

The third component, along with theme and media, is the teaching of technique. This is especially important when introducing a class to a choice-based program, as students may need a variety of skills depending on their solutions to the theme. While the teacher can plan in advance for some of the techniques students may require based on the provided choice of media, other techniques may need to be taught based on the individual student's needs. With this in mind, it is important to understand that a teacher in an Open Art Room will be called on to teach technique in two different scenarios: up-front lessons and back-end lessons.

For example, if the choice of materials includes pen and ink, the teacher can plan up front for a lesson in cross-hatching. However, suppose a student decides to create a portrait as a solution for the assignment, but needs assistance understanding facial proportions. The need to teach this technique cannot be planned in advance and will be taught on the back end of the lesson.

Up-front Lessons

The up-front lesson is the most obvious and easiest to plan. The teacher can develop a set of lessons that revolve around the media choices on offer. Such lessons can be accomplished using several different methods.

Mini-Lessons. A mini-lesson is an ideal way to start a class, especially with a body of students who are new to the materials available in the room. The basic mini-lesson involves presenting a technique or media to the class through a short demonstration. Sometimes the lessons are only demonstrated by the teacher, while at other times the students might be allowed to try out the materials. This would be determined by the amount of materials available. In either case the function of the lesson remains the same: an introduction.

Examples of Mini-Lessons:

- How to use a tortillion stump
- How to use salt with watercolors
- The importance of score and slip with clay
- How to draw an eye
- Understanding one-point linear perspective

Pairing Mini-Lessons. Pairing mini-lessons is an effective method when the teacher is pairing media for a theme-based project. Pairing mini-lessons fol-

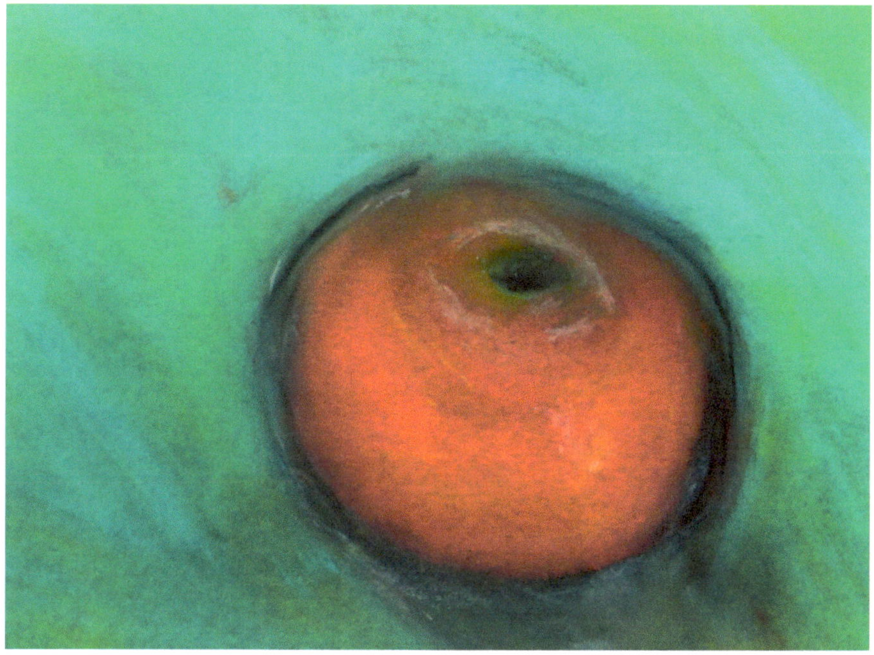

Study of fruit in pastel as part of the unit Artists Observe (p. 164).

lows the same concept as the mini-lesson with the exception that the teacher seeks techniques or skills that are common across the media. In other words, the demonstrated techniques can be used with either of the paired media.

Examples of Pairing Mini-Lessons:

- Cross-hatching using pencil, charcoal, pen and ink
- Creating highlights and shadows using color pencil, markers, oil pastels
- Tints, shades, and gradients for watercolor, acrylic, and digital painting
- Weaving using paper, fibers, or metal

Bootcamps. Mentioned in Chapter Two, Bootcamps are set up as an intense week of lessons. Bootcamps are best utilized when covering a detailed range of techniques within a particular medium that cannot be sufficiently covered in mini-lessons. During the Bootcamp, students are given mini-lessons as well as more thorough exercises in which to explore the media. The goal is for students to gain understanding, not to create a work of art.

Examples of Bootcamps:

- Drawing Bootcamp covering observation skills, value, perspective, proportion
- Painting Bootcamp covering color theory, proper tool handling, brush techniques
- Clay Bootcamp covering score and slip, stages of clay, firing, glazing

Back-end Lessons

There are many opportunities for the teacher in an Open Art Room setting to demonstrate techniques on the back end of a lesson. These opportunities arise when the student has determined an outcome for a project but doesn't yet have the skill set to complete his or her design. Teachers should actively seek out these situations and interject advice as needed. Back-end lessons may be as straightforward as the student who needs a lesson on perspective or proportion. However, they may be as complex as the student who doesn't fully understand the concept behind abstract art or who has never stretched a canvas.

The Exercise/Project Trap

There should be a distinct line between an exercise the teacher provides and the art the student produces. Unfortunately, this line is often crossed by creative-minded teachers.

As an example, a teacher may start by asking his students to mix paints for the purpose of learning color theory. The teacher soon realizes that making little boxes of color is rather dull, so he decides the students should create color wheels. Soon, the teacher recognizes that color wheels aren't creative either, so he decides the students should turn the color wheels into mandalas. Without realizing it, the teacher has turned a simple color-mixing lesson into a complicated teacher-directed project that will take his students a week to paint, when all they needed was an exercise that should have taken a day.

The purpose of an exercise is to provide a method for understanding a concept or learning a technique. Once learned, the student may select to incorporate that concept or technique into the project. However, the teacher should never present an exercise as a project.

Voice and Meaning in Art at the Beginning Level

Finding voice and meaning at the beginning level might sound like a bite too big to chew. However, creating works of art with voice, purpose, and meaning is an important endeavor and one that can be fruitfully explored at the beginning level.

It is important to understand that a student who is not accustomed to choice may have never been asked to create a work of art using his or her own voice. More likely, if they have followed a teacher-directed program, students have explored the voices of famous artists but not developed their own. Likewise, it is probable that these same students have not created art where they had to assign meaning. Perhaps they have designed pieces based on a theme that came with an assigned meaning, but not on themes that they selected on their own.

If this is the case, it is important to handle the situation correctly. Developing voice or determining meaning in an artwork can feel overwhelming to a student who has never attempted it before. Some may soon feel frustrated by what seems to them a difficult task. Others, however, may jump right in with both feet. For this reason, it will be necessary to handle each situation individually.

Building a relationship with your students will go a long way in knowing how far you can push a student. For the student who is reluctant to pursue deeper meaning in an artwork, it can sometimes be best to start slowly. You might begin by asking that they use topics or images that are personal to them. It can be beneficial to find out about their interests and passions and guide them to incorporating these into their work. For those students who seem more willing to explore such topics, the teacher may be able to push back on project ideas that lack meaning or purpose.

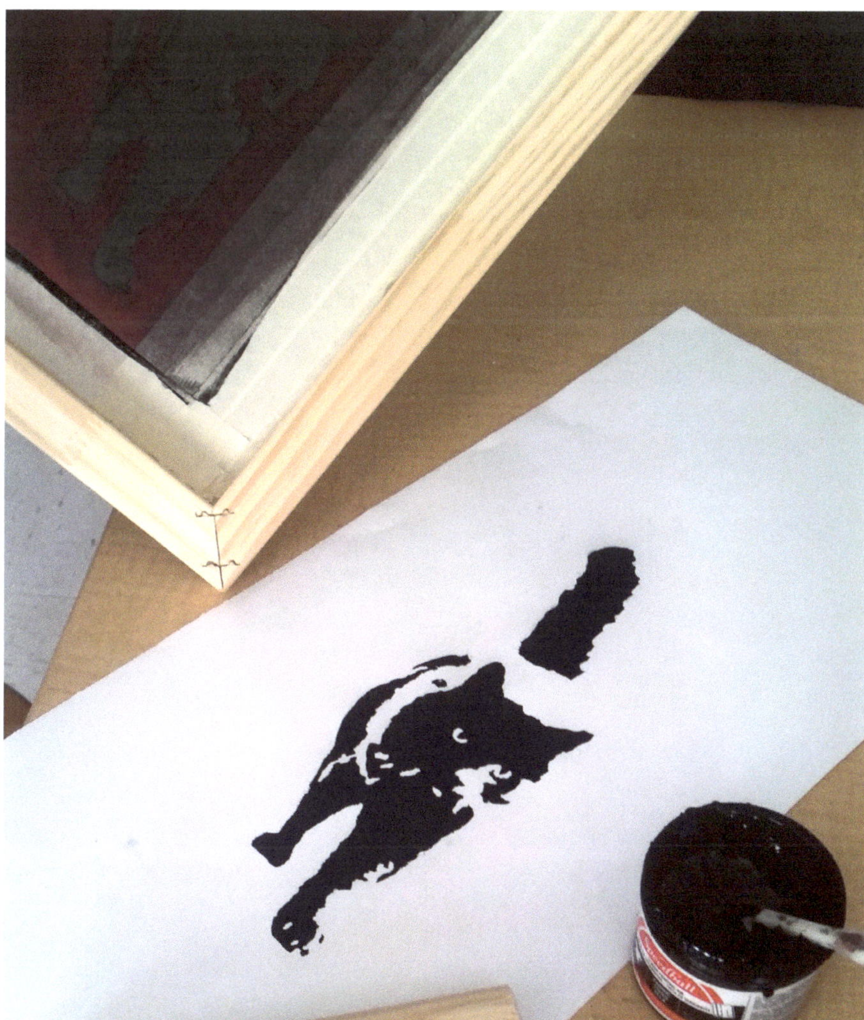

Screenprinted image of a cat.

Emma Z. and Personal Meaning in Art

To kick off our semester, I offered my Art Three class an intermediate level choice-based unit titled Artists Incorporate Text. Emma Z. created a wonderful piece converting an old textbook into a relief image of a girl reading a novel. It had so much meaning and purpose that I anticipated an even deeper solution on her next project, which would be full choice. I sat down next to Emma and asked, "What are you thinking about creating?"

"I'm thinking about painting a peacock like one I saw on Pinterest."

"No," I responded without putting much thought into my choice of words.

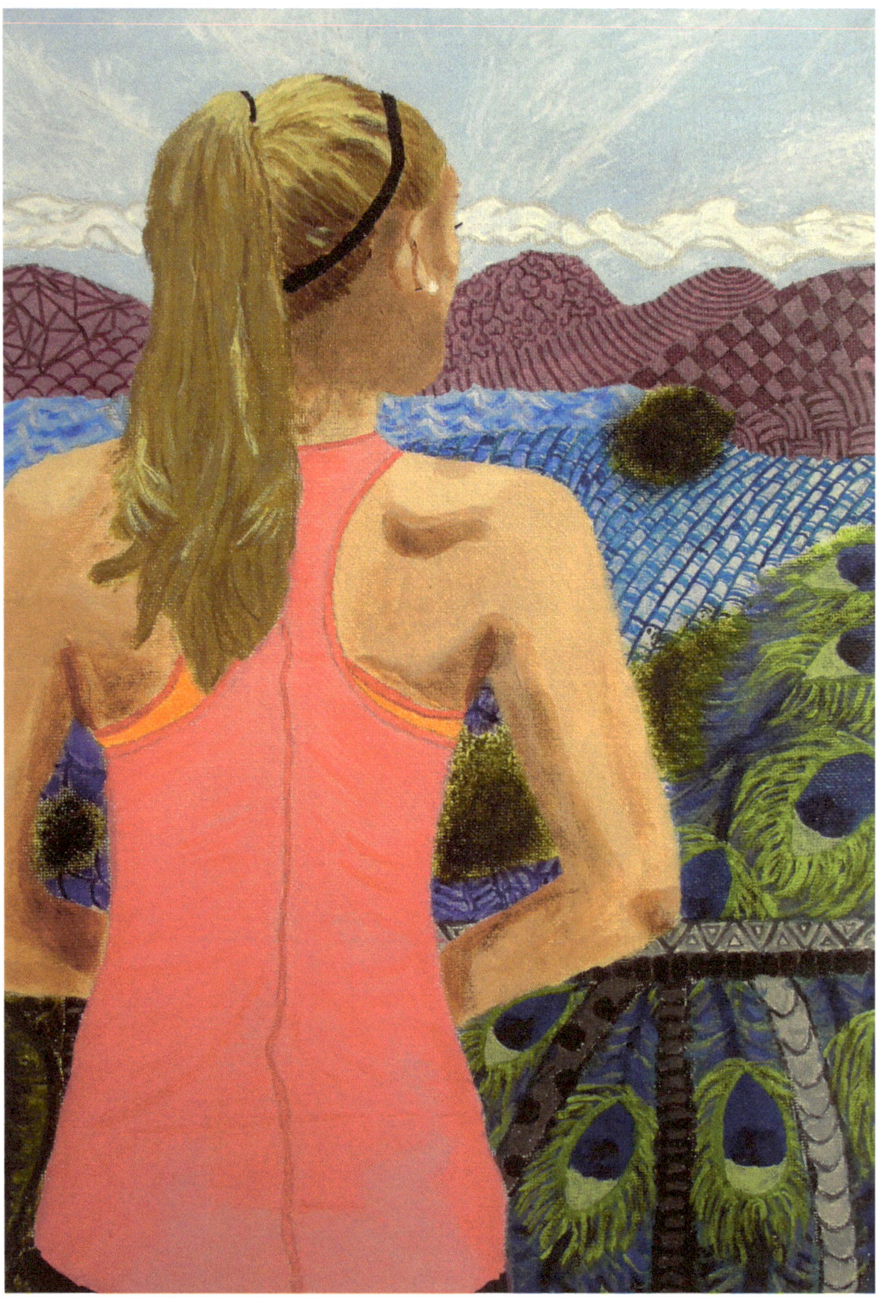

Emma Z's final painting.

"Why not?" asked Emma.

I went on to explain how she had put so much meaning and purpose into her text project that she needed to put in just as much, if not more, for the next. Besides, there already was a peacock painting on Pinterest.

Emma Z. sat there for a week. Every time I asked what she wanted to do she would only reply that she was still thinking about it. Finally, she told me she had an idea.

"I want to create a Zentangle elephant like the one I saw on Pinterest."

"No," I responded in similar fashion to how I had reacted to the peacock idea. Again she questioned why, and again I explained about the meaning and purpose thing and besides, there already was a Zentangle elephant on Pinterest.

Emma Z. sat there for another week. Just like before, every time I asked what she wanted to do she would only reply that she was still thinking about it. Finally, after two weeks, Emma Z. presented a solution.

"I want to paint a self-portrait using a reference taken while I was on a mission trip. The photo is very meaningful to me," Emma explained.

"That's good," I said, satisfied with her solution, but Emma had more to add.

"And I want to turn the foliage in the background into a Zentangle design," she added.

"That's even better," I said, but Emma still wasn't done.

"And I want my palette to reflect the colors of a peacock feather."

"That's outstanding!" I exclaimed. "Make it so."

Emma went on to spend at least a week drawing a rather elaborate black and white Zentangle design in pencil that she used as reference for her background. She then spent the rest of the semester working on her painting. Emma only completed two works the entire time she was in my class, but the combination of time, effort, meaning, and purpose she put into those two works made up for the lack of quantity.

Putting It All Together: Sample Unit

The following is a sample unit, provided as an example of how all the components of a beginning choice-based lesson might be assembled. The sample lesson includes a theme, three choices of paired media, and techniques for each media.

Theme: What's the Point?

To begin the unit, it can be advantageous to start with the theme. In this example, we will use the theme, What's the Point? Students are presented with the theme, followed by a series of idea-generation activities.

An effective brainstorming activity is to provide small groups of students, perhaps four or five, with a large sheet of newsprint paper and markers. Have the groups write down as many ideas about the theme as they can in seven minutes. Set a timer and let them know they should have at least twenty ideas. At the conclusion of the seven minutes, have each group share with the class their top four or five ideas for the theme.

Over the next day or two, the students should participate in other brainstorming activities. There should be a variety of both group and individual methods. The objective is to get students thinking far beyond the first things that come into their minds.

The final step of the brainstorming process is to narrow down the field of ideas to a few choice options. Students should select their top three or four ideas and begin considering how their final compositions will be achieved. Creating a series of thumbnails for each can be beneficial. During this same time, the teacher can begin to present the paired media.

Media: Pencil, Charcoal, Pen and Ink

For this example, students have three choices of media. The choices will each be black and white and will include pencil, charcoal, and pen and ink. One day is required for each medium being presented along with the associated mini-lesson.

Techniques and Mini-Lessons

An associated mini-lesson should be presented each day a new medium is presented. For each medium, several mini-lessons may be presented that demonstrate various techniques that correspond with the material.

For this unit, the following mini-lessons would be presented along with the media.

Media	Mini-Lessons
Pencil	The different types of pencils (H, B, 4B, 6B, etc.) Value scale Blending techniques, using a tortillion
Charcoal	Different types of charcoal Methods for applying charcoal Using a kneaded eraser Fixing charcoal
Pen & Ink	Hatching Cross-hatching Stippling

Additional Skill-Building

In addition to the various media and technique lessons, the teacher might include a presentation on concepts that can be associated with the media and techniques. For this example, since all the media is black and white, a

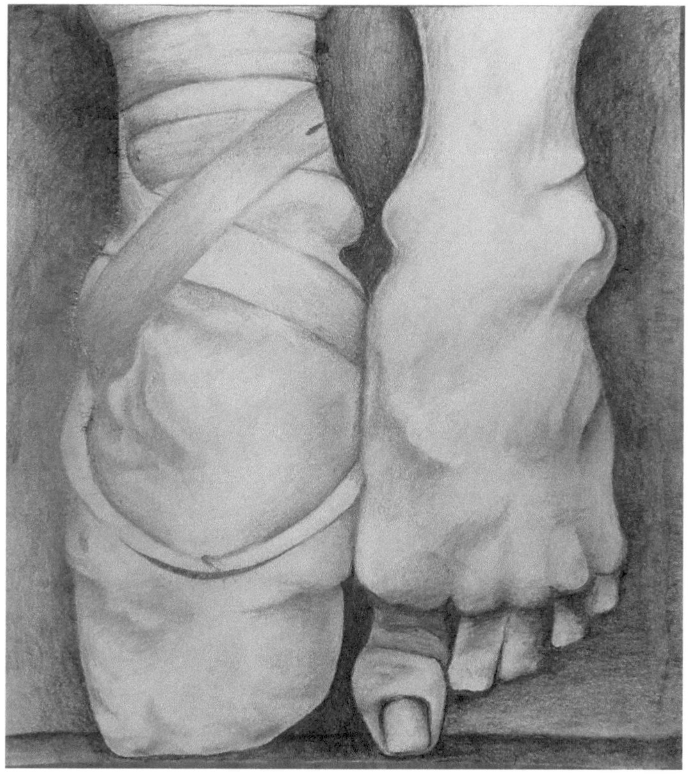

Student responds to theme, What's the Point?

presentation on contrast would be appropriate. The teacher might present the concept of contrast and show a selection of high-contrast artworks.

The Final Project

After the students have been exposed to all the media and mini-lessons, they should be ready to begin their final project. They will have had several days to consider ideas and should have already narrowed their choices down to a few select concepts. They also should have considered possible compositions, possibly by creating thumbnails. Finally, they will have been exposed to the various media and should be able to decide which to use to bring their concept to fruition.

Creation

As the creation part of the process begins and the students start work on their final projects, there are a few things to keep in mind.

Have Materials Ready and Accessible. All media—pencils, charcoal, pen and ink, along with different types and sizes of paper—should be readily available to the students. The teacher should not be responsible for the

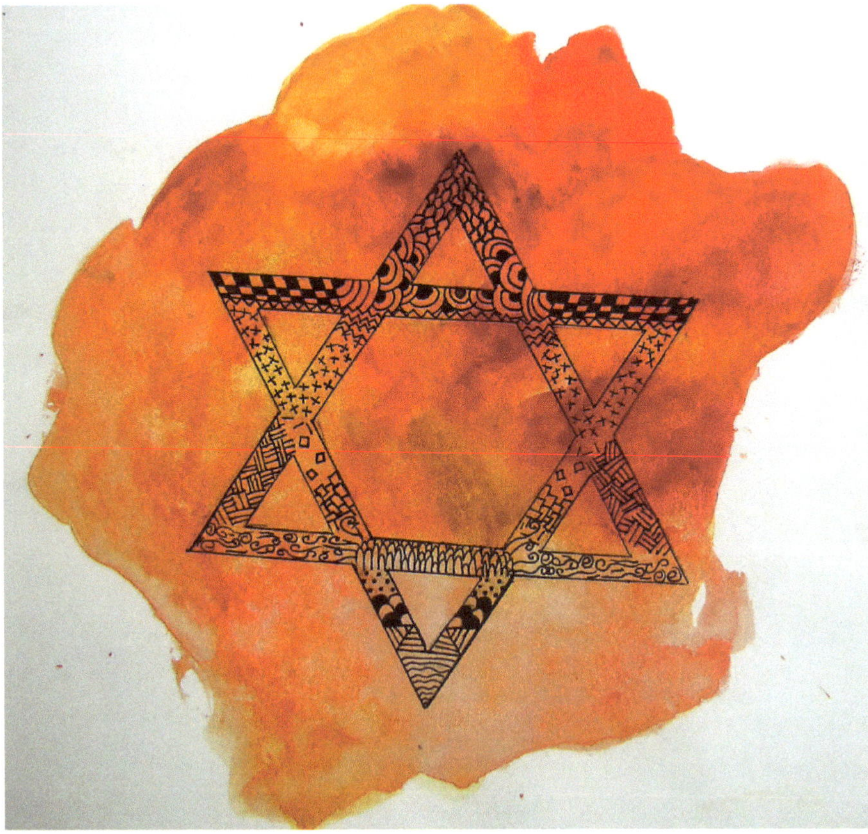

Star of David in pen and watercolor, part of a series about religious symbols.

distribution of materials. Students should understand how to retrieve, care for, and replace all materials in the room.

Continue Conversations and Assessments. During the final project, teachers should be constantly monitoring their students' progress. Different students respond to choice differently. Some will need no assistance at all, while others may struggle to decide on their topic or media.

Back-End Lessons May Be Needed. Conversations with students may reveal needs for further instruction, calling for additional lessons at the individual level. As an example, a student who has used black charcoal on light colored paper might be curious about trying white chalk on dark paper. Another example might be the student who wants to draw a building but isn't familiar with linear perspective. These types of exploration should be encouraged. The teacher may use discretion in determining whether a demonstration should be given to an individual student, a small group of interested students, or the entire class.

Consider Time Tables and Due Dates. A common concern with a unit such as this is how much time the teacher should allot to students to complete their projects. Adhering to strict or floating due dates is another. Due to the similarity in media and scope of a beginning-level choice-based unit like the one described, it is possible to determine how long the majority of students will need to complete their projects. The teacher may set a reasonable time table for completion before moving on to the next unit, while being flexible towards those students who need more time due to individual project scope.

Reflection

As with all units, regardless of level, a time for reflection should be established. This time is used for sharing of completed work and for critiquing. Several types of reflection methods are presented in Chapter Four.

The beginner level is presented as a means for introducing limited choices to assist in the transition towards a more open art room. Deciding on the level of choice in the classroom should be determined by the comfort level of both the students as well as the teacher. The teacher may select to remain using the beginner level with an introductory class. However, the teacher with upper-level students who have learned to take ownership of their creative decisions may resolve to progress to the intermediate level of choice.

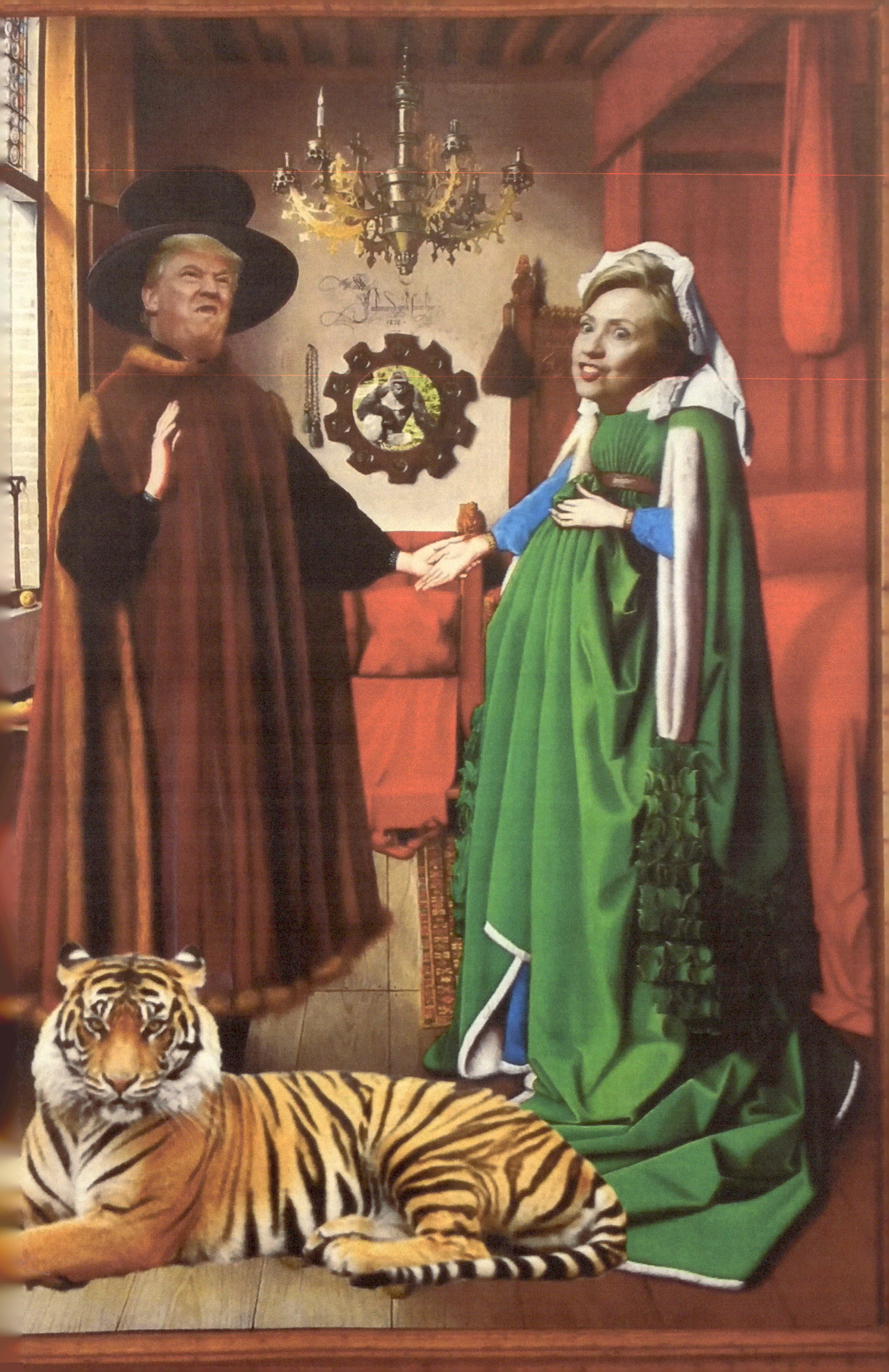

4 | Implementing Choice at the Intermediate Level

If you ask art teachers who say they offer choice, most will describe their practice as "modified," but what is modified choice? The answer to this question is as wide as the number of choice teachers. Some teachers would describe choice as giving the students a range of colors to select from when completing a project that otherwise looks very similar to all the other students' projects in the class. Other teachers would describe modified choice as permitting the student to determine the theme and medium of a project with a fixed due date. So, what is modified choice?

For our purposes here, we can define modified choice, or the intermediate level, as the ability of the student to make most decisions within the framework of a class unit. That is to say, the teacher provides a theme or topic but the student has the freedom to determine how to respond to the proposed prompt. This differs from the beginner level where the student selects from a controlled range of media, and it differs from the advanced level where the student either chooses from a list which topic to pursue or determines the topic altogether.

In this context it is easy to see why most teachers consider themselves modified choice. This intermediate level can address the student body as a whole. It meets the needs of the timid student seeking a starting point, but can also accommodate the student who wants to control the entire process. This flexibility makes the intermediate level program most advantageous for teaching the Open Art Room at the high school level.

Key Differences Between Beginner and Intermediate

The key difference between the beginner and the intermediate choice program is not simply the increasing availability of choices. While widening the number of choice options does increase the student's experience of working in a choice-based situation, by itself it doesn't necessarily extend the student's experience beyond the beginner level. Students are still making choices based on limited selections, and are not yet fully making their own decisions and fully working like artists. In order to accomplish this next step in the student's growth, the teacher must make the following further changes:

- Move away from paired media and towards open media
- Move away from themes
- Move towards Artistic Behavior Units

Moving Towards Open Media

One of the benefits of pairing media is that it facilitates an experiential understanding of the different characteristics of various materials. When we as the teacher present the media, we offer techniques and instructions on how to use the material. We also provide instruction on how to retrieve, handle, and store the material. Once students have been introduced to a pair of media, we hope to expect that they will able to use either one independently on future projects. Thus, once the foundation has been laid, there is no need to continue limiting media selection.

Students who are ready to work at the intermediate level should be able to determine the media that is right for their project. Materials should be stored where students can easily access them. Along these lines, labeling and grouping materials is beneficial.

Moving from paired media to full media choice does not mean that every student will necessarily have been introduced to every media now available. There will likely still be many different materials that the teacher has not presented to the students. There are several methods that the teacher can use for presenting these materials.

Bootcamps

Mentioned in Chapter Two, Bootcamps are set up as an intense week of lessons. Bootcamps are best utilized when covering a range of detailed techniques within a particular medium that couldn't be sufficiently covered in mini-lessons. During the Bootcamp, students are given both mini-lessons

Examples of Bootcamps:

- Drawing Bootcamp → observation skills, value, perspective, proportion
- Painting Bootcamp → color theory, proper tool handling, brush techniques
- Clay Bootcamp → score and slip, stages of clay, firing, glazing

as well as more thorough exercises in which to explore the media. The goal is for students to gain understanding, not to create a work of art.

Mini-Lessons

Many elementary choice-based teachers are familiar with the five-minute lesson. The basic idea is to present a five-minute or less demo on a new skill or technique before students move to their centers. Students watch the demo lessons and the teacher presents, hoping to inform and motivate. Once the lesson is over, the students can decide if they want to try the new skill for themselves or move on to the center of their choosing.

In this same manner, the high school teacher can present a mini-lesson at the beginning of class. The teacher might present a new material or technique, providing both a demo and a hands-on lesson. Since high school students have more class time and hopefully longer attention spans, the mini-lessons can be longer than five minutes. However, they should still only take up a portion of the class. The point is to take the least amount of time to present the information without taking time away from art-making.

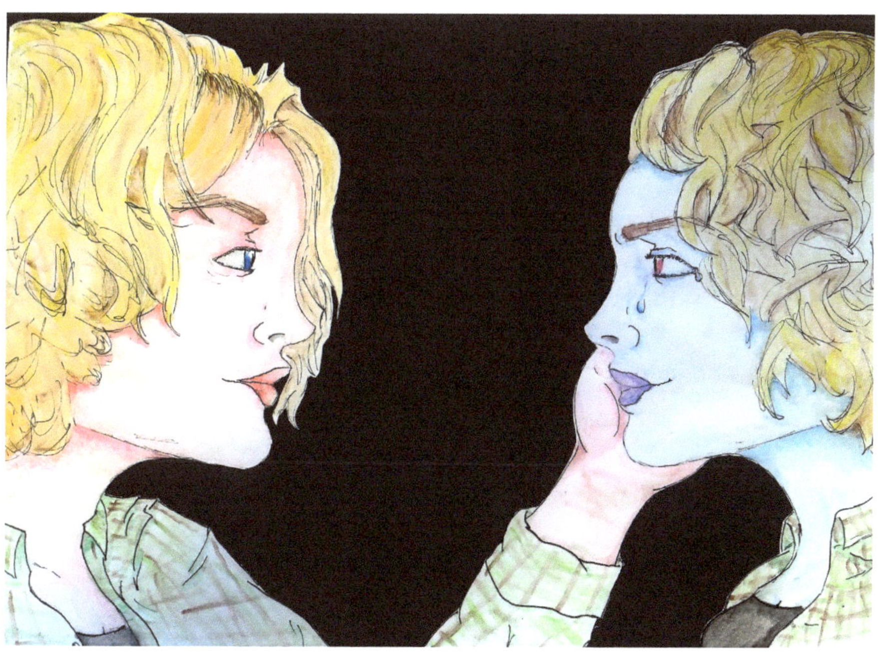

Una re-imagines the yin-yang symbol as a mirror-image portrait.

Self-Educating

Sometimes the student will want to try a material or a technique that the teacher doesn't know how to do. In a teacher-led class this issue might not arise, but in a student-led class it can be quite common. Instead of relying on the teacher to know the answers and teach the student, the teacher can tell the student that she doesn't know either but together, they can find out.

Student-led research puts the burden of finding the answers on the student. Self-educating, especially by trial and error, is one of the best ways to learn.

Transitioning from Themes to Artistic Behavior Units

There is perhaps no better way to transition from a teacher-based learning environment to a student-directed program than with themes. Themes can be concrete to provide a starting point for the student who struggles to come up with ideas, or themes can be more fluid to accommodate outgoing, choice-centric student desires. Though themes can be used even in an advanced choice-based program, to truly be immersed in choice is to let go of themes and let students determine the entire direction of their art.

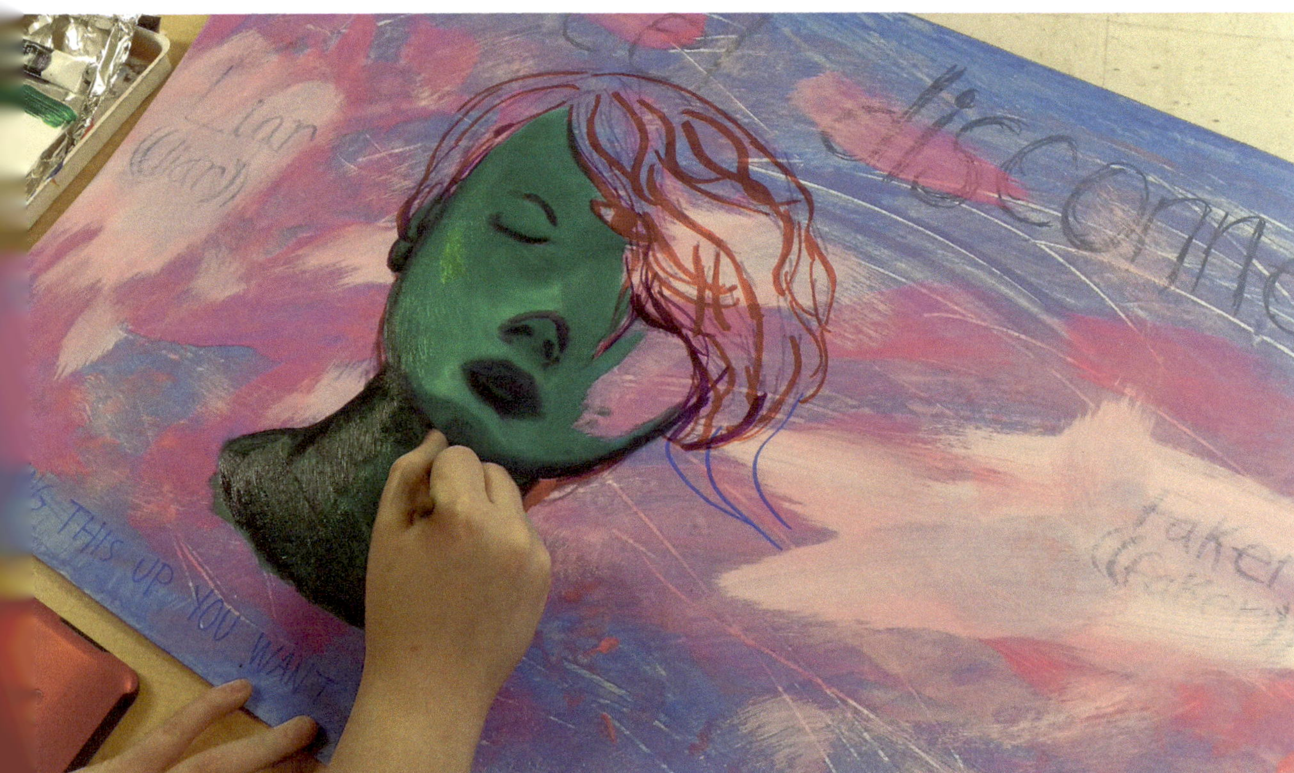

res mental health issues with oil pastels in this expressive work.

The question then becomes, How is this goal to be accomplished?

Since the students are still not advanced in their ability to independently create art, there still needs to be some structure for them to build their art around. This is where the introduction of Artistic Behavior Units comes in.

What Are Artistic Behavior Units?

The best way to understand Artistic Behavior Units is to consider the things artists do in order to create art. For example, artists observe, artists solve problems, artists collaborate. These are all good examples of how artists work. Each of these artistic behaviors can be presented to students as units. Creating units based on Artistic Behaviors is an ideal place for the high school art teacher who wants to advance from the beginning to the intermediate level.

Why Are Artistic Behavior Units the Next Step?

Themes, especially themes with paired media, open the door to choice-based teaching. The students learn to make decisions about what they want to create and how they will create it. However, as art teachers, we know a secret that, at this stage of the game, the students still don't know. We understand that we have limited the students' selections in order to help them make selections. By pairing media and providing a theme, we have opened the door to choice. However, choice by itself isn't the end goal of the art teacher. The art teacher isn't solely interested in the student making art. The art teacher wants students to think, design, and create like artists.

When art teachers present an Artistic Behavior Unit, they are allowing their students to move beyond the limitations of the theme-based program. The students will still be making decisions about what media they will use and they will still be ultimately deciding their final product outcomes, but now they will also be exposed to a third element: the thinking and working as an artist. In doing so, the students will continue to grow, taking ownership of their creative decisions from ideation to completion.

Themes and Artistic Behavior Units: What's the Difference?

What's the difference between themes and *Artistic Behavior Units*? This is an important question, especially for those teachers wanting to incorporate choice at the high school level. Though both can be used to implement choice, understanding the strengths and weaknesses of each will assist in developing a strategy to guide your curriculum.

Themes

Teaching through themes has become increasingly popular, with websites such as Art21 promoting this practice. Common themes include topics such as Identity, Boundaries, and Place, and are generally presented as a starting point for students to generate ideas.

Pros

Themes are especially helpful with students who have not had much experience in a choice-based classroom. The level of choice in a theme lesson can be modified to provide more direction for those students who need it.

Cons

Theme topics are still decided by the teacher. Whereas this is an advantage with beginning-level students, for more advanced-level students you may want to challenge them to design their own theme topics.

Artistic Behavior Units

Artistic Behavior Units are designed to teach students to think and work like artists. Common Artistic Behavior Units include Artists Solve Problems, Artists Are Self Learners, and Artists Answer Essential Questions. Each unit presents a new process that can be applied for developing art.

Pros

A well-designed Artistic Behavior Unit will contain many examples of the specific concept. Students gaining an understanding of the presented process have a wide, and yet targeted, area in which to work. The knowledge gained from Artistic Behavior Units may also be applied to all future art-making processes.

Cons

Students who have not had a solid foundation in a choice-based class can become overwhelmed in Artistic Behavior Units that offer high levels of choice. In that situation, the teacher must either provide solid ideation strategies, or use a theme-based teaching method.

The Structure of an Artistic Behavior Unit

Perhaps the best way to understand an Artistic Behavior Unit is to click the latch and see what's under the hood. Artistic Behavior Units begin by looking at a particular way that artists conduct artistic affairs. In other words, the behaviors, actions, or steps an artist performs, accomplishes, or fulfills in order to make a work of art.

For our first example, we will look at a behavior that all artists perform at one time or another: the act of observation. To gain a better understanding of how this Artistic Behavior Unit will unfold, we will first need to understand the format of the lesson plan. The following lesson plan format illustrates the four-part structure that all of the lesson plans in this book follow:

Inspiration

Our first task is to get buy-in from the students. The inspiration sections may use videos, artists, or examples of artwork to hook the students. These inspiration pieces should be properly selected to pique interest and elicit excitement about the unit that is about to be presented.

Design

The design phase of the project presents challenges, mini-lessons, or group activities to help the students further understand the concept being presented. The challenges may be short, one- or two-day projects that build an understanding of the concepts being presented. Mini-lessons may contain demonstrations of techniques for the various media associated with the unit. Group activities may include brainstorming or other methods of eliciting ideas. All these activities together build a foundation of understanding for the unit.

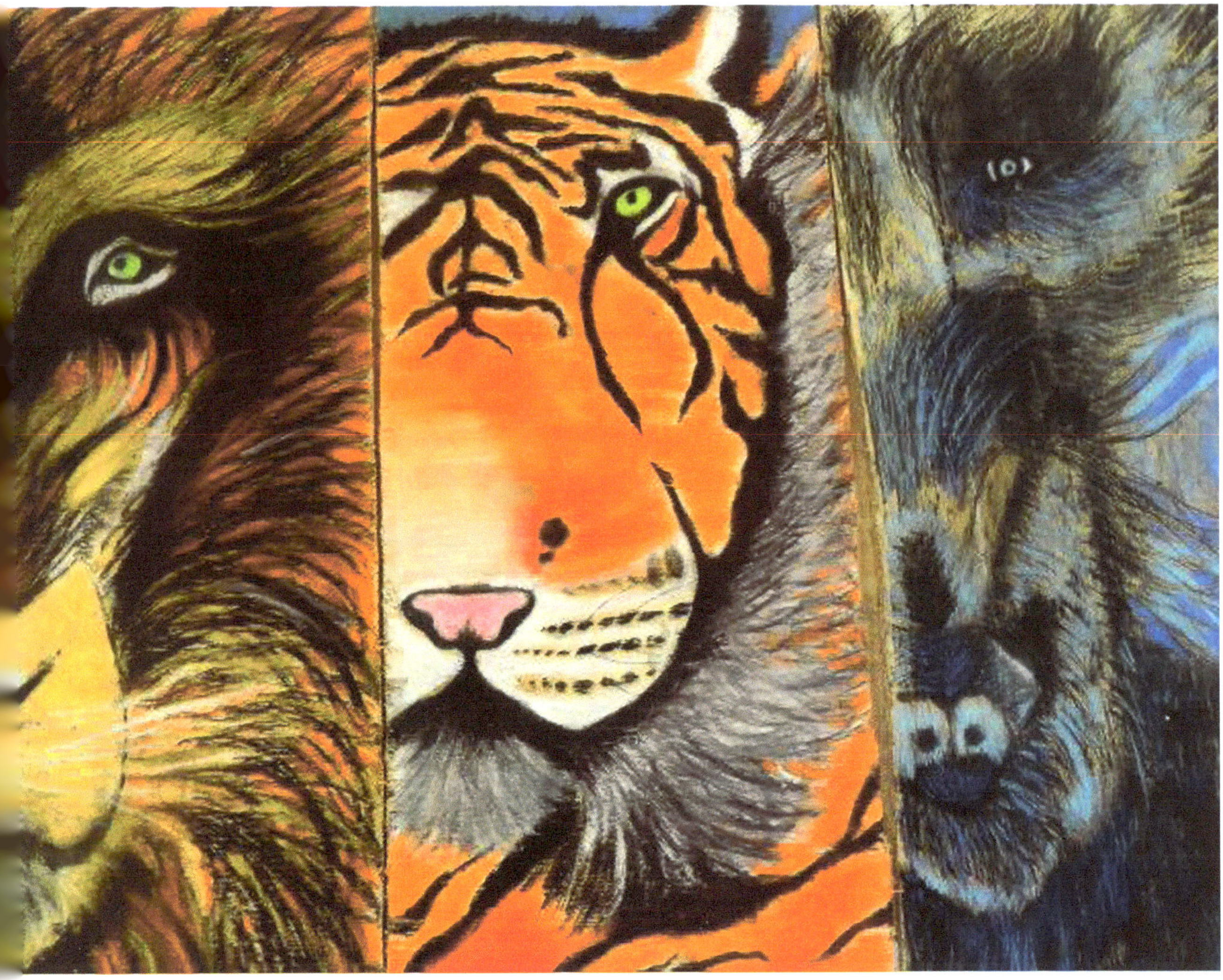

el on wooden panels.

Creation

The third phase of the lesson is the point at which the students understand the concept and will demonstrate their knowledge by completing a final project.

Reflection

Even though the art has been created, the work isn't done. Students need to reflect, critique, and assess their art in order to recognize and understand their individual work's strengths and weaknesses. Reflection is an often overlooked, yet vital, part of the process. Critiques from fellow students provide suggestions for improvement or give insight into areas of merit that have may have gone unnoticed by the creator. Self-assessment that is used to gain an understanding of the steps accomplished to complete the final artwork can often be a benefit for the success of future works.

Example Artistic Behavior Unit

The following is an example unit titled Artists Observe. As the title suggests, the objective of this unit is to introduce students to a variety of methods utilized for producing art that is based on observation. The example proceeds through the four phases as described in the structure of the Artistic Behavior Unit.

Inspiration

All artists observe, whether it is at first hand, such as when creating a still life or plein air painting, or whether it is as abstract as the work of Chicago-based artist Deb Sokolow, who is known for observing people and then documenting what happens. To kick off this unit, you might start by presenting these ideas along with images of various types of artists' works. Searching YouTube might find a video of one of the artists talking about their work. The PBS series Art21 has many contemporary artist videos and is a good place to start.

It is important to present the information in small, comprehensible bites. It is easy to fill a slide presentation with image after image of artworks that fall under the genre of observation. The concern is that too many images become an image dump. They just become too much to process and the point is lost.

It is best to introduce a few key images that make your case and move on. If you find you have too many images even after you have stripped out all the nonessential pictures, then you might want to consider breaking your presentation into several smaller slideshows and presenting them over the course of a few days.

Design

An Open Art Room unit on observation might begin with three or four challenges that only take a day or two to complete and that teach students about different concepts in observation. For example:

Challenge One: Exploring Scientific Observation. Discussions revolve around how naturalists such as John James Audubon used observation. Natural items such as shells, bones, insects, and leaves can be set up at different centers in the room for students to observe and sketch. Allot students ten to fifteen minutes at each center before rotating to the next.

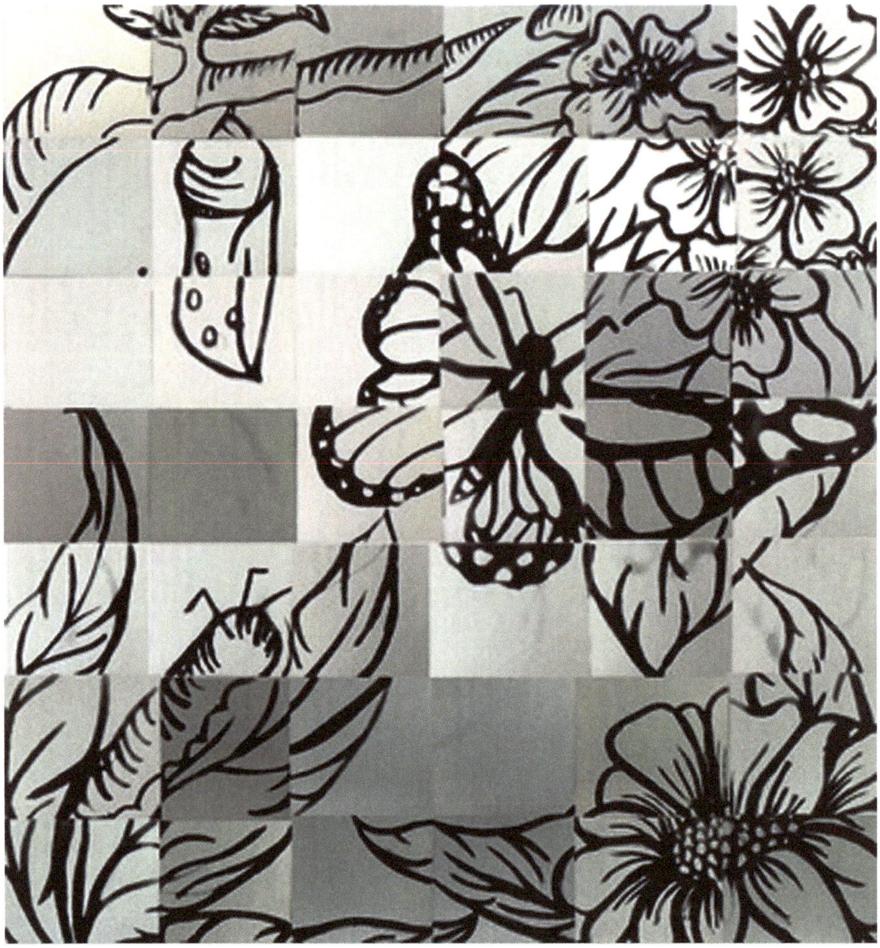

A student drew one part each day on a Buddha Board to create a work of art that never existed as a whole.

Challenge Two: Contemporary Observation. Have the class review the work of Deb Sokolow, who is known for observing people and then documenting what happens. Have the students set up objects in unusual settings around school where people can come into contact with the objects. Have your students observe people as they come into contact with the object and ask the students to document what happens in some way. Their documentation could be photos, sketches, or writing. After completing the task, ask students to share results with their peers and compare notes.

Challenge Three: Perspective and Urban Sketching. Demonstrate one- or two-point linear perspective to your students. As part of your demonstration, make sure they have an understanding of how buildings can be drawn using perspective. When the students understand the concept, bring them to an outdoor courtyard where they can observe and sketch the school building using perspective. You might also include bringing small packs of watercolor paints so students can color the sketches while still outside.

Creation: Final Project

Once students have completed several different types of observational challenges, they will be ready for a final unit project. The objective would be for students to create an observational work, but the media, direction, and scope of their projects would be left entirely up to them.

Some students may have ideas of what they want to do right away, but most students will need some time to think and plan about what they might observe. It is best to start with a few group ideation activities to get the wheels turning.

Suggested Ideation Activities. Provide a large sheet of newsprint and a marker to a group of four or five students and have them write down as many responses to a set of prompts on a particular question as they can think of in five minutes.

Sample questions may include:

- Name all the different items that could be used for a still life.
- Write down all the different type of scientific objects you could bring to school to draw.
- Where would you need to use linear perspective to accurately draw a location?
- What are all the different methods you could use to document an event?

Follow this up by having each group pick their top five answers and share them with the class.

After group activities, try individual ones by having each student write down ideas in a sketchbook. Next, have them select their top two ideas and create three thumbnails for each.

Another possible activity is to have students pick a found object for making an observational drawing and then answer questions about it on a worksheet.

Here is a sample worksheet questionnaire. Have students answer questions 1-4. Then, ask students to partner up to share their results. Have the partner respond to number 5.

1. What is your object?
2. What is interesting about this object that made you select it?
3. What elements of art or principles of design might you need to explore when drawing this object?
4. What medium do you plan to use?
5. Comments and suggestions

Reflection

Now that the art has been created, the students should engage in the process of reflection. Reflecting on their accomplishments will help students grow as they identify their works' strengths and weaknesses.

Written assessments allow students time to reflect on their thoughts as they try to respond to their art using words, not images. Offering students prompts gives them important starting points that can help them better reflect on their work.

For a unit on observation, you might ask that students select from a series of questions, such as:

- Did you learn new techniques or processes as part of the work for this project?
- Did you gain skill with familiar materials?
- During this project, when did you step back and analyze your work?
- Did you consider how your ideas would work before you tried them?

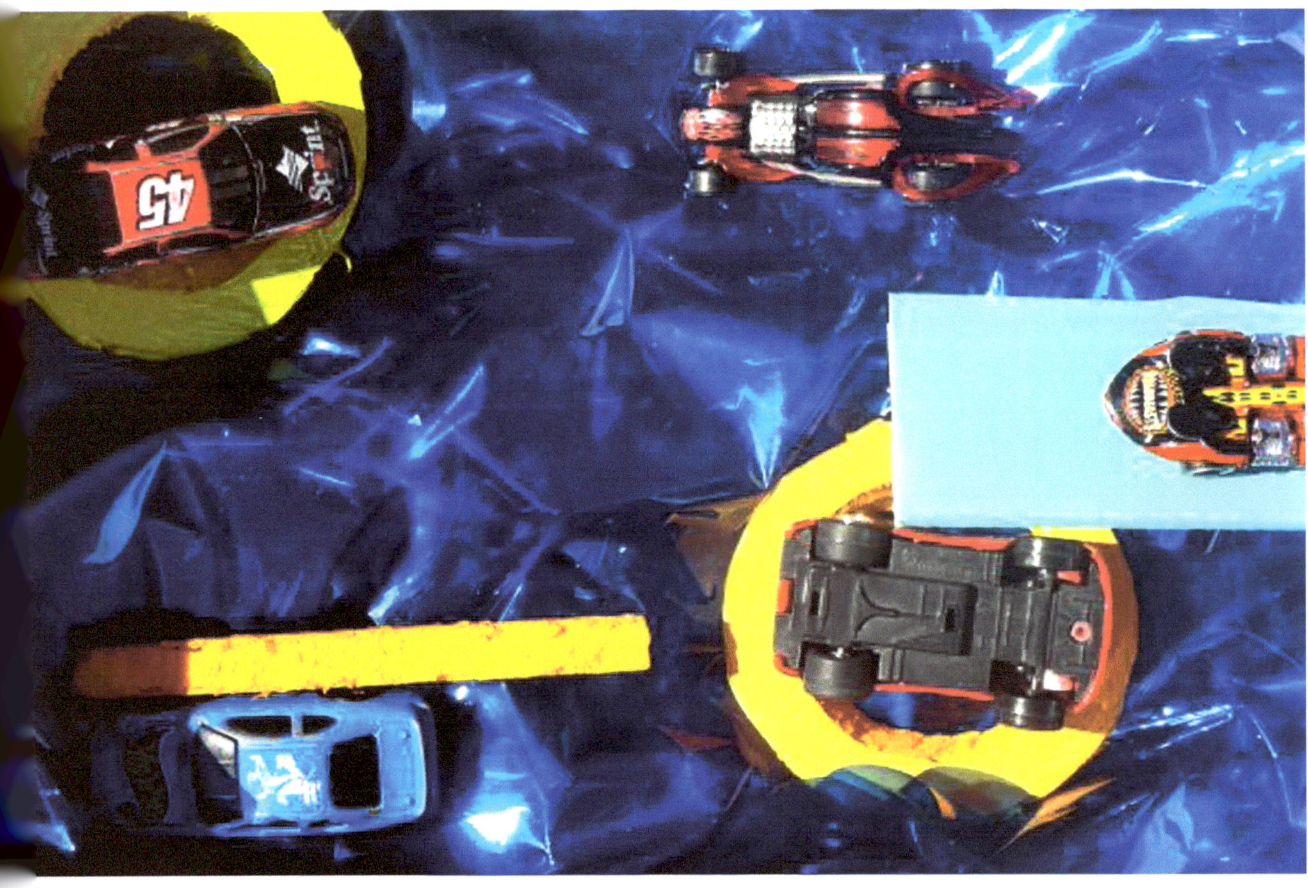

erpretation of the term "carpool" for the Artists Steal unit.

Addressing Challenges

When students are working at the beginning level and are all working with similar materials, most will complete their assignments around the same time. However, when the teacher moves the class from the beginner to the intermediate level and the student media choices start to vary, the time they need to complete their projects will vary. You can expect that some students will finish in a few days and others may take weeks. Students finishing projects at varying times isn't an issue as long as you have strategies in place to deal with the situation. Here are a few possible solutions for students who finish early or those who take longer:

Work in a Series. Sometimes a student's idea can be completed quickly. This doesn't mean he rushed through it, it just means his solution didn't take much time to create. One solution is to ask the student to consider creating a second or even a third solution. Many artists work in a series, creating several works of art with a similar theme or technique. This should be explained in a manner so as not to diminish your student's first solution but rather to encourage him to see how many solutions he can achieve.

Alternative Projects. One method for dealing with students who finish early is to give them an alternative project to work on while the others finish the unit project. Journals and altered books (a used book that has been converted into a sketchbook for mixed-media projects) are great examples of alternative assignments as they can be worked on continually throughout the year.

Exploration. Another solution for students who finish early is to ask them to explore a new medium or technique that they haven't yet explored. It could even be a material in the room that the teacher is not familiar with. The teacher can ask the students to figure out how something is done through research and exploration. Afterwards, the students can report back to the teacher or, better yet, present their findings to the class.

Moving Forward. Sometimes it is not the student who finishes early that is the issue but rather the student who needs more time when the rest of the class has completed their projects. The student in this situation truly needs more time. One solution is to move forward with the next unit and leave the student to complete her previous work. The student may only need to skip the beginning challenges and may be able to pick up the work mid-unit. It is also possible that the student needs all the time dedicated to the next unit. In this case, the teacher may choose to exempt the student from that unit entirely.

Perhaps the biggest advantage of implementing the intermediate level of choice-based art teaching is that it provides the student a guideline from which to create without specifically instructing the student on *what* to create. There is enough framework to formulate cohesiveness within the unit while still allowing for a plethora of final creations. Artistic Behavior Units build on concepts that students can incorporate in any future project. They also address life skills such as problem solving, collaboration and risk-taking which go beyond the Open Art Room.

Blackout poem created as part of the unit Artists Steal.

Ariel, Never Give Up

Ariel was consistently exploring geometric vs. organic shapes through a series of small acrylic paintings. As her teacher, I wanted to see her push past these exercises. I could have assigned her a project, but that would have been my solution. Instead, I gave her the materials and instructions for building a 4′ x 4′ canvas, which she applied gesso to and placed in a corner of the room.

For about a week, Ariel didn't paint but rather stared at the canvas. I joked with her that she was afraid of it. To some extent I was right, but toward the end of the week, Ariel started painting her organic shapes. A few days into the painting, Ariel was (in her words) "having a bad day." Dissatisfied with the results, she took a palette knife and covered the canvas in muddy, brown paint. The painting remained in this state with Ariel not picking up a paintbrush for several days. It was now mid-May and I was starting to second-guess my teaching. If I had just given her a project, she would already have a successful, completed product.

Then, on her own, Ariel changed course. She started cutting out magazine images in geometric shapes and gluing them to the canvas. Next, she applied paint to create thick, black, organic lines. Ariel realized she was onto something. Throughout the month and into June, Ariel continued to work on her art. By the end of the school year, she had almost completed a well-balanced composition that incorporated both geometric and organic characteristics.

Ariel was thrilled with her results, as was I. She had spent many weeks not simply painting, but contemplating, struggling, engaging others in conversation, and eventually, following her own voice.

Another teacher could easily argue against my teaching philosophy. It could be pointed out that Ariel wasted two months on this project. She could have completed at least four teacher-directed projects in the same time. Teacher-led projects could have also incorporated more concepts with less ambiguity. If my focus was still on making art, I would agree. However, I believe the process that Ariel went through held the most value. It was something I couldn't tell her.

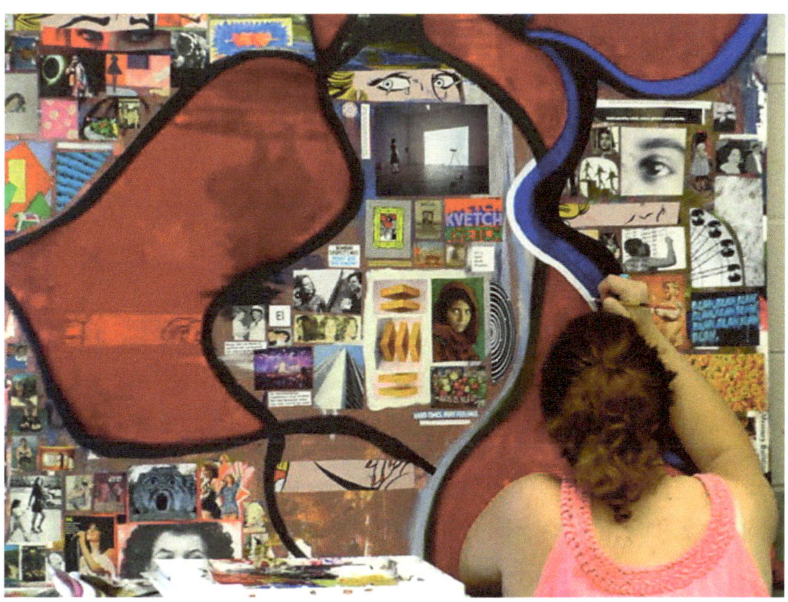

Artistic Behaviors

- Artists Steal
- Artists Solve Problems
- Artists Use Nontraditional Materials
- Artists Collaborate
- Artists Tell Stories
- Artists Communicate
- Artists Seek Inspiration
- Artists Are Self-Learners
- Artists Engage
- Artists Synthesize
- Artist Have a Style
- Artists Impact Their Communities
- Artists Are Global
- Artists Support Other Artists
- Artists Collect
- Artists Research
- Artists Experiment
- Artists Make the Viewer Think
- Artists Repurpose
- Artist Solve Problems
- Artist Persevere
- Artists Make a Difference
- Artists Educate
- Artists Document/Record
- Artists Take Risks
- Artists See
- Artists Share Themselves
- Artists Explore a Theme
- Artists Are Self-Promoters
- Artists Develop a "Flow"
- Artists Reflect
- Artists Are Attuned to Their Environment
- Artists Play with Materials
- Artists Work with What They Are Given
- Artists Curate
- Artists Observe
- Artists Create Original Art
- Artists Develop Art-Making Skills
- Artists Communicate through Work
- Artists Have a Global Awareness of Art-Making
- Artists Develop a Style
- Artists Question
- Artists Transform
- Artist Are Entrepreneurs
- Artist Create Temporary Art

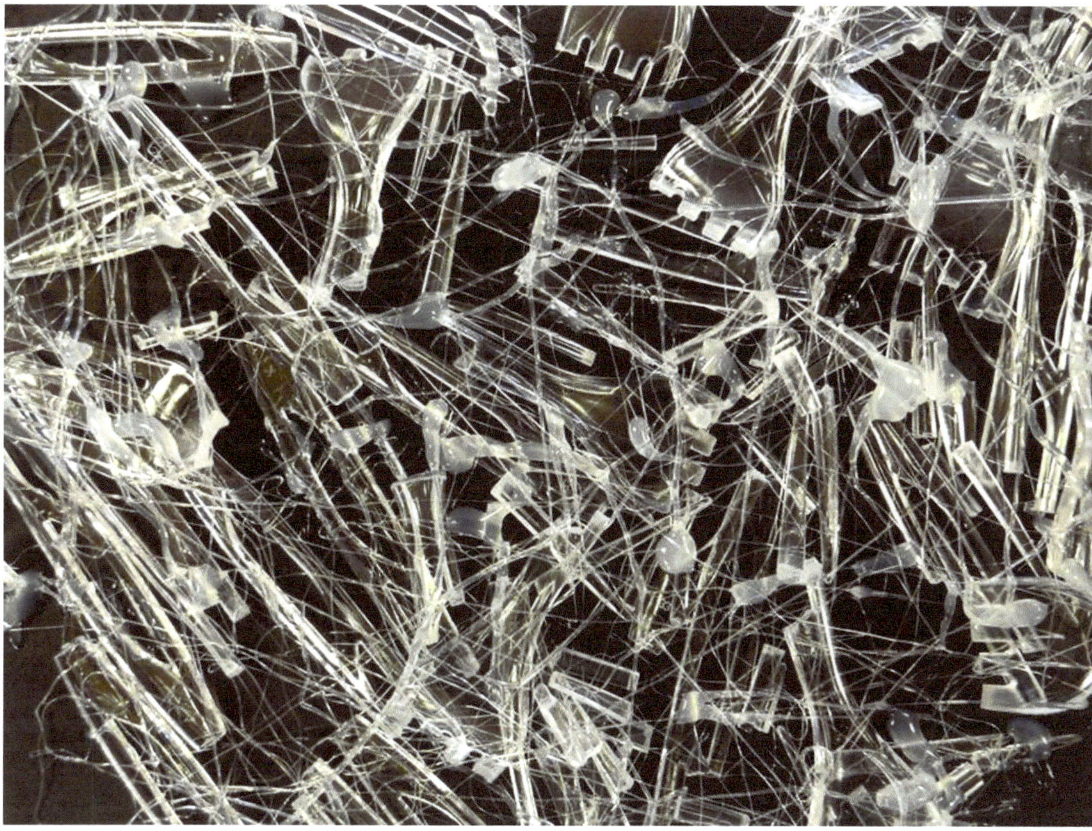

Finding new ways to demonstrate line and movement in art.

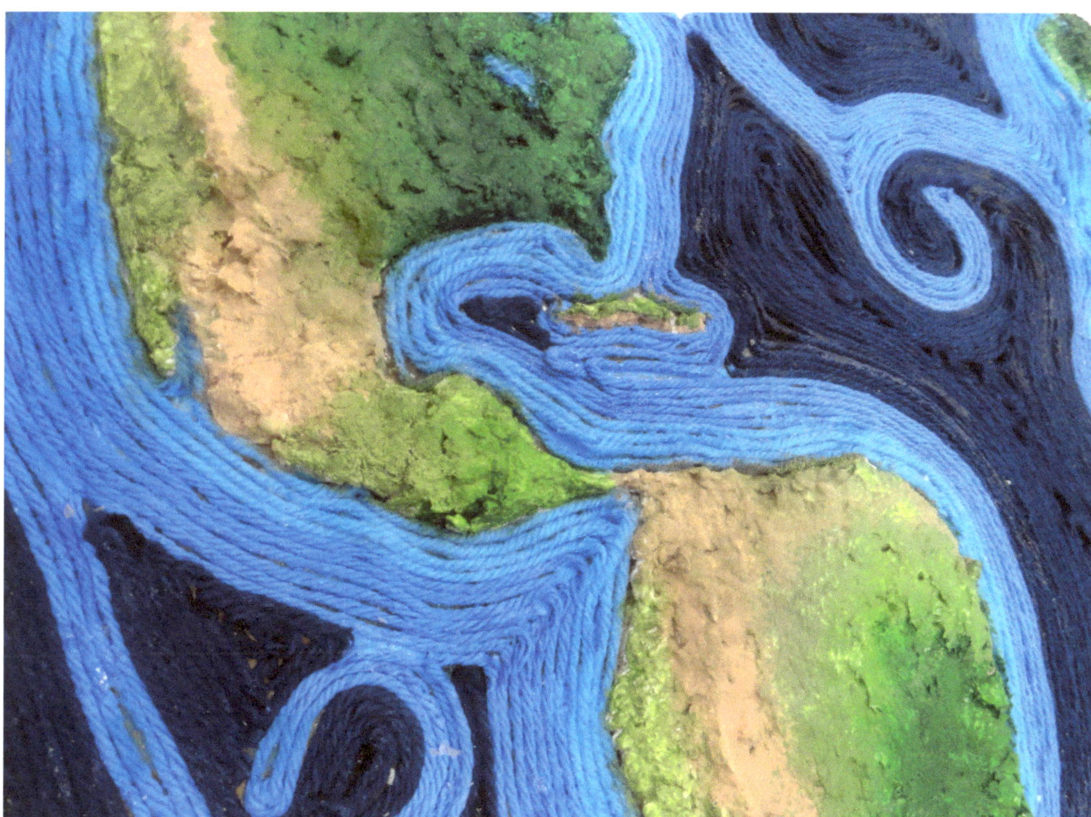

Emphasizing line and texture (detail) as part of the unit Artists Emphasize the Elements.

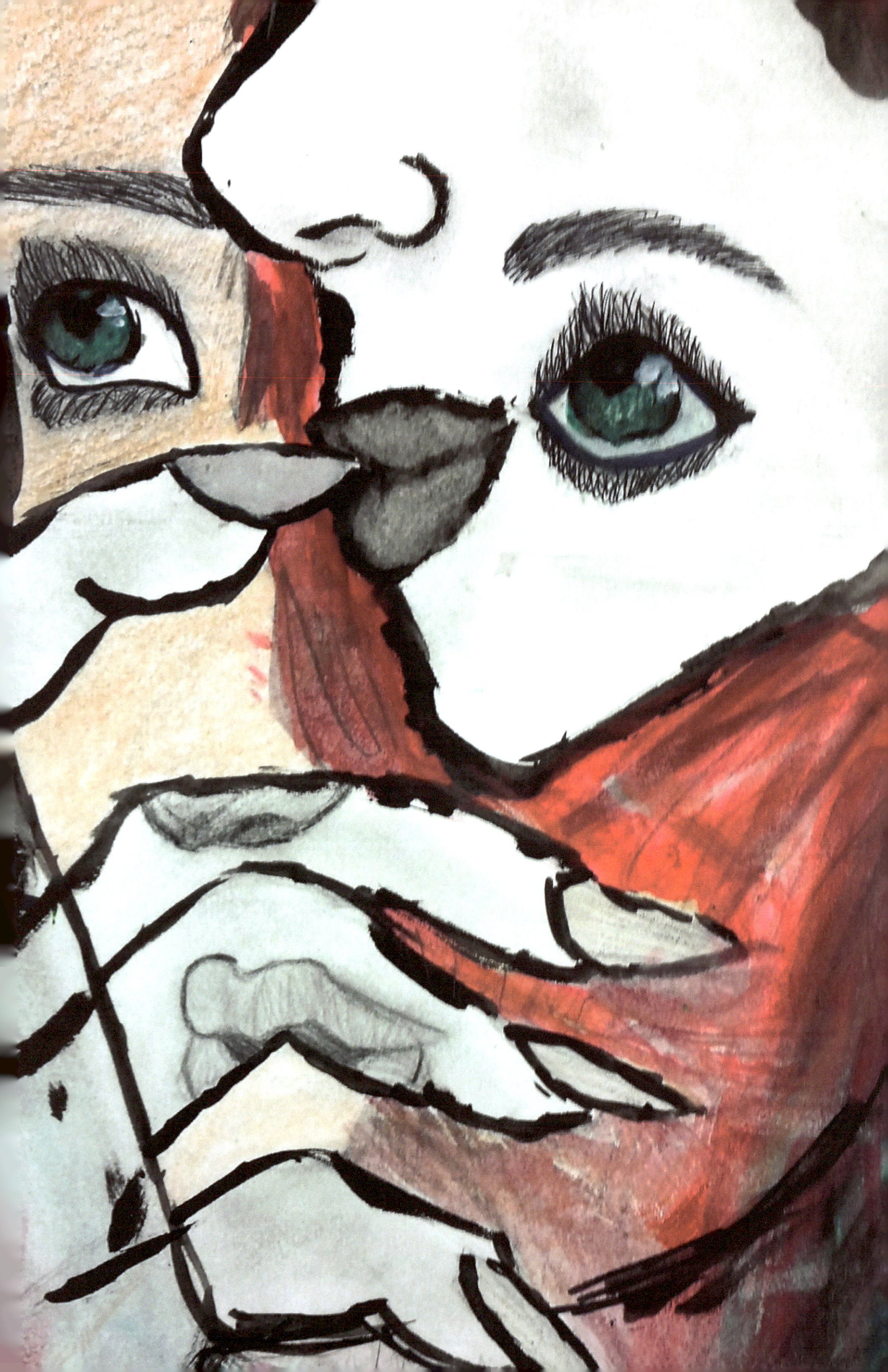

5 | Implementing Choice at the Advanced Level

There are two types of people you interact with when you go to a restaurant: the host and the waitstaff. The first person, the hostess, is there to help you get a table. She looks at her plans, decides what she thinks your seating needs will be, and then leads you step-by-step to your table. This is a type of leader. This is a type of leadership.

The second person you interact with is the waiter or waitress. This person is there to present you with the menu, take your order, and bring your food. However, good waiters do much, much more. They tell you about the specials the chef has prepared. They make suggestions, both about the food, as well as recommendations about beverage selections that will best complement your dinner. They answer all your questions and are there to make sure your dining experience is superb. This also is a type of leader. This also is leadership.

As teachers, we need to decide if we will be the hostess or the waiter. Will we look at our plans and tell our students what to do, or will we show them all we have to offer and let them decide? Will we make our students go step-by-step through our lessons, or will we make suggestions and offer recommendations so their art experience is superb?

To continue with the restaurant metaphor, advanced students in the Open Art Room are already connoisseurs of good art dining. They already know what's on the menu; they want to know about the specials. They are familiar with the beverages but would like a recommendation as to which goes best with their meal. They aren't looking for a hostess to show them their seats; they already know where they want to sit. Instead, they are seeking a great waiter to help make their fine art dining experience superb.

Full Choice

Offering full choice at the high school level can, in some ways, be much more challenging than at the elementary level. Insecurities about ability, indecision over what to accomplish, and uncertain knowledge of technique will often hinder the high school student's art-making process. While offering a center with access to materials can sometimes be enough to keep an elementary student motivated for weeks, the same scenario can stop high school students in their tracks.

High school students are often unaccustomed to being offered full choice. They have come to expect a series of directions that they are to follow. A class that is offered full choice without scaffolding first through beginning and intermediate levels will struggle with questions such as: What do I make? How do I know how to make it? How do I begin?

Because of these challenges, art teachers who decide to move to full choice need to prepare even more than art teachers who are offering choice at the beginner level. They will need to prepare a system to guide students through the design process to ensure that they can develop ideas, handle and learn new skills and techniques, understand what to do when they get stuck, and reflect and assess their own work.

To begin this preparation, there are two methods that may be considered when moving to the advanced level: Nonlinear Pacing and Student-Proposed Assignments.

Nonlinear Pacing

A nonlinear pacing program is a method of offering Artistic Behavior Units without the teacher-directed element. In other words, the units—including all inspirational materials, exercise, mini-lessons, and final projects—are available in a menu form for the student to access. However, the student decides which units to complete and in which order.

What Units Are Available?

Before beginning a nonlinear pacing program, the teacher needs to prepare all the information that students may choose to complete. There should be more units designed than there would be time for a student to process over the course of a semester. That is to say, if the average student can complete six units per semester, the teacher should design at least eight units. This gives students a choice in the order of the units as well as over which units they will select.

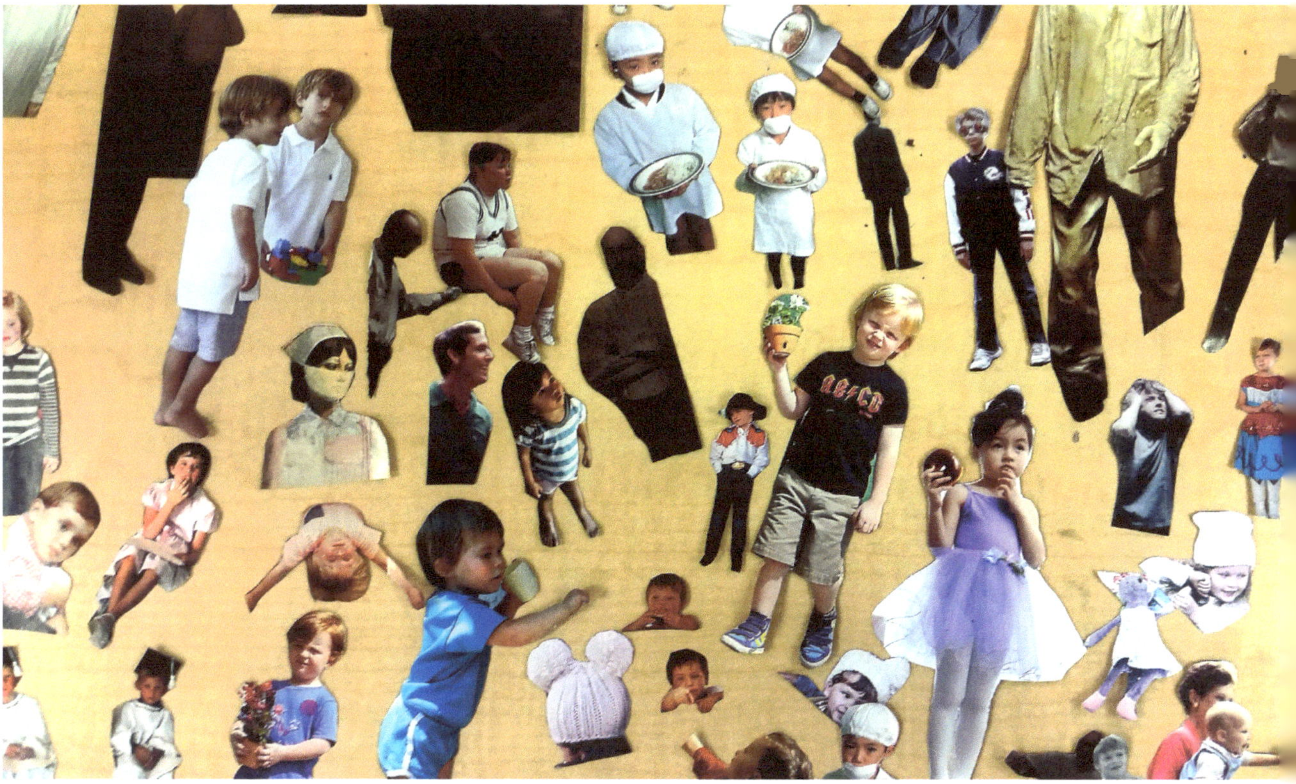

Morgan collects images for a collage.

What Information Is in the Units?

The units need to provide everything that a student will need in order to proceed through the design process, from inspiration to assessment. Think of these units as if they comprised an online class or a chapter in a textbook. Each section of the design process is offered to the student in small sections, allowing the student to move step-by-step through the unit.

How Do Students Access these Units?

Unit information needs to be presented in a simple manner, using a technology that students can easily access. The simplest method may be to use printed handouts. Alternatively, students can access printouts from a file system and return them once the unit is completed. Other options may include using online or cloud technologies. Consider technologies such as Google docs or videos on YouTube. Many schools have access to online content or learning management systems, such as Blackboard, Schoology, or Moodle, that offer additional features such as online forums.

How Many Units Should Students Complete per Semester?

This has a lot to do with how much time you are able to spend with your students. It also will depend on individual students and the scope of their projects. As a general rule, establishing a set number of units per quarter or semester is advisable. Try to find a reasonable number of units that will keep students working through the entire semester. However, flexibility is key. It is preferable that a student complete two solid units in a quarter than to rush through a third unit simply to satisfy an arbitrary number.

For example, you might assign students to complete three units from the following list per quarter, for a total of six units per semester.

- Artists Observe
- Artists Steal
- Artists Solve Problems
- Artist Tell Stories
- Artists Answer Essential Questions
- Artists Use Nontraditional Materials
- Artists Develop Style
- Artists Collaborate

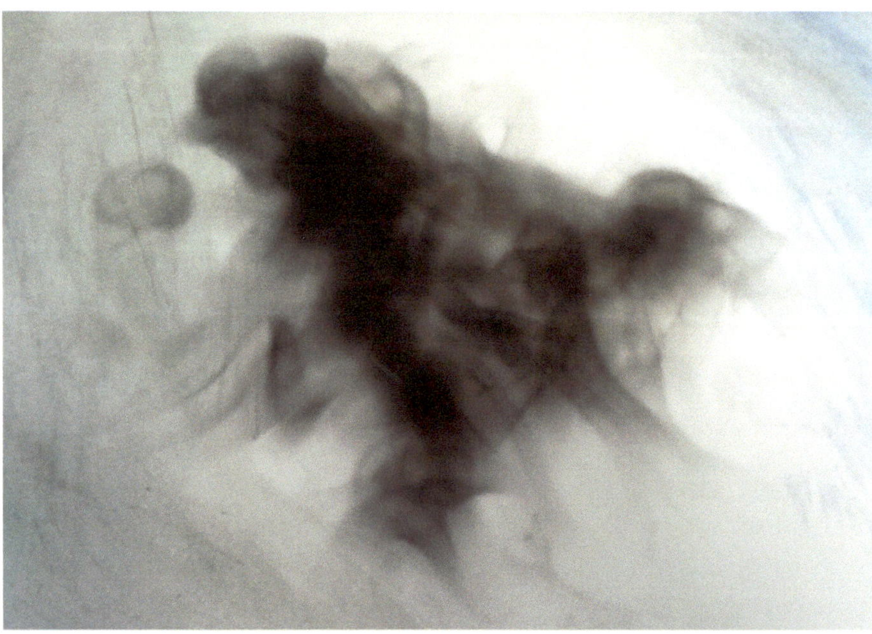

For the Artist Answer Essential Questions unit, this student asked, “Can art be created with fire?” (p. 190).

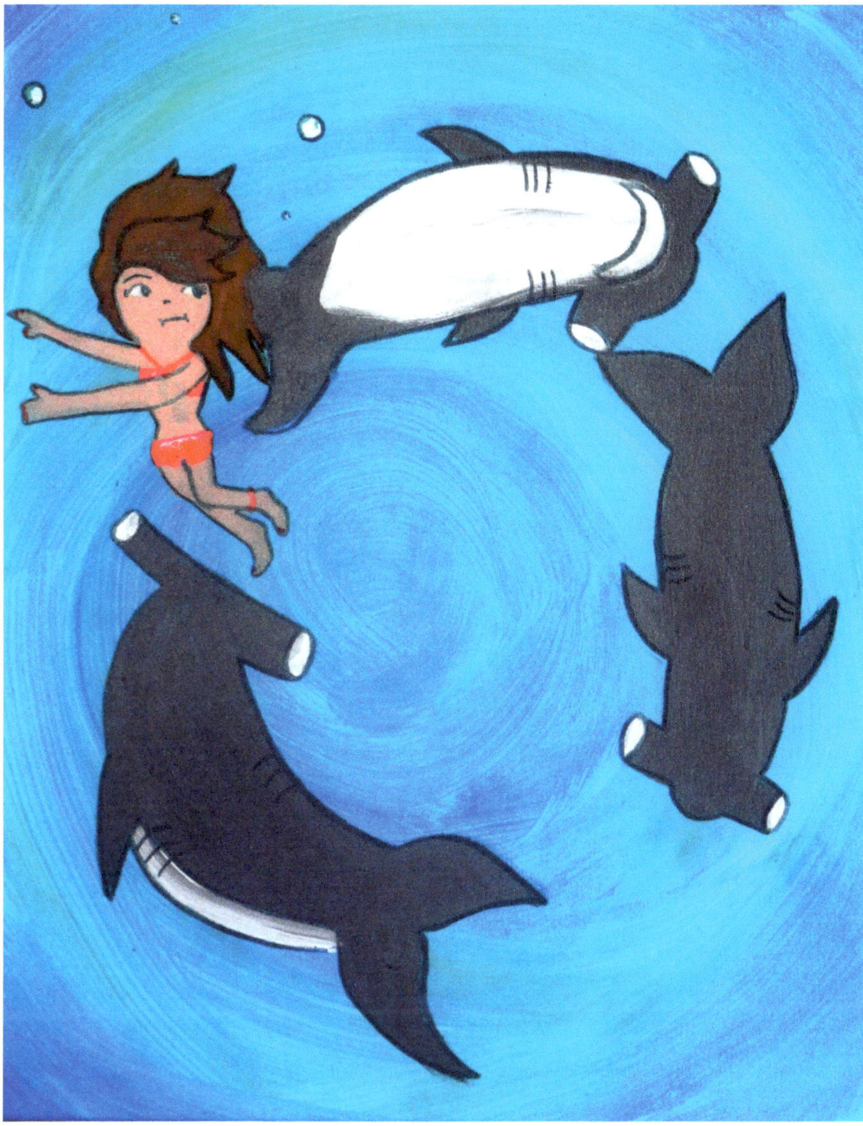

Acrylic painting based on a student-generated theme.

Student-Proposed Assignments

The most advanced level of choice is student-proposed assignments whereby students independently develop their own lesson plans. In this situation, there are no themes or Artistic Behavior Units. Instead, these are replaced by proposals that students create in order to outline their learning goals.

Most proposals ask students to describe what their intentions are as they relate to media, content, inspiration, and timeframe. Students write their individual plans on paper and submit them to the teacher for review. The teacher and student discuss the plan together and consider any possible pitfalls along with solutions. Once a proposal has been reviewed and the teacher approves the plan, the student moves forward with the design, creation, and reflection process.

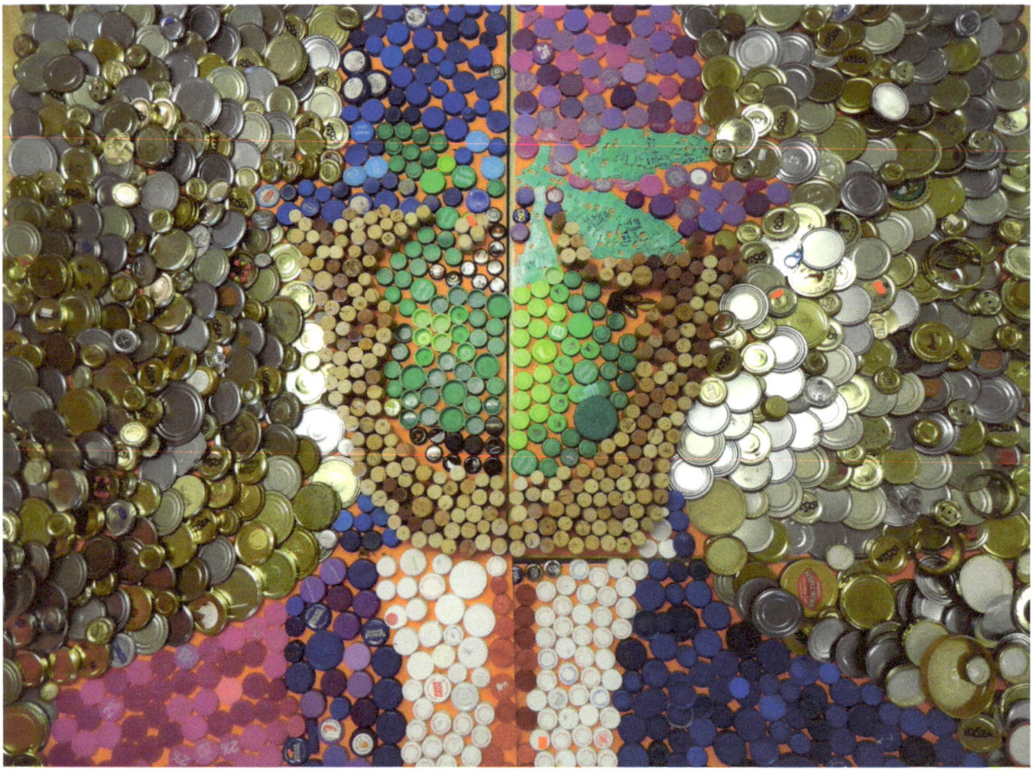

Completed temporary bottlecap mural inspired by Magritte's *The Son of Man*.

Student Inspiration

Perhaps the biggest challenge a student faces when considering a proposal is finding inspiration—in particular, finding inspiration that goes beyond a basic Pinterest search. Teachers understand the difference between true inspiration, appropriation, and copying. Students often do not. It is not uncommon for students to find art pinned on Pinterest that they wish to emulate. Though recreating art that was created by someone else can have some value towards learning a technique or skill, it is not true inspiration. True inspiration comes when a student borrows an idea or concept or even a technique and then extrapolates that idea to form something new. The reluctant student will need to have this explained. It will also help if there are methods students can use for finding inspirations that are less prone to mere imitation. Here are several ideas to get started.

Mini-Lessons. Even in an advanced-level choice classroom, mini-lessons should still be presented. Demonstrating new techniques or media is an ideal way to inspire students, especially if the demo is hands-on. Asking students to keep a record of what they accomplished or to generate a list of ideas that they thought of while working with the technique or material can boost inspiration.

Inspiration Books. Having students keep an inspirational sketchbook is another method for generating ideas. Teachers can offer weekly prompts that students must use to create ideas to be recorded and kept in their inspiration sketchbooks along with their doodles, thumbnails, and other visual methods of recording.

For example, prompt suggestions might include:

- Create five sketches based on something you saw on TV.
- Write ten sentences that all start with the word "Sometimes" or answer the question, What's inside a tree?
- Find a color that matches each of the following words: Internet, time, fancy, spacey, fraud, and hungry.

Students can also use their inspirational sketchbooks to track ideas on their own. They might sketch places they go, cut and paste images from magazines or images they print, or use their sketchbooks as a place to take notes during and after mini-lessons.

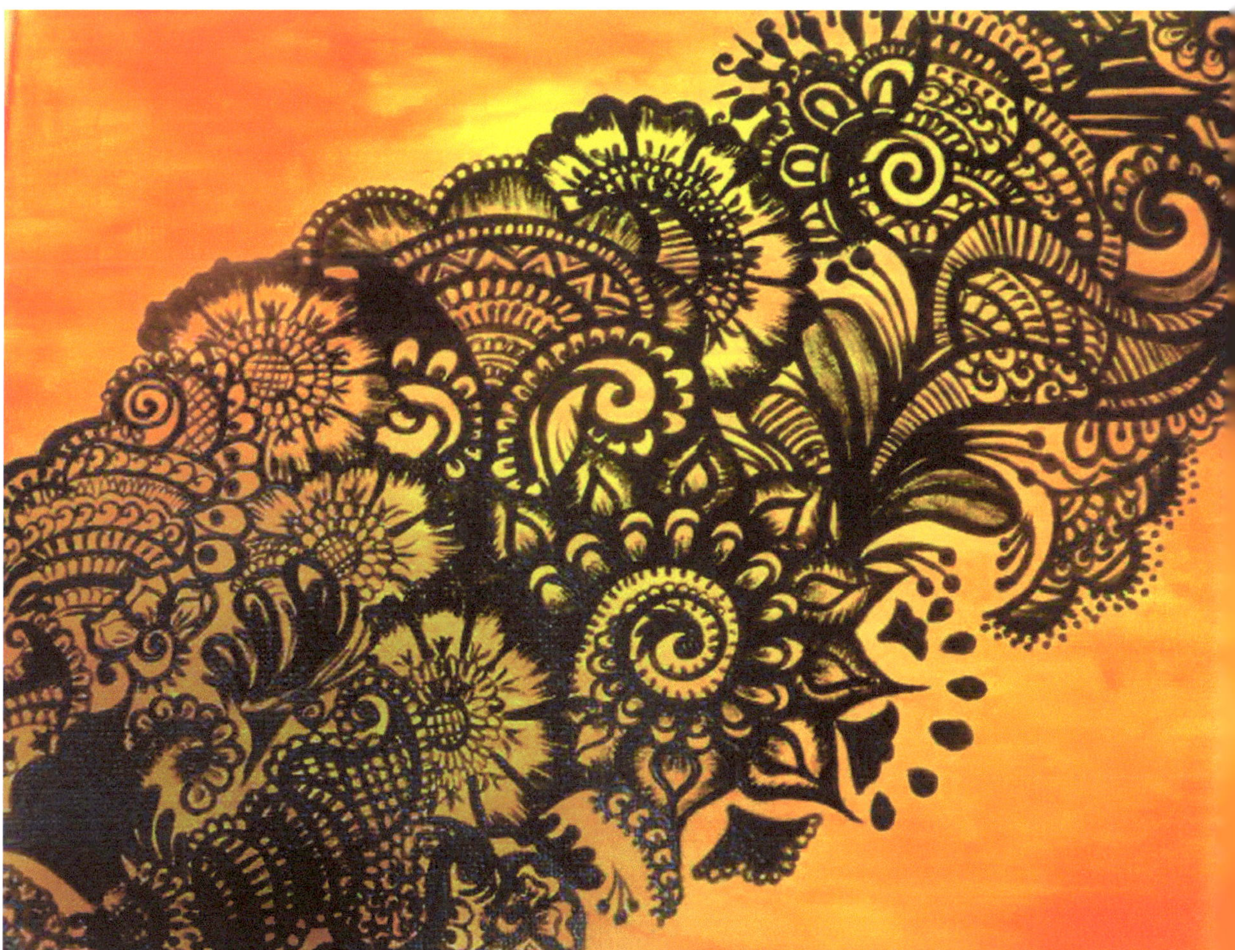

This acrylic painting expands on the student's interest in henna.

Idea Cards. For the student who is truly stumped, the teacher can suggest reaching into the idea box and selecting an idea card. Inside the box are index cards, and on each index card is listed one idea. Card ideas might include things such as:

- Create an abstract painting based on an actual landscape.
- Draw the reflection in a doorknob.
- Create a print using the theme, Washed Away.
- Learn how to reverse tie-dye using a black shirt and bleach.
- Create a sculpture using only items you have found while walking around the school.

Inspiration Center. Just as it is common for teachers to have a part of the art room dedicated to painting, drawing, or ceramics, having a place for inspiration can be just as important. Setting up a center for ideas can be as simple as maintaining a file cabinet with reproductions of famous works of art, how-to cards that provide instructions for learning new techniques, or newspaper articles about local artists. A more complex inspiration center might possess a full bookshelf, a computer with access to the Internet, and a comfy chair for perusing art-related magazines.

Self-Learning: Techniques and Skills

Students in the advanced level of a self-directed classroom have choice in almost every aspect of their work. They have choice in media, scope, and concept of their projects and often will have rolling due dates. The one area that student-artists need to fulfill in order to make the complete switch from student to artist is the ability to self-learn.

While some group demos or mini-lessons can still be advantageous, the beginner- and intermediate-level technique and skill-teaching methods will no longer be relevant. Instead of starting with a familiar medium or technique and building a project around a given concept, students may be designing art that is be beyond the teacher's skill level or even completely unfamiliar. In a teacher-directed class, the student would not be able to proceed beyond this point. However, as students become self-learners, their art can grow beyond the abilities of their teacher.

Keys to Self-Learning

Some students are born self-learners. It is not uncommon to meet students who learned to play guitar by ear or to code on their own, without the assistance of an instructor. However, other students will need a system in place that walks them through a process. Here are five keys that will help students become better self-learners.

Take Time to Research. Finding videos online that explain how to do something is quick and easy. However, finding a really good video that explains exactly what you need to know, in an economical manner, with the correct information, can be a challenge. Explain to students that researching doesn't simply mean finding the first video in a Google search. Rather, it means watching many videos on the same topic and comparing and contrasting their differences until the search can be narrowed down to one or two videos that meet one's needs.

Play. The word "play" is often misinterpreted to have negative connotations. We can envision the cliché of a father yelling at his son, "Stop playing around. This is serious work!" However, play *is* serious work. It is the art of

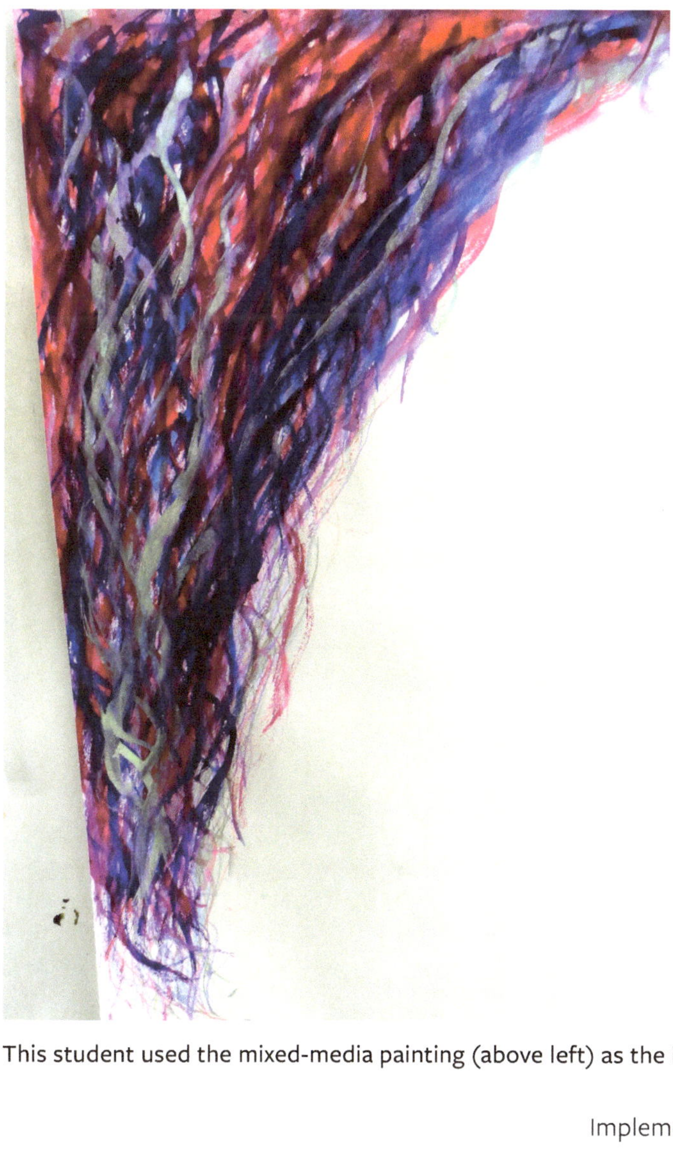

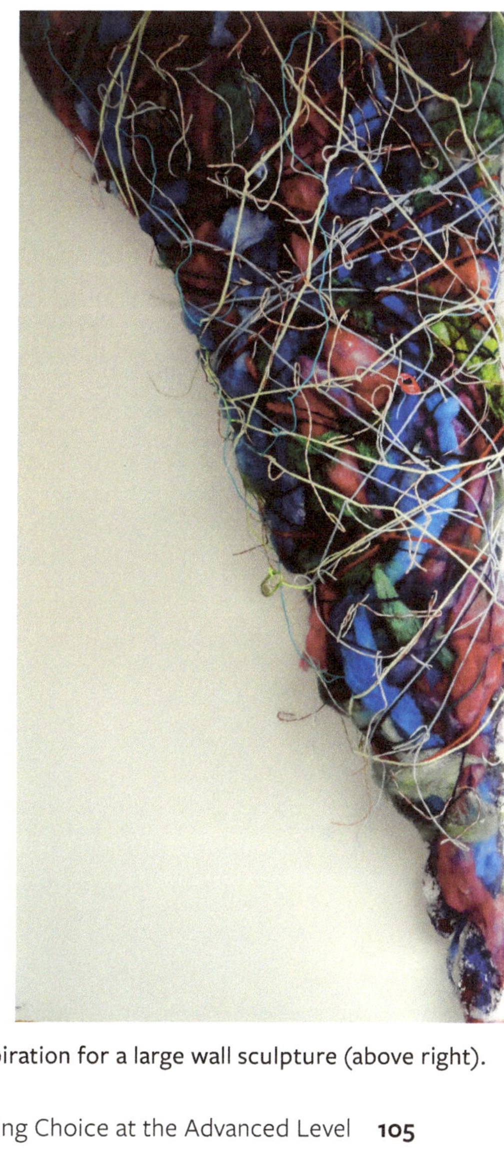

This student used the mixed-media painting (above left) as the inspiration for a large wall sculpture (above right).

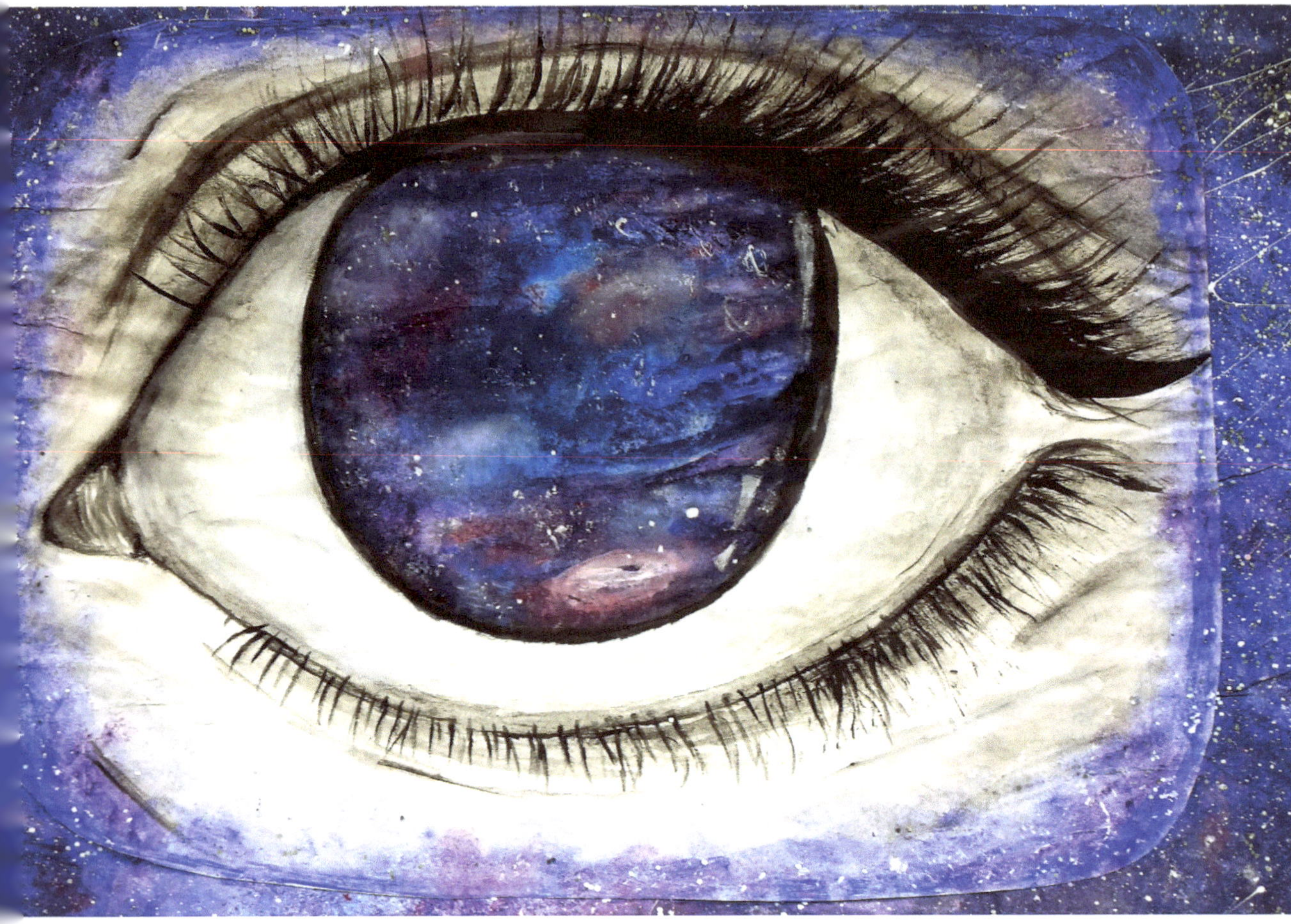

ıted to take this drawing further, so she used charcoal and acrylic paint to make it more interesting.

experimentation. It is finding out how things work. If a student asks how to accomplish something and the teacher is not sure, the best response may be, "I don't know. Let's find out."

Allow for Trial and Error. Like play, trial and error is a form of experimentation. The key difference is the understanding that sometimes, perhaps most often, the objective being attempted may fail. Failure is a good thing. When we fail, we learn what doesn't work and often gain an understanding of why it doesn't work. This puts us on a path to find a solution that does work.

Crowd-Source Knowledge. Just because neither a student nor a teacher knows how to accomplish a task, it doesn't mean that everyone in the room doesn't know. It is quite possible that someone in the room, in the next room over, or somewhere in the school knows how to accomplish the task. When one student teaches other students, or when students teach teachers, for that matter, it helps solidify their knowledge in their own minds. Seeking information from other students is a win/win for everyone involved.

Persevere. "If at first you don't succeed . . ." is a saying that students don't often subscribe to. In an era of instant gratification, it isn't uncommon for a student to give up after one try. "Get it right the first time" may be a wonderful saying, but it doesn't have much basis in reality. "Try, try again" is the conclusion to the opening saying and is the one that yields results.

Potential Challenges

It takes the trained eye of a teacher to not only see the potential in a student's art, but also to recognize the direction the student is capable of taking.

In this scenario, the teacher notices that the student is exploring an area of interest. The exploration may appear as play and, if the student is questioned about the work, a common response the teacher may hear is that the student is just playing, or bored, or experimenting, or messing around. However, if pressed further, the student will most likely be able to convey an actual explanation as to what and why she is doing what she is doing.

At that point, it is important for the teacher to realize that there is something that the student is interested in but is reluctant to share with others, perhaps because it may seem silly or irrelevant. Keep in mind: When

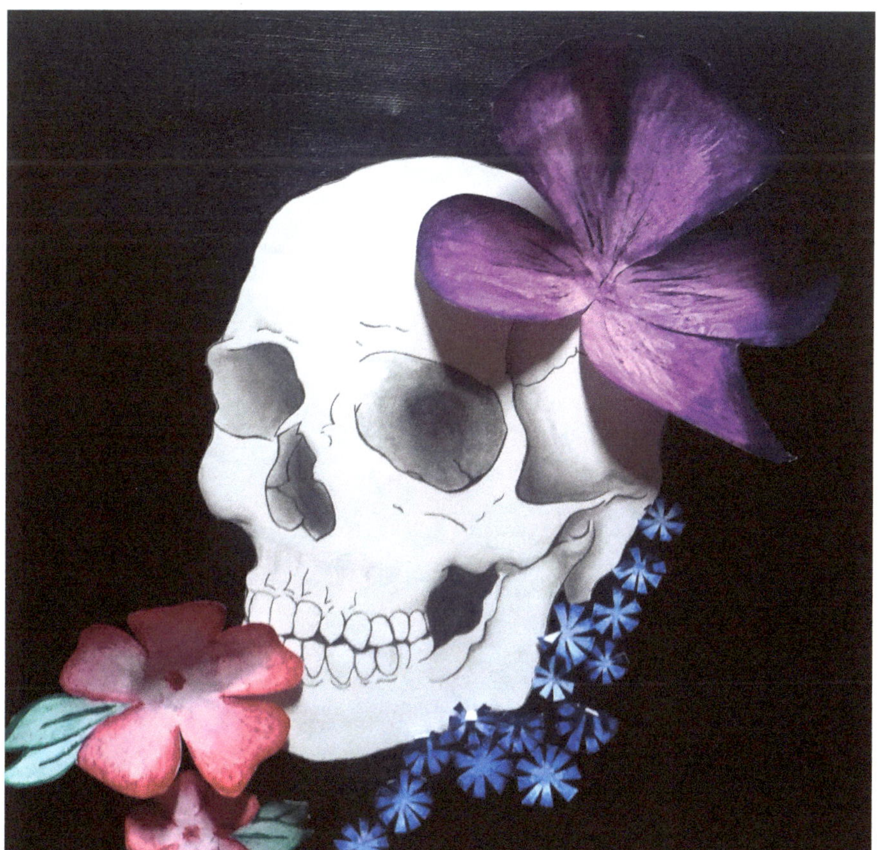

Tori created this mixed-media piece as a response to the theme Identity.

teachers let students know that they are interested in their thoughts, students become more comfortable about sharing what they are attempting to accomplish.

Once students see that a teacher is receptive to their ideas, they will start to open up and explore their own thinking. The teacher may hear responses such as, "I like the way the colors mix," or "I'm trying to make a pattern."

It is important to listen and try to understand what students are saying. Often simply listening and then encouraging the student to continue is best.

The next step for the teacher is to decipher what the student is truly trying to accomplish and then to gently point towards possible directions the student might go, especially those directions that the student doesn't yet recognize as available.

Such new directions might include everything from introducing a new medium, technique, or process, to researching new artists and exploring other artworks. Such new directions should legitimize the students' experiments and guide them towards growing as an artist.

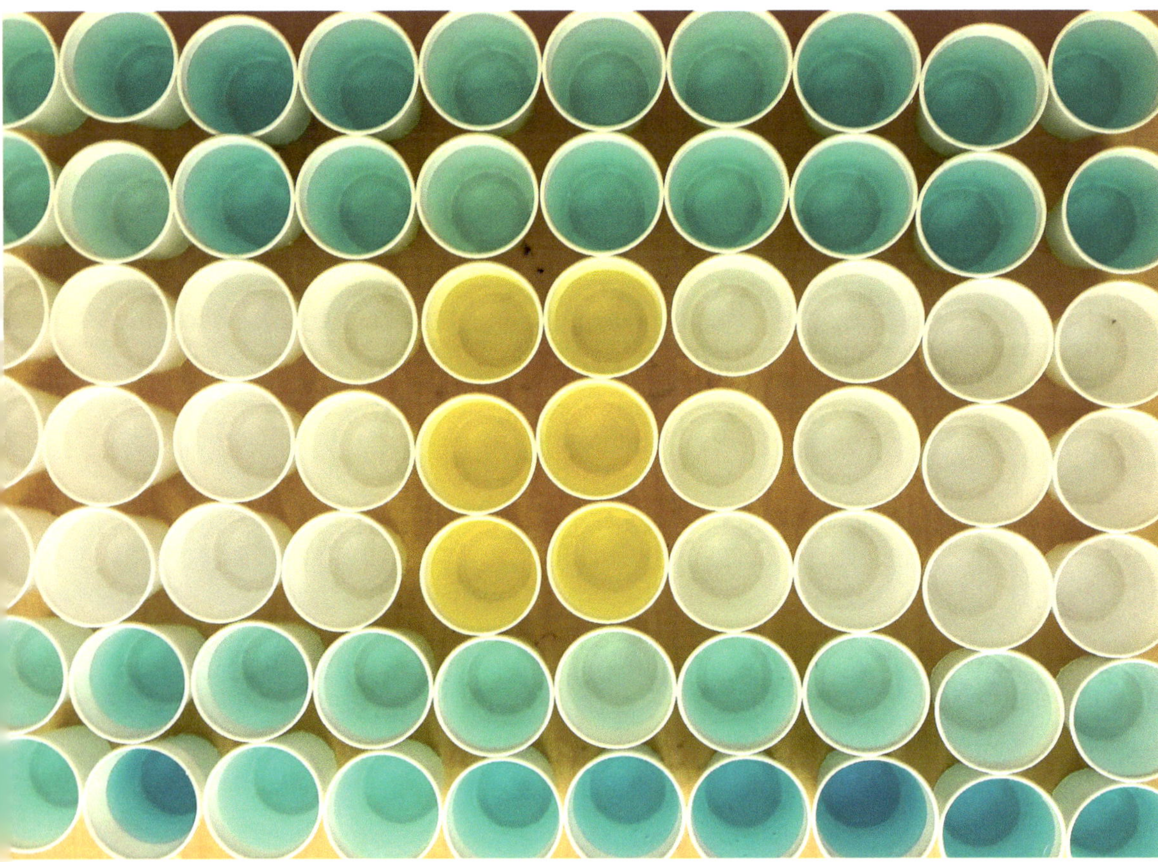

Cups filled with dyed water are arranged to create an image.

Emma D.: Choice Increases Evolution of Style

Besides the obvious "No!" I wasn't sure what to say when Emma D. asked if she could photograph her friends' butts with the word "cheeky" painted on them. She was seeking a solution to a unit on incorporating text and art and she was adamant about her idea. After several days of listening to her pleas, I finally offered a compromise: If she could get an administrator's approval, then I would sign off on the idea. The next day, Emma informed me that she was scrapping the photograph idea and replacing it with a painting.

It turned out that Emma was really interested in painting butts. She was less interested in painting text. She was, however, very interested in the thick texture she was producing with acrylic paint. Thus, our discussions turned from butt photographs to techniques to increase texture. We explored adding gesso and then cotton, which transformed the 2D painting into a relief.

When this project was complete, Emma decided to pursue the concept of texture. She found a Styrofoam square that was about the same size as a ceiling tile, and again our discussions turned to techniques and materials that could be used to increase texture. Emma explored gesso and canvas, which produced some texture, but the medium that truly satisfied her needs was Sculptamold. This paper-based sculpting material was perfect for shaping lumpy structures that clung to the canvas and Styrofoam.

The final result replaced one of the art room ceiling tiles, allowing the long stalactite-like sculpture to suspend seemingly precariously from above. This project was a far cry from the original photography idea. However, the choices that Emma was allowed to pursue contributed to the evolution of her personal style.

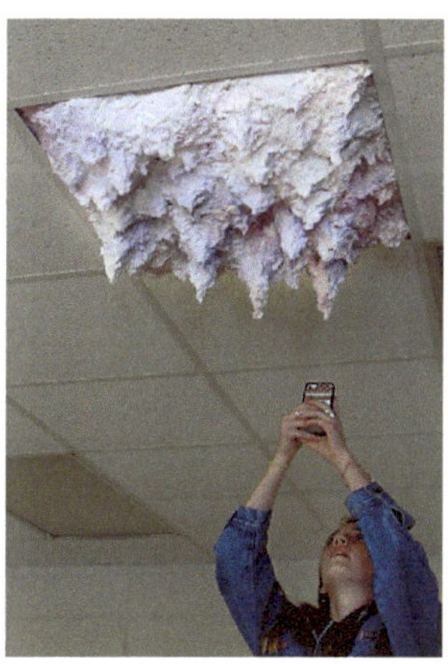
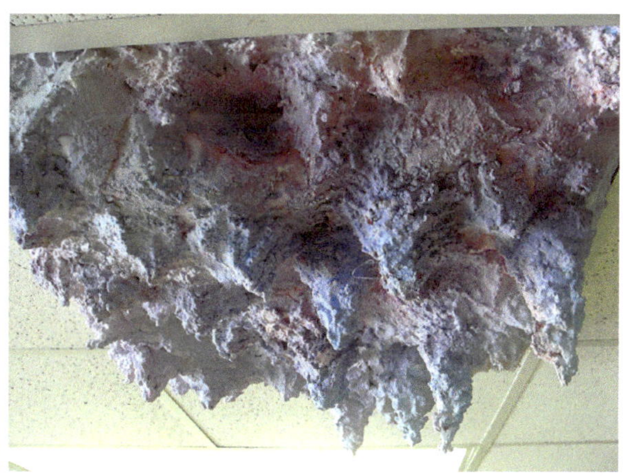

Emma's sculpture installed in the classroom ceiling.

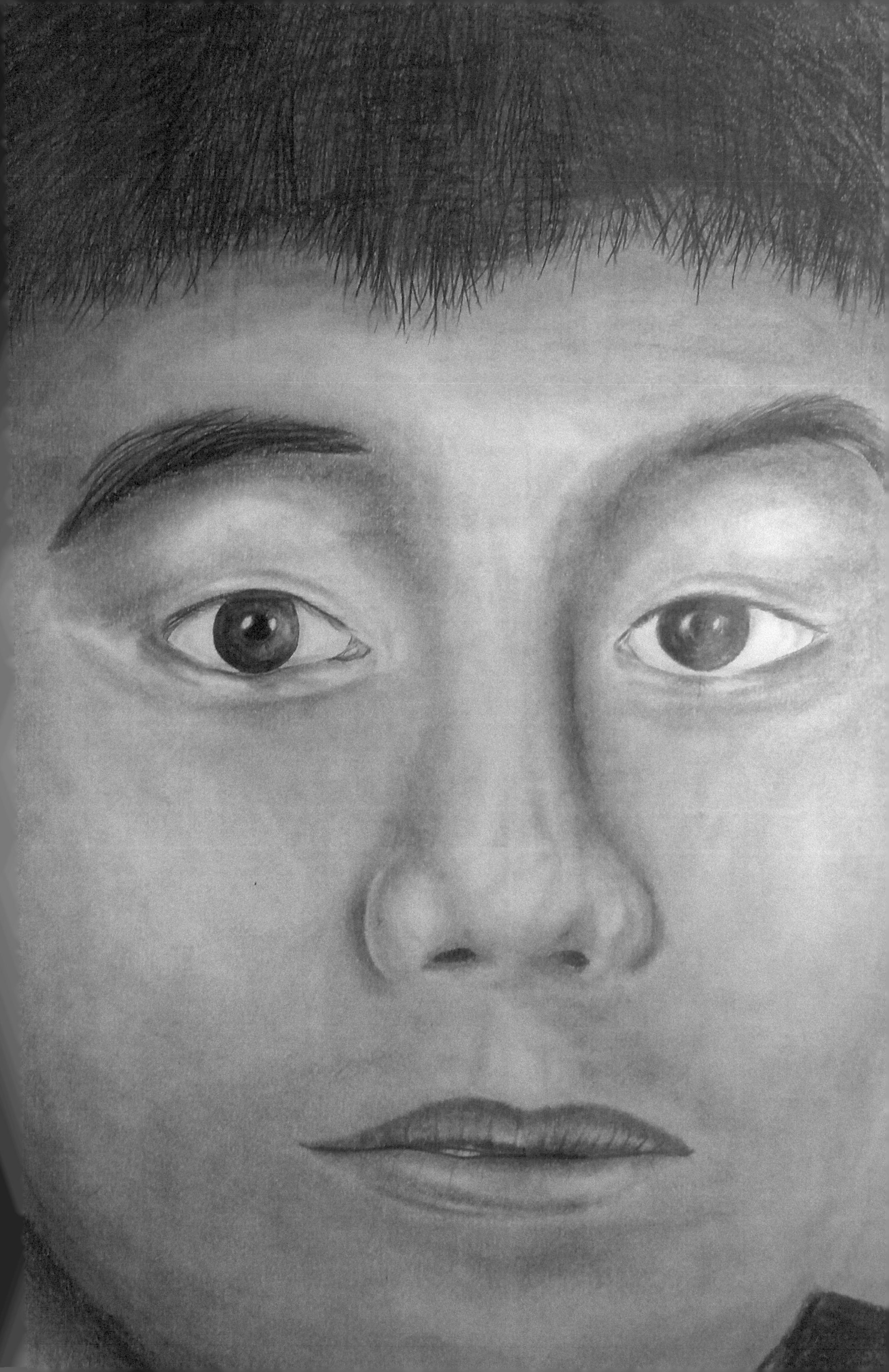

6 | Assessment

What do students know and what do they still need to learn? Answering this question is the core mission of assessment. Assessment is something good teachers are doing constantly. Every question students ask and every observation we make of them at work provides us with valuable information that can be used to help steer the course of the class. We gather information from every interaction with our students and use it to inform how we guide each individual to the next level. The relationship between the student and teacher that brings about this "leveling up" is essential for a choice-based classroom to flourish.

Assessment is essential for teaching and learning. However, when it's tied to grading, sometimes it can feel like a burden. The high-stakes, do-what-it-takes-for-the-A culture that permeates school life works against the intrinsically motivated artists we want to create, threatening to reduce anything that earns points to another hoop to jump through. In our ideal world, students would have the opportunity to create because they want to, making decisions based on personal vision, not on grades. Our goal in the Open Art Room is to use assessment to provide the best support to students and create grading policies that foster intrinsic motivation. We can make things less about point value by reducing the number of grades we give and by simplifying our grading systems to reflect what we value.

This chapter will focus on how to collect information using formative and summative assessment, and how to use such assessments to guide individualized instruction with the goal of fostering growth in every student. Grading comes at the end, where we will describe two approaches of tying assessments to grades and the philosophy behind our thinking.

Just Tell Me How to Get an A

I was so excited about moving up from elementary to teach high school. I had this beautiful vision of eager students engaged in their work, appreciative of the freedom and flexibility that would be part of my instruction. That first week of school was a rude awakening. They looked at each other warily as I described what the choice-based course structure I planned would look like. I finished my review of the course syllabus and asked, smiling, if anyone had questions. One brave Art 1 student raised his hand and asked what they all must have been thinking.

"So, what do I have to do to get an A?"

Formative Assessment

Formative assessment refers to the guiding and monitoring that teachers do every day as they teach: observing students at work, asking questions, giving feedback, and using this information—along with previous experiences with each student—to formulate the best way to teach. This might sound complicated to someone unfamiliar with teaching, but it is second nature to most teachers and foundational to the profession. For those who incorporate a high level of student choice it is even more important; it's the driving force behind almost all instruction, and how we individualize content and move kids from point A to B.

Formative assessment is best used diagnostically to develop a plan that helps students learn at their full potential. Developing this plan is contingent on the specific needs of individuals at any given time. Most students fall into one of three levels of engagement: Stuck, On Track, or Ready for a Challenge. Knowing the engagement level of students helps teachers respond with the right sort of support. The levels discussed here should be viewed as generalizations to customize and build upon, not as a set of steps to follow. How they are applied in the classroom will depend on one's teaching style and the specific needs of individual students.

Three Levels of Engagement

Recognizing how students are engaged with their work will help teachers decide how to support students, with the goal of keeping them on track and enjoying making art.

Stuck. The student isn't progressing forward at an ideal rate. This could be due to a variety of factors, such as behavioral issues, personal problems, lack of ideas, misunderstanding of next steps or unexpected challenges. Students who are stuck can appear like they don't care or even seem defiant. It takes

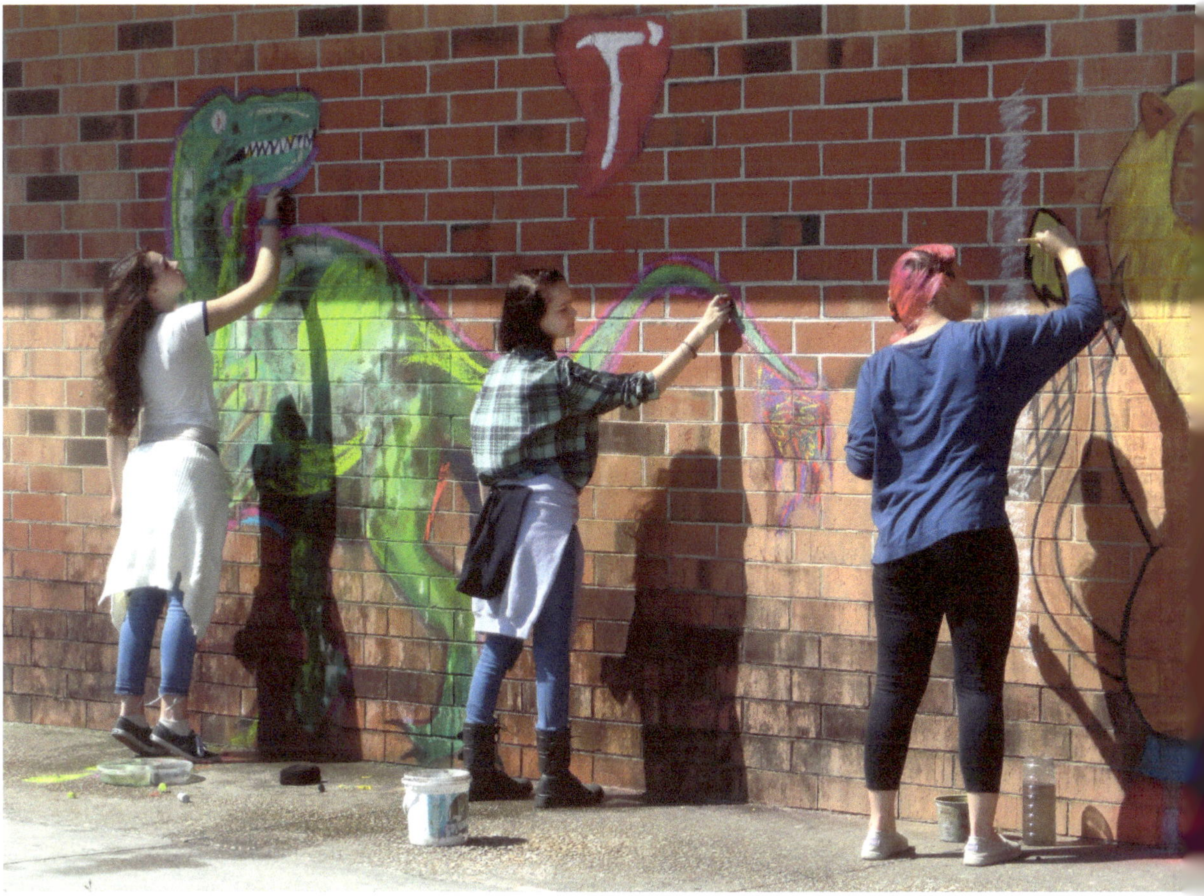

Collaboration can be a big part of the Open Art Room.

asking questions and really listening to find out what's going on. The student is unengaged, either actively or passively, by being on the phone, not working, talking, getting off-task, or being disruptive. How to respond? Find the cause of the issue and work to redirect, support, and engage the student.

On Track. An on-track student is working through the task at hand successfully with the resources provided. This is the behavior that you want to see in your classroom: The student is doing focused work for the majority of class time and is interested and engaged. With on-track students, teachers should maintain momentum with a minimum of a once-daily check-in, asking for questions and providing feedback.

Ready for a Challenge. The student at this engagement level might normally function at a high level and has interest and developed ability, but has plateaued. A student who's ready for a challenge is one who has been making similar projects or using the same supplies again and again without new discoveries or connections. If you have a student who seems to be always working in a particular style or scale, encourage him to break out of his comfort zone. Offer specific suggestions for new things to try.

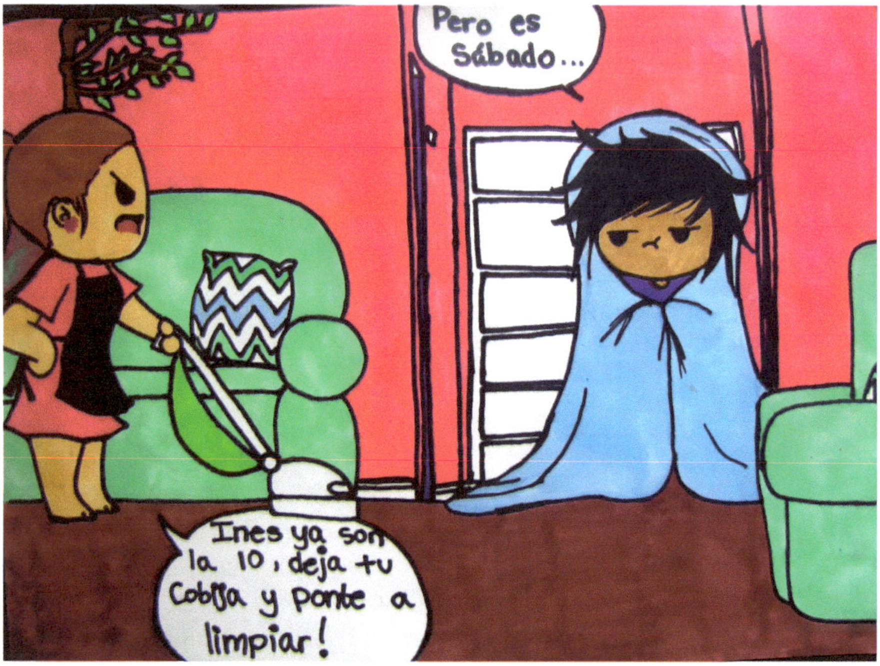

Inez drew this comic to capture how she feels on Saturday mornings.

Formative Assessment Types and Uses

Formative assessment helps identify existing gaps in knowledge or ability and how to fill them. Formative assessment should be used as a diagnostic tool and not necessarily as a grading tool.

Pre-Assessment. Pre-assessments are used at the start of a learning experience to determine what students know going in. For example, before teaching a painting Bootcamp, it makes sense to see what students know about color theory. Think about the information you would expect students to know at the beginning of the Bootcamp and what you would like them to know at the end. Questions that might be asked include: What are the three primary colors? How is the color orange mixed? Is pink a tint or a shade?

Starting a unit or a Bootcamp with a short pre-assessment gives the teacher valuable information to use in planning instruction. It also provides a data point to compare to the summative assessment at the end of the unit (discussed below). This comparison allows teachers to reflect upon the effectiveness of their teaching and provides useful data for conversations with administration about what students are learning.

Designing a pre-assessment is straightforward: Just think about the key ideas you want students to leave the learning experience with. Use these key ideas to write questions that can be given as a short quiz or used as the basis of a class discussion. Plan on revisiting the questions you use in your summative assessment.

Observation and Conferencing. The method of formative assessment teachers tend to use almost constantly is observation, or simply looking and thinking about students learning as they watch it happen. Observation has extra importance in art because the idea of looking and being seen is essential to the discipline. When observing students, think about how they are using the Artistic Thinking Process and consider what the artwork looks like, how comfortable the students seem with the assignment, and their general demeanor. These observations will guide you in providing differentiated support to each student.

Conferencing, or informal conversations with students, works hand in hand with observation. Daily conferencing, even just for a quick check-in, with every student is the key to keeping all students on track in the Open Art Room.

Providing Feedback. Ideally, when conferencing with students you observe them at work, think about which of the three levels of engagement they fit in, and combine that information with your previous knowledge of them. Next, ask them questions to find the right sort of feedback to give them about work in progress and to determine how best to support their learning. The following guide gives examples of what to look for during observation, matched with conferencing questions for each of the three types of engagement.

Feedback on the Artwork. *What to look for:* Is the work they are producing successful and what you would expect based on your understanding of their current skill level? Are they developing new skills and learning different ways of art-making, or are they re-creating similar work again and again? *What to ask:* How do you like your work? What area is the most successful? Are you experiencing any challenges?

For a student who is stuck, try something like this: I really like how you [compliment a successful area of the work] but I notice that [mention an area they seem to be struggling with and why they are having a challenge]. Would you like me to [give you some suggestions or demonstrate]? I notice you aren't moving forward with your work. What can I do to help you?

With a student who is on track, try: I notice you seem very comfortable with this assignment. Is there anything I can help you with? I really like how you [give the student some positive feedback, followed with suggestions, if needed].

For a student who is ready for a challenge, try: You did a great job with [name something she did well]. I think you're ready to [something she might try now].

Stuck in Graphite

Alex was talented, of that there was no doubt. He spent hours outside of class sketching the cartoonish figures he'd created, developed from his friends and experiences. Of course, he wanted to use this work he was so passionate about for class assignments, so I let him. Over time, however, his lack of progress made one thing abundantly clear: Alex was stuck. His ability to draw his figures had improved over time in Art 2, but we were halfway through the course and he hadn't produced anything that looked finished. He just wanted to draw in his sketchbook.

"Alex," I told him, "I love the expressions on your figures' faces and the action that you're drawing but your work doesn't look done. Let's come up with a plan to turn some of these sketches into finished art."

Alex was resistant. He liked what he was doing and didn't want to change. I didn't want to push too hard and risk ruining his love of the work he was producing, but I clearly saw how much a bit more detail and thought about composition would make his images shine, so I kept making suggestions. He liked some, like my tips about composition or taking reference photos for the poses he needed, and ignored others. Finally, after weeks of suggesting that he use color, he came to class clutching a case of high-end markers. "Mrs. Purtee, I'm in love!" he told me, beaming, as he showed me his gleaming work.

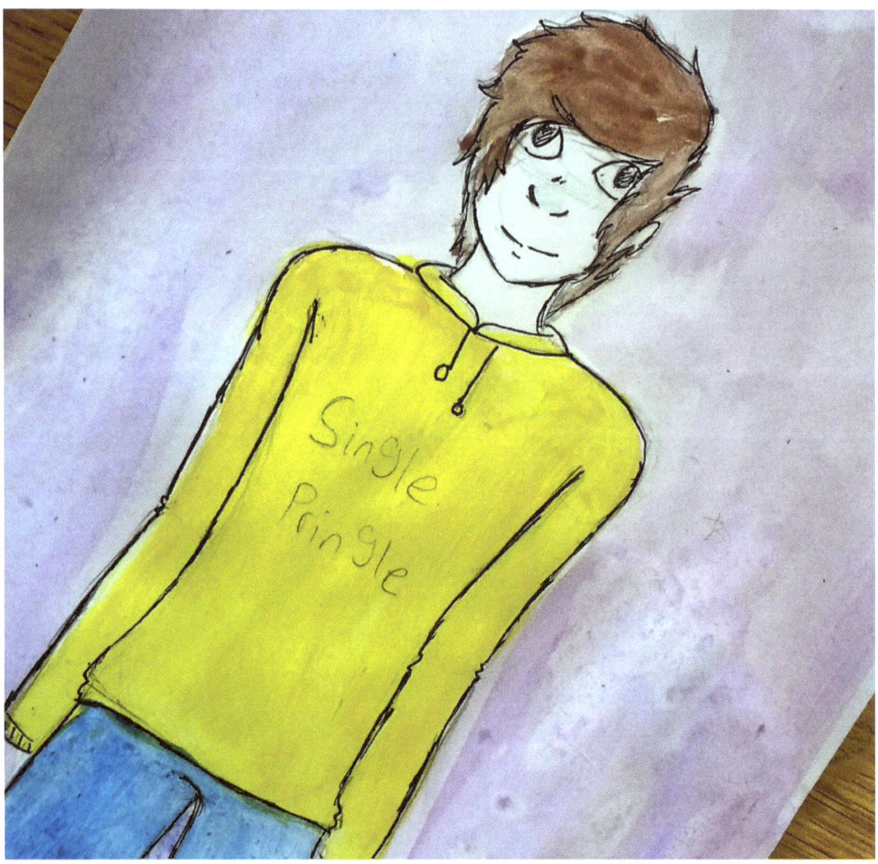

Alex's sketches are transformed with color.

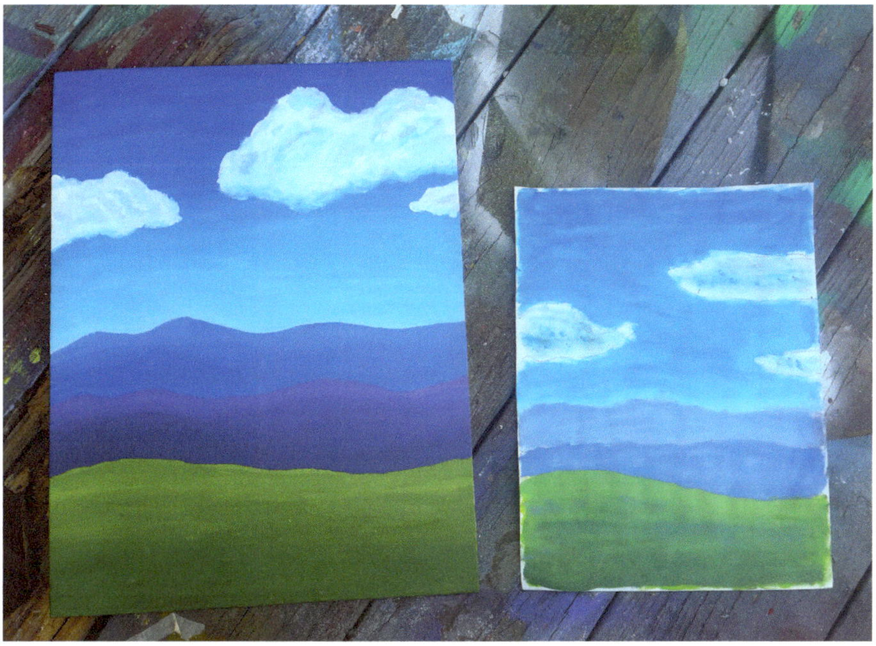

This painting from the beginning of the year was recreated by an Art 1 student to show how her skills had improved.

Feedback on Work Habits. *What to look for*: Are they moving forward and using the Artistic Thinking Process to work through tasks, or are they floundering? What is their behavior like: engaged, compliant, or disruptive? *What to ask*: Tell me about what you've been working on today.

For a student who is stuck: I see that you aren't moving forward with [the task at hand]. What is going on? How can I help you?

For a student who is on track: It looks like you know what to do with this assignment. Do you have any questions for me?

With a student who seems ready for a challenge: You don't seem that into this work. Let's brainstorm and see if we can come up with something that will be more interesting for you.

Teaching with Empathy. When a student is experiencing emotional difficulty, it impacts work. Teaching with Empathy will help resolve these issues. When you notice changes in behavior, or a student is in a bad mood, it never hurts to ask if everything is okay. *What to look for*: Is the student engaged in the work or do they seem sad, tired, bored, or angry? *What to ask:* How are you today?

If the student is stuck: You seem [tired, upset] today. Is there something going on?

If the student is on track: How are you feeling about your work? Are there any parts that are difficult?

If the student is ready for a challenge: It seems like you are finished working on this. Have you tried [suggest something to try]?

Taking the Time to Ask

Justin was new to the school and had an attitude. Likable and funny sometimes and withdrawn on other days, he was in my most challenging class and his mood determined how the day would go. One day, he was especially out of sorts and making comments that got the whole class laughing while I was trying to introduce a unit. I told him to knock it off more than once but he kept on going, so finally I snapped.

"If you can't listen, then leave."

"Fine, I'll leave," he said, and stormed out.

Part of me wanted to let him go because I was so sick of dealing with interruptions, but I knew that if he left, the situation would be worse the next day. I took a deep breath and walked outside the door, where he was calling a ride.

"Justin, I'm sorry I snapped at you," I said. "I don't want you to leave and I shouldn't have said that. You don't seem like yourself today. Is anything going on?"

He told me about how he wasn't getting any sleep because he was sleeping on the couch in his dad's house and his toddler stepbrother kept him up crying all night. He was also fighting with his dad and missed his friends in Florida.

"That sounds really stressful," I said. "Maybe you need some space today, so what if I agree not to bug you and you agree not to disrupt class?"

"Okay," he said. We went in the room and finished the lesson. Justin was never a model student, but he was never disruptive like that again. Knowing that I cared about him enough to ask and listen made all the difference.

Feedback on Content. Content is best addressed during the inspiration and design phases of the Artistic Thinking Process, before it's been decided on. *What to look for*: Is the content of the work appropriate for the age and ability of the student? Is it original or is the student recreating an image she's found? Does the student seem excited about the content and invested in the outcome of the work or does he seem unengaged?

If the student is stuck: Tell me about your concept for your artwork. You don't seem to be moving forward. How can I help you make your idea work? I think I've seen things that are similar to this. Let's talk about some ways to make it more original.

If the student is on track: Can you explain what your work is about? Do you have questions about how to move forward with your idea?

If the student is ready for a challenge: You don't seem too excited about this idea. Can I help you find something you like better? Have you thought about [using a material that might be a good match, looking at specific artists that might be inspiring]?

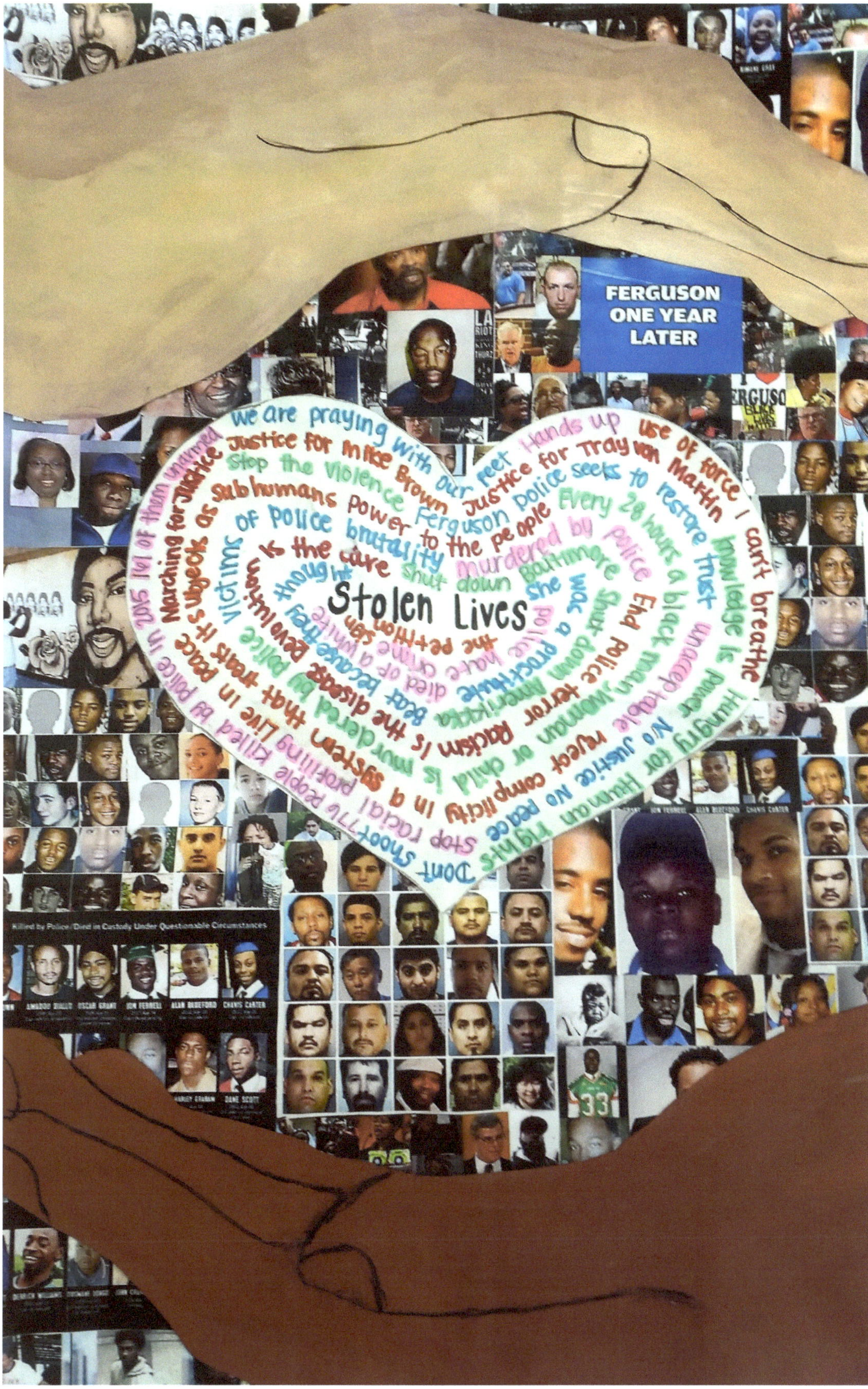

Mixed-media work created for the Artists Take a Stand unit (p. 206).

Drawing the Line, with Respect

I love to include topics related to world events and social justice issues in my class because they are engaging and meaningful to students. Of course, I know it can be risky to ask kids to delve into this sort of subject matter. What if topics cause arguments? What if they produce something that goes too far? What if parents or other students get offended? Developing some guidelines for content can reduce much of this risk. The most important guideline I use is that everyone in the classroom will be treated with respect. I tell my students that disagreement is fine, but offensive language or personal attacks are not.

This guideline has come in handy more than once. It helped me the one time I really objected to a student's work. Chris wanted to incorporate a Confederate flag made out of guns in his art, but it was an extremely volatile issue at that moment due to recent mass shootings and the displaying of the flag by a few state capitals. Complicating matters further, a few students in the class were making art in support of the Black Lives Matter movement.

I talked to Chris. I started by telling him that I understood that hunting and gun rights were important to him and that I realized that the Confederate flag was a symbol of Southern pride to him. Next I mentioned some of the recent events and told him that, because of the current social climate, I felt like combining guns and Confederate flags would cross the line between making people think and being deeply offensive. I offered to help him think of another way to make work about the ideas he wanted to talk about and he agreed. He ended up taking a series of photos during a hunting trip that made a much more eloquent statement about the cultural value of guns than the work he was originally considering.

Summative Assessment

Summative assessment occurs at the end of a unit or Bootcamp to evaluate the learning that has taken place during a specific timeframe. Critiques are an important traditional form of final assessment. In the Open Art Room summative assessment also takes place when we ask students to assess and reflect in blog posts, conferences, and presentations. These activities provide students the chance to step back and look at the growth they have made, to enjoy the work others have made, and to celebrate everyone's accomplishments. Summative assessment helps teachers understand more clearly what students know and can do. Furthermore, as we ask students to reflect on what they've learned, we can also use their responses to evaluate the effectiveness of our teaching.

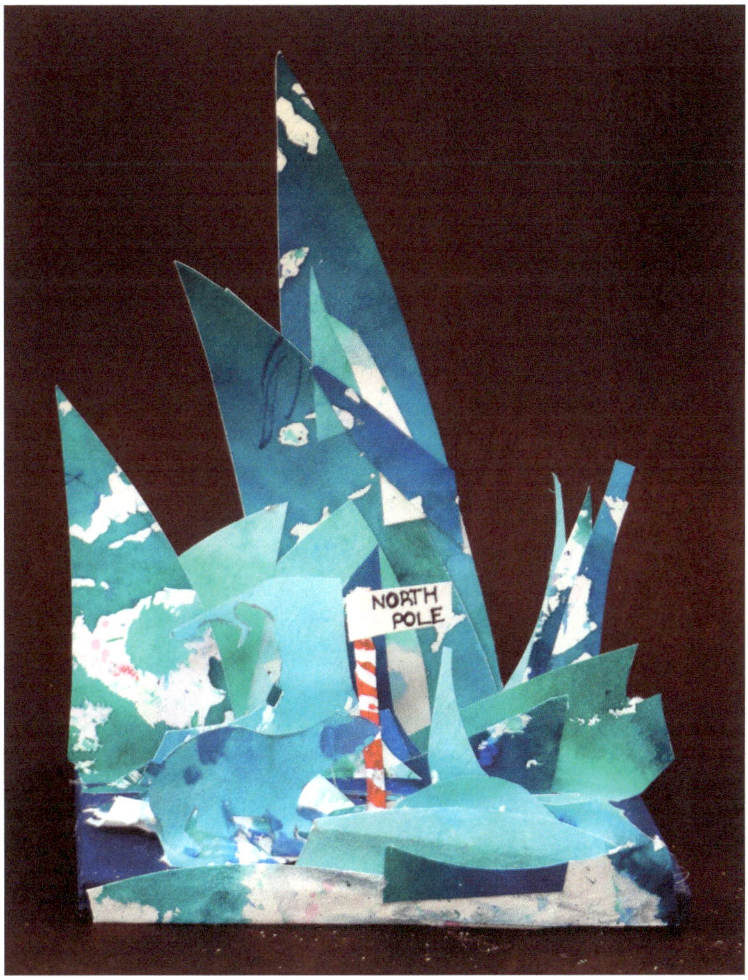

Paper sculpture created in response to the unit Artists Emphasize the Elements.

Types of Summative Assessments

Summative assessments using presentations, conferences, and blog posts are similar in content but different in delivery. Reflective questions for all three types should assess what you wanted students to learn during the lesson. Typically, some questions are about the Artistic Thinking Process, while others are related to Artistic Behaviors. Ordinarily, questions are designed to assess a specific Artistic Behavior or standard. Alternatively, students may choose questions from the Artistic Behavior Rubric.

Presentations, conferences, blog posts, and critiques are all ways to evaluate what students have learned during a given period of time. Each method has different strengths. Teachers can select which method to have students use or offer the methods as choices.

ction Tool and Rubric

Behavior	Questions	Rubric
eate Original Art tively riginal ideas	How did you use your own unique ideas in your work? Did you use a source for inspiration, then combine it with your own ideas to make it original?	1. Artist's ideas are unoriginal, copied, or plagiarized. 2. Artist's attempts to use original ideas are somewhat unsuccessful; low level changes are made. 3. Artist's ideas are original, unique to the artist, or borrowed ideas are merged/changed to create something new. 4. Artist's ideas are original and creative. A personal style develops.
velop Skills niques sses edia	Did you learn new techniques or processes as part of the work for this project? Did you gain skill with familiar materials? Explain how your skill grew.	1. Artist stays at current skill level. 2. Artist attempts to learn new skills but gives up when presented with challenges. 3. Artist puts forth needed effort to develop new skills successfully. 4. Artist's development/effort exceeds expectations.
mmunicate ssion rsonal interests nportant issues	What is this artwork intended to say? What issues are you examining through your artwork? How is this artwork about who you are or what you like?	1. There is no original message or meaning in the artwork. 2. An original message is attempted but it becomes lost or confused. 3. The work has a discernible message that is accessible to the viewer. 4. The work has impact and makes a personal connection with the viewer.
e Risks edia/ processes t	Did you try something new or unfamiliar as part of this project? Did you pick a material or technique that was new or different over something that was familiar?	1. Artist selects familiar options with predictable outcomes. 2. Artist takes limited risk or the outcome is somewhat predictable. 3. Artist selects options where the outcome is unsure. 4. Artist embraces the potential of risk to take work to the next level.

Presentations. Presentations work well for students who like to share ideas publicly. They are also appealing to kids who dislike writing, whether because of preference or skill deficit. Since they are done in front of the class, students who present get immediate feedback and are able to interact with class members in a discussion. Also, all students get to hear more details about the work that is being discussed, which helps build a supportive classroom culture. A plus for teachers is that presentations are easy to grade as they are watched. However, they do require everyone's attention, and they reduce work time.

Artistic Behavior	Questions	Rubric
Artists Collaborate share ideas and knowledge teach help critique	Did you use feedback during your work process? Did someone help you understand important information or inspire you? Did you work with a group to make something you couldn't have made on your own?	1. Artist works alone. 2. Artist collaborates passively. 3. Artist actively collaborates. 4. Artist takes on leadership roles within groups.
Artists Solve Problems try alternative solutions use mistakes as learning opportunities plan	How did you respond to challenges that occurred as you worked? Did your work take an unexpected turn due to a mistake or did something happen that was unplanned?	1. Artist gives up when confronted with problems. 2. Artist can solve problems with help. 3. Artist is self-directed in seeking out and attempti solutions. 4. Artist generates solutions to problems independ
Artists Reflect analyze work and process plan	When did you step back and analyze your work during this project? Did you consider how ideas would work before you tried them?	1 Artist does not reflect. 2. Artist needs help to analyze work. 3. Artist can independently understand strengths a weaknesses of artwork. 4. Artist can independently analyze artwork and ap observations to past, present, and future work.
Artists Use Personal Voice develop an individualized style make art that expresses personal ideas, values, or opinions independently develop and select themes	How did you use ideas that are personally meaningful as part of the work you created? Does your work express your ideas, values, or opinions? Give examples. How did you select and develop your own theme?	1. Artist mainly replicates the work of others. 2. Artist needs step-by-step support to plan and cr original work or borrows heavily from the ideas of 3. Artist has elements of an individual style and ma related to personal ideas, values, or opinions. 4. Artist has a clearly defined personal style and w thematically to create personally meaningful work.

In presentations, students stand up in front of the class and share their artwork, then answer reflection questions that they have selected or that have been assigned. After the student shares, students in the class can ask questions and provide feedback. As an alternative to oral presentations, students can make videos and post them on their blogs.

Conferences. Conferences appeal to students who prefer one-on-one conversations. They are a great option for building positive relationships with students and getting to know them on a personal level. The best part

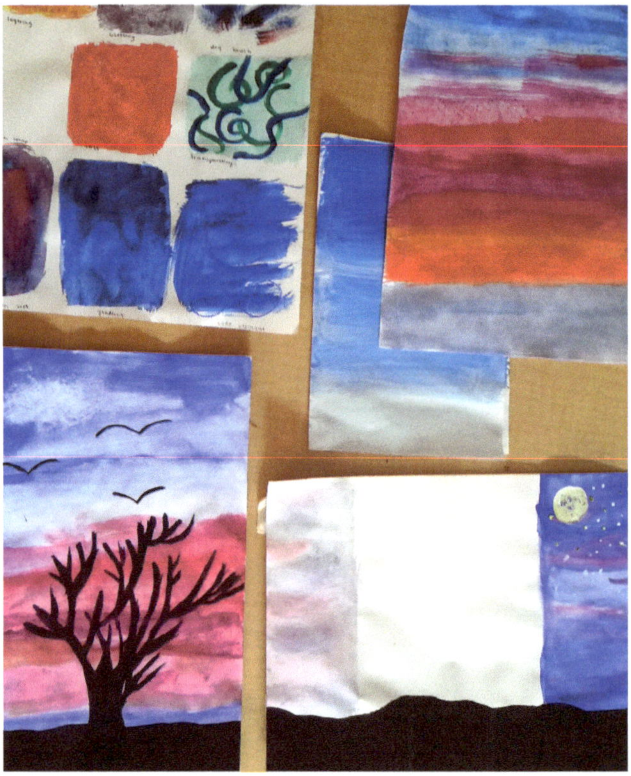

Design stage of Emma's watercolor painting. The assignment was to depict a sequence of events.

about conferences is that they are more distinctly individual. Questions can be modified to flow with the conversation. Conferences also work as modifications for students who are unable to write due to special needs, such as a learning disability or ELL status. One huge plus of the conference assessment method is that personal feedback can be given quickly and easily. However, conferences take time away from circulating around the room and talking to students about work in progress.

During a conference, the teacher and the student sit down and talk, normally during class work time. The teacher verbally asks the reflective questions that have been assigned, or the student answers the questions that he or she has selected. The artwork being discussed is shared and the teacher gives feedback. Another option for conferences is to have them in small groups instead of one-on-one. This option reduces the pressure that students may feel when speaking in front of the whole class, but still permits the exchange of diverse viewpoints and group discussion.

Blog Posts. Blog posts are an especially effective form of assessment for keeping a record of student work. First, a student creates a personal blog. When a summative assessment is assigned, the student can write responses to the assigned or self-selected reflection questions on the blog and post

One on One

Emma was shy, so shy that she often responded to questions with just a shrug or a one-word answer. I didn't get much more on her blog posts. She'd write the absolute minimum, and it always felt as though she was merely trying to say what she thought she was expected to say. Personal conferences made a big difference in the quality of information she was able to communicate. Sitting over by my desk with me gave her enough privacy from the group to feel less self-conscious. When I'd ask her a question, she would initially respond with a vague, generic answer. I'd follow up with questions until she was able to explain her thinking clearly. This conversation gave me a chance to know her better. After our first conference she began to respond more to the questions I asked when she was at her seat working, and by the end of the class we could joke and laugh together. Conferencing really helped develop our relationship and improved how we worked together.

images of artwork to accompany the writing. Blog posts create a digital record of the learning that has taken place during the class. Student blogs can be continued in subsequent art classes and serve as online portfolios of work and learning. They are easy for the teacher to access and grade with a link. However, they can be a challenge for students who have difficulty writing due to disability or preference. They can also prove time-consuming for teachers who provide written feedback.

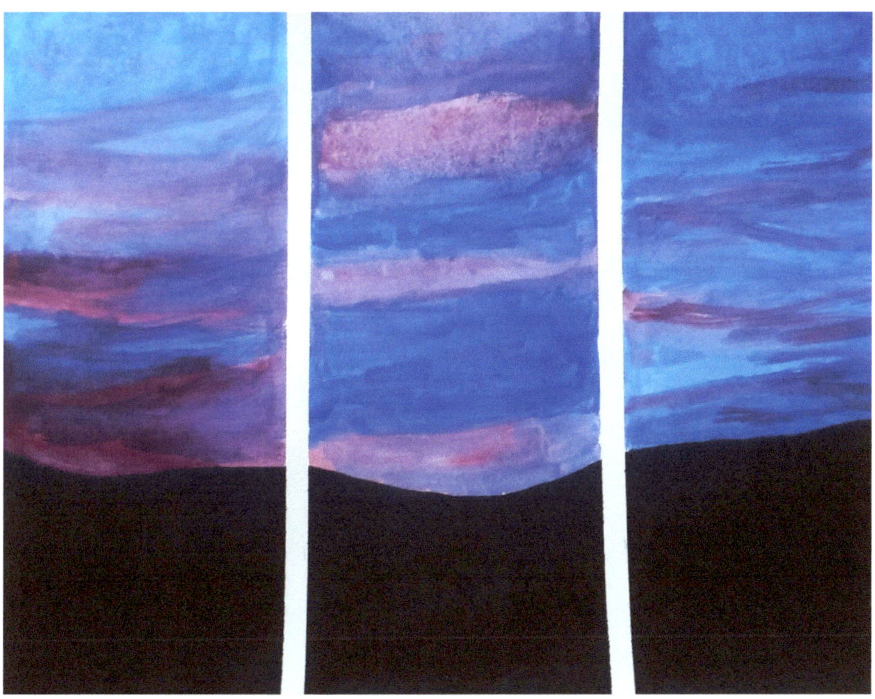

Emma's finished work shows enormous growth.

Thinking Is Thinking

Brittany hated writing blog posts, so much so that she would almost rather fail the class than write. However, she loved to talk about her work. When she presented to the class she really opened up, sharing her struggles with autism and explaining the symbolism in her work. Her drawing of two figures represented two sides of her, she said, while she described the manga storyline that inspired her. She was able to express so much more verbally than she could in writing, and the class loved learning about her ideas. No one had known that both figures in the artwork were her, and learning that made the whole class think about using symbolism. Writing is a good thing to ask kids to do, but it was not the best assessment method for Brittany.

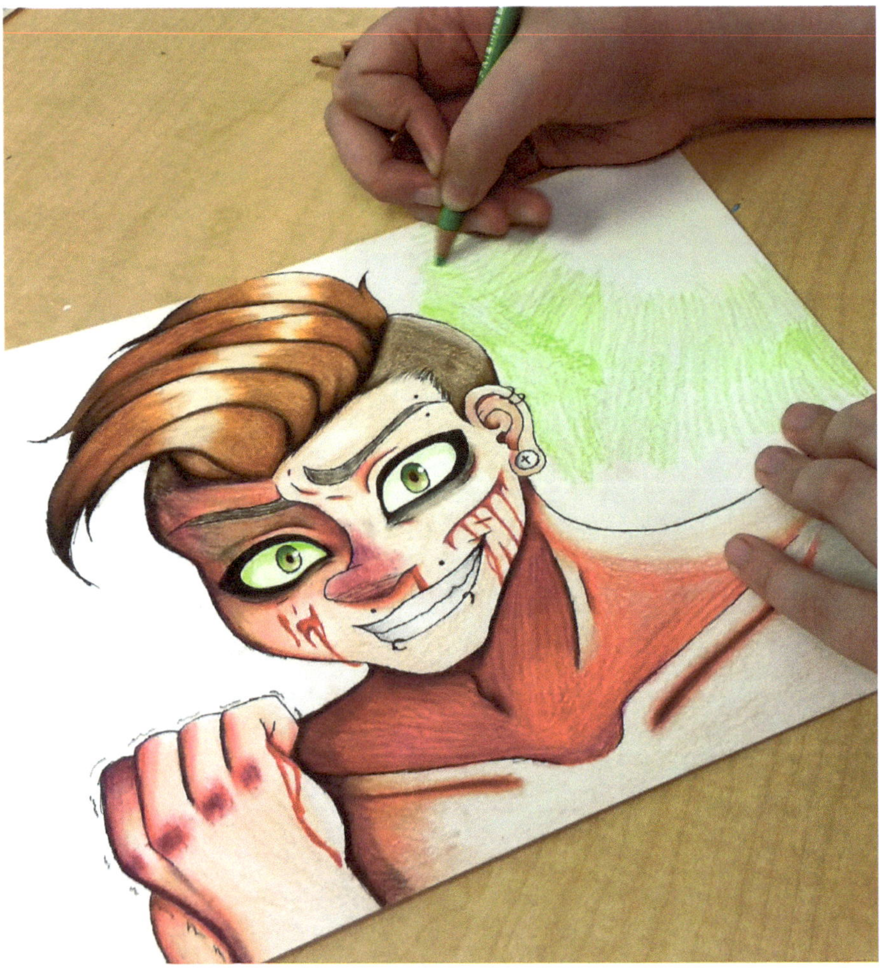

Self-portrait exploring mental health issues.

When Writing Works

In the following blog post, Jenna reflected on how she planned her artwork and developed her ideas. As part of this project about current issues, students were asked to come up with an essential question. Jenna chose to focus on the issue of violence against women. She originally started with the question, How does sexual assault affect the United States? and then narrowed her focus. She wrote about figuring out how to translate her concept into a powerful visual image:

"The issue that I chose to portray in my artwork was violence against women. My piece is titled "One in Three" because one in three women in the United States have been victims of rape, beating, and/or stalking. Women are assaulted at a much higher rate than men, and while the assault of men is just as important to address, violence towards women happens much more frequently across our country and across the world. I selected this issue because many people in our country, men and women, believe that women have full equality and respect, so they don't have to be feminists. However, with such a high percentage of women in the United States, statistics show that we aren't even close to having equality in this country. I wanted to convey with this piece that we have a long, uphill battle to fight before we eliminate violence against women, but we have to fight it because women are people too.

"The first thing I did to plan was research my issue to find the statistics of violence against women. I wrote down a question in my notebook and answers that I tried to base my artwork off of. Another thing I did to plan was brainstorm with a mind map. The last thing I did to plan was look up reference images."

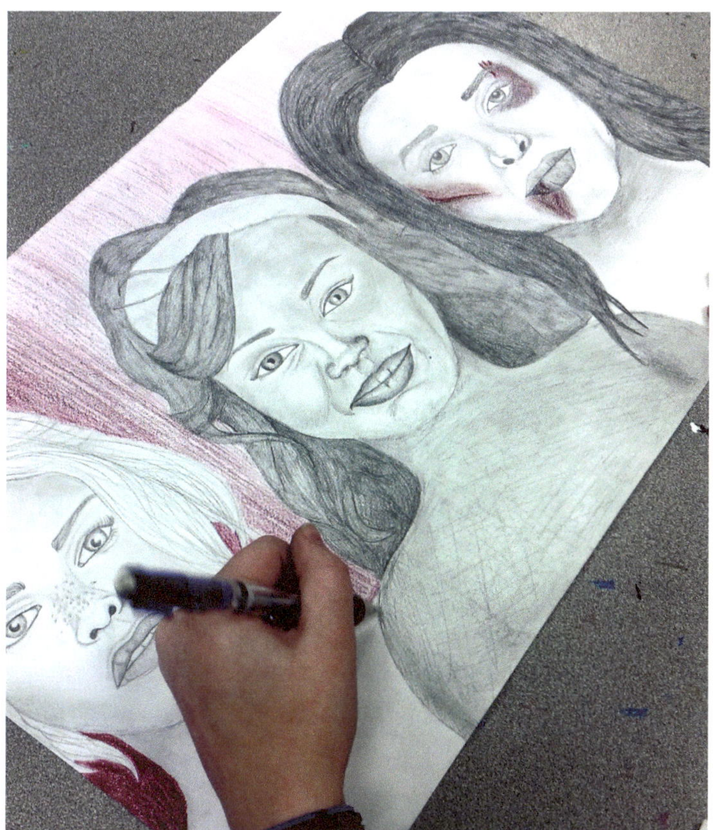

Jenna works on her drawing for Artists Take a Stand (p. 206).

Critique

Critique is an essential part of artistic development and it provides necessary closure to the learning experience. In the Open Art Room, we use and value critique, but it might look a bit different than it does in many other settings.

What is the value of critique in the art room? Traditionally, critiques are conducted by guiding students through a process of describing work and analyzing its formal use of the elements and principles. Only after this process takes place do we ask students to form a judgment. Sometimes, however, this sort of academic perusal of artwork causes kids to disengage. In the Open Art Room, we want students to connect, form personal responses to work, and think about what stands out to them. Usually, criticism about mistakes and shortcomings is best saved for more private, individual critiques. We want group critique to be fun and engaging to celebrate the learning that has taken place. We do this in two main ways: Critique Games and Fun Fridays.

Critique Games

Critique games counter the potentially tedious and intimidating nature of some traditional critique methods. Critique games are fun, short, and participatory. Work is interacted with instead of passively viewed. These games are also a good way to build a positive classroom culture and encourage students to get to know class members who don't sit nearby.

A good critique game asks for analysis and lets kids share thoughts, respond to one another, and collaborate.

Critique games can be used to scaffold critical thinking. The following examples are listed from beginning to more advanced. Before you play a critique game with your students, it helps to share the following expectations with the class:

- Participate in activities and conversations.
- Use "art-specific vocabulary" when possible, like the names of media and processes and the elements of art and principles of design.
- Respect the thoughts and opinions of others.

Each game starts with placing students in groups or teams. Assigning them places instead of letting them pick helps make sure that students are connecting with people they may not have gotten to know and that they are experiencing new work and ideas. Team placements can be done by preplanning the groups, numbering kids off, or handing out colored cards as students walk in the door. If you incorporate the expectation that students will work in groups that you create from day one, students tend to accept it, but if you try to start mid-year, expect some pushback.

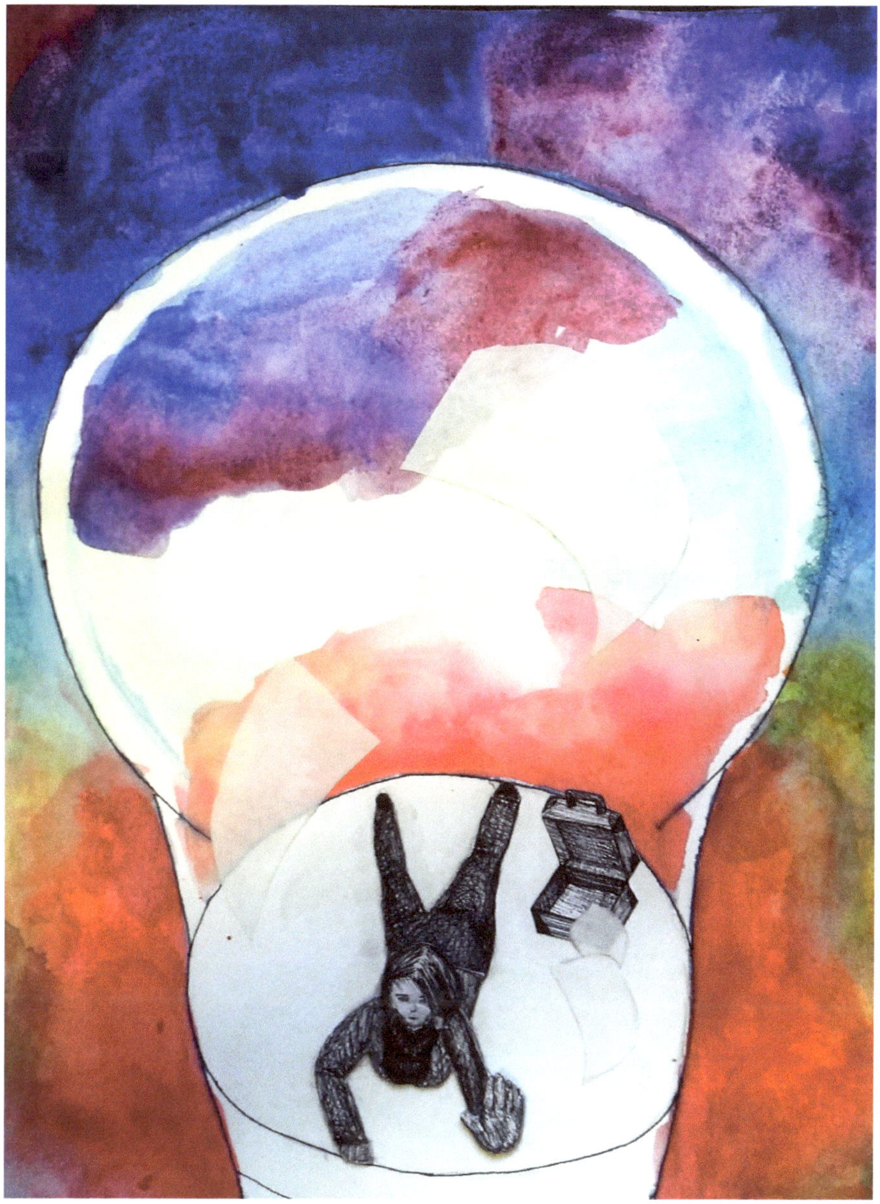

Finding new ways to demonstrate line and movement in art.

The Title Challenge Game. In this game, student teams analyze the artwork to think of an appropriate or funny title, and then justify their reasoning when they present.

Have students bring artwork to their groups. Next, pass out strips of paper and ask kids to write the title of their artwork on it. The rules are that the title can't include their name or be too obvious (like titling a picture of a chicken "The Chicken"). Have them place title strips face down in the center of the table while displaying the artworks around the perimeter. Add a fake title or two to each pile and instruct groups to rotate to another table. The task is for each group to match the titles to the artwork at the table they've moved to. Give them no more than five or ten minutes to do this, then have each student share an artwork with the title they gave it and explain why their group matched it that way. If any are mistitled the artists can explain what the correct title is.

This game is also fun when played by giving each group another group's work to title.

The Theme Mashup Game. In this game, students describe their artwork, analyze the components of the work in their group, and apply new information to make a new piece of art that works as sort of a visual summary. Next, they justify their decisions and describe their process in a presentation.

Have students bring artwork to their groups. Explain that they will be making one piece of artwork that somehow includes content from each group member's art. Instruct groups to start by having each person share their work. Next, give groups a time limit and a few material options, and then have them create. They will need support deciding what to include, so make sure you confer with each individual group, helping them brainstorm ideas if needed. When the time is up, have each group share their new work and explain how it represents the work that inspired it.

The Love Note Game. In this game, students describe their work, analyze the work of another student, and summarize observations in a response piece.

For this critique game, have each student bring an artwork, and then pair students in groups of two. Instruct each pair to share about their work with one another. Next, have the class return to their seats and write a "love note," with text and illustrations, to their partner's artwork. Encourage the

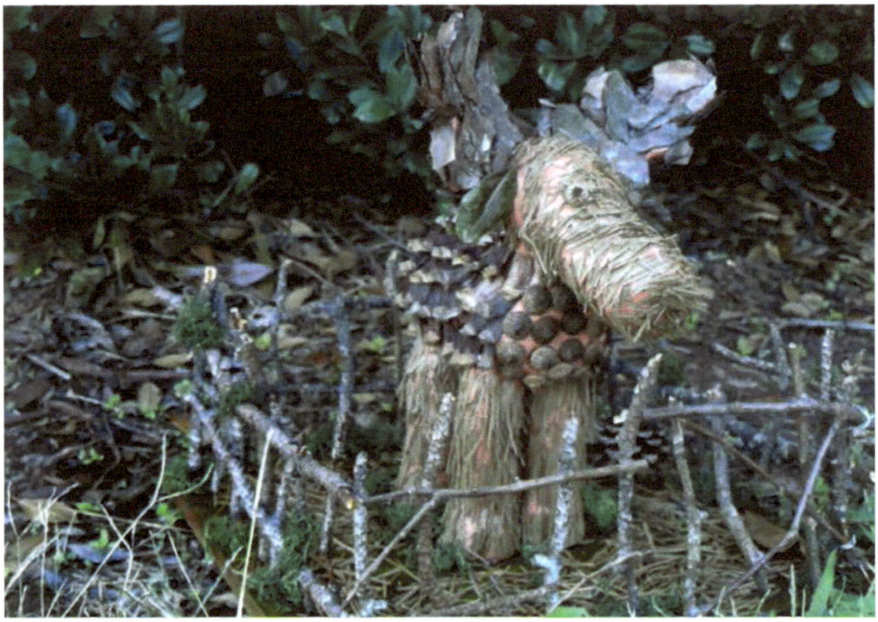

This sculpture was created using all natural materials.

use of cheesy poems, glitter, and crayons. Notes can then be read to the class or in groups. This is a fun activity around Valentine's Day.

The Performance Piece Game. In this game, students describe their artwork, analyze the components of the work in their group, and apply new information to make a new piece of performance art. Next, they justify their decisions and describe their process as part of their presentations.

In this activity, students are asked to make a story, song, or skit that incorporates an element of each group member's artwork. Requiring props is a fun addition to this game. Be warned: Students really complain when you give the directions for this game, but they unite in talking about how dumb it is, and end up really getting into it by the time the performance part rolls around, which happens in front of the class.

Fun Friday

Fun Friday is the Open Art Room's version of formal critique. This event often occurs at the end of the week, hence the name, and is a celebration of student achievement that is saved for the end of units. Students are encouraged to bring in food to share, which is set up on tables to be enjoyed. Students display their artwork on a table and place a comment sheet next to it. Kids stroll around the classroom, listening to music, enjoying snacks, and studying the art. As they look at work, they write feedback statements on the comment sheets. After everyone has had a chance to enjoy some food and finish writing comments, all students sit down, read through the responses to their work, and pick a favorite comment to share with the class.

Through this activity, students experience presenting their own art and viewing the work of others. They are asked to develop opinions about the work they see and share their own work for consumption. Through Fun Friday students see the presentation of artwork as the communal and celebratory sort of experience it often is in the art world.

Fun Friday has a number of learning goals, including: to develop and share constructive opinions about artwork; to apply art vocabulary to work; and to select work for presentation.

Here's a good rubric for the feedback:

1. Comments are not specific to the artwork, are sarcastic/mean-spirited, or are missing. For example, "It's nice."
2. Comments include some art vocabulary but are generic and might apply to any artwork. For example, "Good value."
3. Comments are specific, include correct usage of art vocabulary, and explain opinions or talk about the meaning of the work. For example, "I like how the value makes the tree stand out."

4. Comments include more than one usage of art vocabulary and analyze cause and effect in the artwork. For example, "I like how you created contrast between the tree and the sky by using a range of values in your drawing."

Grading

Grading can be a complicated subject for teachers. We worry about the validity of letter grades and their effect on student motivation. Some of us might prefer to teach without grades, but often this isn't feasible. Schools and principals have expectations for grading student work that most of us have to abide by. The Open Art Room seeks to minimize the amount of grades to increase intrinsic motivation. We also strive for grades that are flexible and take into account student growth and the process of art-making. When thinking about grades, the final product is one type of evidence among others, not the focus. This grading philosophy is holistic in nature and flexible. We firmly believe that teachers have to develop assessment and grading policies that work for their individual settings.

Below, we share our grading processes. But the bottom line with grading is that it should work for you, your students, and the expectations of your school. Take the information we have provided in this chapter and use what works for you, making changes to fit your situation.

How We Grade: Melissa

Grading is something I've struggled with. I want the grades I give to reflect and support what I'm doing in the classroom, not to create busy work or extra hoops that students have to jump through. Developing this grading system took quite a bit of trial and error. However, I've created a system that works for me in my current setting. This system:

- keeps the number of grades I give to a minimum.
- communicates progress weekly with students and parents.
- allows for recovery when kids slip up.
- reflects students' learning about the art-making process.
- meets the grading requirements of my school.

Class grades are composed of three parts:
40%.........Artistic Thinking Process
40%..........Summative Assessments
20%...........Final Portfolio

The Artistic Thinking Process

I grade students' use of the Artistic Thinking Process weekly. I do this because it gives both students and parents a good indication of how students are doing in the course. Typically, when students earn a low grade in my classroom, it is because they are refusing to work or putting minimal effort into work. The Artistic Thinking Process grade captures the importance of a student working through the design process to create work daily, but it's not a participation grade. Instead, the grades give students feedback about how they are using the Artistic Thinking Process to complete work in class.

I formulate this grade based on the formative assessment I do every day in class. As I observe students and confer with them, I gauge how they are using the Artistic Thinking Process and I provide them feedback about what I see. This weekly grade is never a surprise. Instead, it's a document of our conversation. It is worth up to twenty points, which makes it important to do well on. At the same time, the point value is low enough that students can recover from a few bad weeks.

I keep track of Artistic Thinking Process grades by making notes in my grade book of outliers. Most of my students tend to be at the "Accomplished" level. I record students who I notice are above and below that. Since I base grades on the week's work, I look for work to be in the same category more than once to determine the grade. This is especially true for the "Incomplete" grade. When I see students meeting the description for this category, I call them over to my desk for a conversation. I politely tell them what I've observed and ask what's going on. If there is an issue that's affecting them, like a breakup or other personal issue, I try to cut them some slack. Next, we come up with some ideas for improvement together. I only give Incompletes when conferring with them doesn't work to improve class work.

Artistic Thinking Process Grading Scale

Category	Point Value	Description
Exceeds	22	ATP is used to work through obstacles or to bring about advanced ideas, showing skill or growth beyond what is expected.
Accomplished	20	ATP is used to develop ideas, plan, and create artwork.
Advancing	18	ATP is used most of the time, but parts of the process are not observable, skipped, or incomplete.
Incomplete	10	ATP is not observable or infrequently used.

Grading Policies

- ATP is graded at the end of each week and is final.
- If ATP is incomplete during class, the teacher and student will work together to brainstorm possible solutions.

Summative Assessments

I grade summative assessments at the end of units, which tends to be every three to four weeks. In the beginning of each course, I have each student set up a blog and make one post. In the next unit, I teach the expectations for presentations and conferences. After all three options have been experienced, students may select how to do their summative assessments from the three options. I've found that providing this choice makes it more likely that students will be able to connect with the activity they select. Also, it's easier and more fun for me to grade when I'm evaluating different forms of assessment.

Summative Assessment Grading Scale
Options: Conferences, Blogs, Presentations

Category	Point Value	Description
Exceeds	100	The student can demonstrate learning beyond the concepts or learning goals.
Accomplished	95	The student can demonstrate mastery of concepts or learning goals through artwork, art-making process, or verbal/written reflection.
Advancing	85	The student's work shows progress towards the demonstration of mastery but is not yet there.
Incomplete	60	The student cannot demonstrate progress towards mastery of learning goals or concepts.

Grading Policies

- Missing assignments are graded as an Incomplete.
- Work can be redone and missing work can be turned in for full points until one week before semester grades are due.

Final Portfolio

I am required by my school district to have a final exam that is worth twenty percent of the final course grade. To meet this requirement I have my students create a final portfolio. The number and content of works required differs by class level but the goals are always the same:

- Demonstrate growth
- Use Artistic Thinking Process independently to create a self-directed collection of work.

This collection of work is shown on Portfolio Day, which is sort of a pop-up art show in the school's media center. Students bring in food and I invite a few classes to visit. We set up the work, have the show, and take work down in one class. Knowing that this event is coming is very motivating for students and pushes them to stretch to have to the best work possible to show. It's a very positive experience and a great way to show off the art program to students and staff. I require that they prepare artist statements and post images of their portfolios on their blogs. They also write short statements to be displayed next to their work at Portfolio Day.

Final Portfolio Grading Scale

Category	Point Value	Description
Exceeds	100	The collection of work is outstanding in the amount of growth shown, content, technical skill, or understanding of concepts.
Accomplished	95	The collection of work shows clear evidence of growth in the understanding of concepts and skill development. The work selected demonstrates knowledgeable application of ATP.
Advancing	85	The collection of work shows some growth in understanding of concepts or skill development. The work selected demonstrates some understanding of ATP.
Incomplete	60	The final portfolio is missing or incomplete. Work does not show growth or mastery of concepts. ATP is not evident in work.

Grading Policies

- Images of work and artist statements must be posted on blogs.
- Finished work and condensed artist statement are required for Portfolio Day.

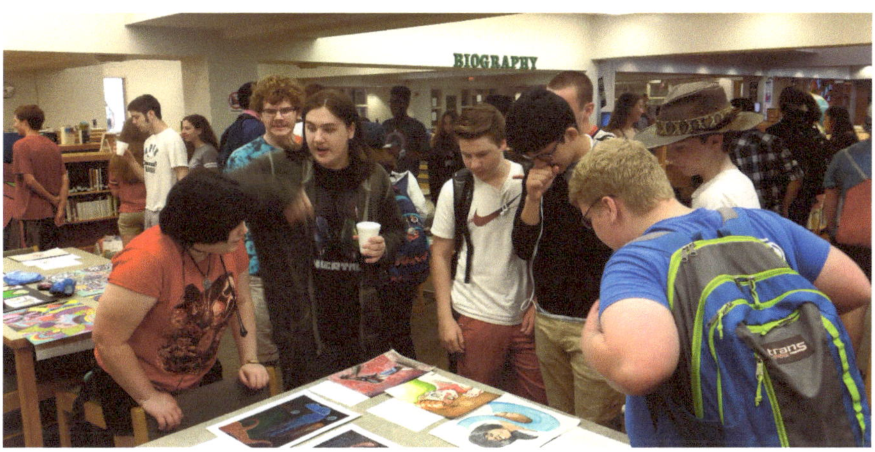

Students discuss each other's work on Portfolio Day.

How We Grade: Ian

Assessment and grading are two different words. I see great value in assessment to communicate with my students, to evaluate their work and help them grow as artists. In grades that assign an alphanumeric symbol to a work of art, however, I see little value. A grade cannot tell students that they need to go darker to create more contrast, it cannot help them understand why their work looks balanced, and it cannot explain why their idea is genius . . . or not. Although they shouldn't, grades can be used as rewards and punishments to manipulate students. Grades also provide two of the worst reasons for making art. First are the students who want a grade because they made art. "What is my grade?" they ask. The second are the students who will make art to raise their grade. "What will my grade be if I make this art?" For these reasons, I do not like grading and have made a conscious effort to eliminate grades from my class.

I'm not the first to feel this way. There are other teachers who have been feeling this way for years. Many of these teachers have been successful at throwing out grades. However, for some, grades cannot go away entirely. Still, the significance of grades can be diminished. The question then becomes, how can I reduce grading so that it plays little to no role in my students' art-making process?

The first step is to reduce the grade conversation. The focus in my class is on the process of making art. Concepts are presented, skills are learned, plans are designed, evaluations and assessments take place, all without the mention of the G word. When students ask the questions I mentioned above, I ask them if they are making art for a grade. I explain why this is the worst reason to make art. They usually agree and more than likely they only want to know where they stand. Again, this can be accomplished without assigning an alphanumeric symbol.

More importantly, I want students to accomplish their learning goals. The units in my class, and in this book, are designed so that the student meets the learning goals by moving through the process. This allows students to accomplish the goals, even if their final project fails. By completing all the objectives of a unit, students will have successfully met their learning goals and, at this point, a completion grade can be assigned.

Sometimes students will not meet all the requirements of the unit. There are various reasons why this occurs, including lack of participation or engagement. However, students who have not completed the requirements have not failed; they are only missing work. Students should be given the opportunity to complete the missing requirements. Until the requirements are met, a final grade cannot be entered. In the system used at my school, we have the ability to enter the words "Incomplete" or "Missing." I use these as placeholders until the unit is completed.

When asked how this works, I provide the following analogy. Pretend you are sitting in a room. On the other side of the room is a box. Your objective is to touch the box. You have three choices: (1) You can get up and touch the box and accomplish the goal. (2) You can get up but not touch the box. You have advanced towards your goal but not accomplished your goal. Something is missing. (3) You can stay in your seat. Your goal is still incomplete.

For grading purposes, this is presented as follows:

Learning Goals Grading

Accomplished Learning Goal	98
Advancing Towards Learning Goal	Missing
Incomplete	Incomplete

I apply this model at the end of each unit. The students will have completed the process including the mini-lessons, Bootcamps, or design challenges. They will have completed a final project, and they will have reflected on their experience through a blog post. Those students who have met all the learning goals receive the grade of 98. For those who worked towards completing the learning goals but haven't yet done so, I enter Missing. In the unusual circumstance when the student hasn't worked at all, I enter an Incomplete.

Notice there is no "Exceeds." Returning to the box analogy, the objective was to touch the box. While it is true that one can pick up the box and in theory exceed, the learning goal was only to touch the box. The grade is only given for accomplishing the learning goal.

Some ask, why do you give 98? Why not 100 or 95? To be honest, it is totally arbitrary. Others ask what to do at the end of the semester if the student still has a Missing or an Incomplete. At some point, depending on the grading software, these words will most likely have to be translated into numerical grades. Missing could be converted into an 88, and an Incomplete could be translated to a 50 or 0 depending on school policy. Again, these numbers are arbitrary, which I consider to be the biggest downside to alphanumeric grading. Remember, the objective is to give the student every opportunity to accomplish the learning goals. A persuasive teacher using this system should have a grade book predominantly filled with 98s.

Some would argue that it is unfair that all students receive a 98. Some students work harder or are naturally more talented and therefore should receive a higher grade. This is reward/punishment thinking. Furthermore, it is not a system that most teachers prescribe to for themselves. Many teachers are paid using a steps method, all receiving the same pay scale for the level they are at, regardless of how talented they are or how hard they work. For students, meeting the learning goal should be the objective and their grade should reflect this accomplishment.

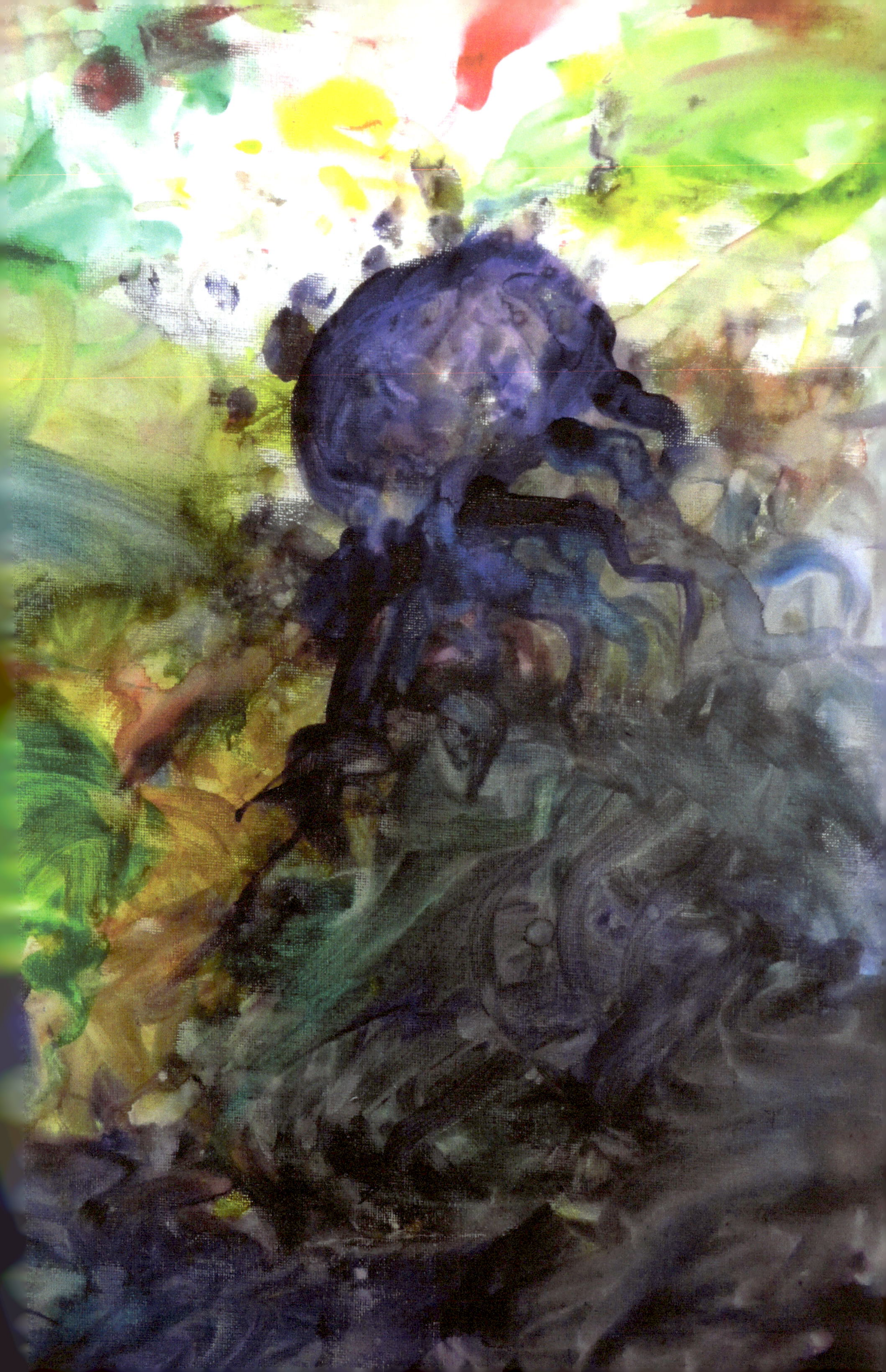

PART THREE | Unit Plans

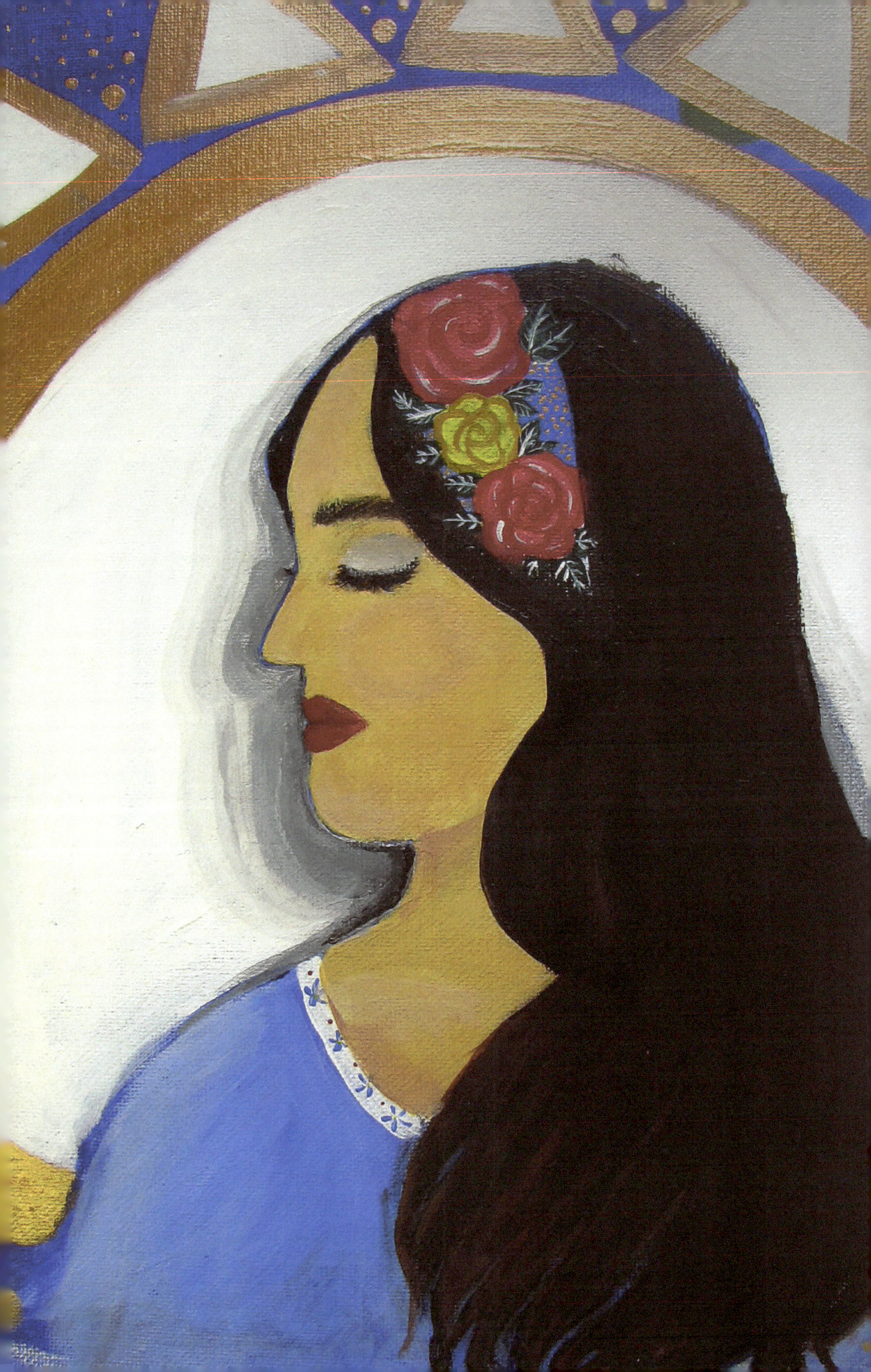

7 | Introduction to Art Bootcamp

The structure of the Open Art Room can be very different from the art experiences that students are used to. They will be expected to make independent decisions and use their own ideas, which is new and challenging. The following unit is designed to do two things to support the transition to the Open Art Room: teach students the Artistic Thinking Process as a framework for independent decision making, and provide key information about available media.

Use this bootcamp unit to introduce the Open Art Room to a beginning art class, or with more advanced classes when transitioning from a traditional teaching style. This unit provides the foundation, but we don't linger here. The really good stuff, where the majority of your time should be spent, is in the next section, Artistic Behavior Unit Plans.

National Standards

- VA:Cr1.1.Ia
- VA:Cn10.1.Ia
- VA:Cn10.1.IIa

Learning Goals

- Know how to select and use the materials of the art room to create art.
- Understand how to apply the Artistic Thinking Process to develop ideas into finished artwork.

Bootcamps are designed to teach students the skills needed to make choices independently by developing a working understanding of available media and knowing how to apply a process of developing ideas into finished art. Bootcamps are organized by media. Techniques are taught in short, focused lessons that often involve group work, and are then applied in student-directed projects. Over the course of the Bootcamp unit, students learn a variety of methods for developing ideas and developing them into finished work.

Mini-lessons are a key aspect of Bootcamps. We use them as quick skill-building activities that introduce media and provide a working knowledge that supports later choice. These one- or two-day experiences typically start with whole group instruction and guided practice, followed by group work. New information is introduced and processed in whole group instruction, then interacted with by students in guided practice. Group work cements new learning as students work together to accomplish the assigned task, talking through concepts and correcting misunderstandings.

Short projects refer to art activities that follow a group of mini-lessons. These experiences are for applying new skills with media and learning components of the Artistic Thinking Process.

Drawing

The goal of this drawing Bootcamp is to build a working understanding of a variety of drawing media in a short timeframe. This knowledge builds the foundation for later choice. Understanding the basics of value can be hard for students to master, so a combination of guided practice and group work is used to provide students with multiple opportunities to interact with key ideas.

MINI-LESSON 1: *Value Study*

Timeframe: 1 90-minute class
Media: Graphite, charcoal
Learning Goal: Understand the basic concept of using value to create form with graphite and charcoal.

Whole Group Instruction and Guided Practice

Briefly discuss the importance of value in creating contrast and form. Explain that graphite is a drawing medium that is used to create drawings in value, and introduce weighted pencils and blending stumps if you plan on using them. Show a value scale and explain the importance of pressure in creating a range of shades. Demonstrate creating a scale or play a video showing how, showing more than one option for mark-making. Give students five to ten minutes to create their own scale, focusing not on neatness but on creating a range of values with their preferred type of mark-making.

Next, explain that value can be used to make two-dimensional shapes, like circles, appear three-dimensional. Show an image of a shaded sphere and point out the stages of value. Next, demonstrate shading a sphere or show a related video. Ask students to work along with you, then ask them to share challenges they noticed.

Group Work

Ask students to work together in groups of three or four to create a giant sphere with all the stages of value labeled. Tell them that they will be using charcoal and briefly explain how it works. Have students work to create their sphere, making sure to ask guiding questions as they work, such as: "Where do you plan to place the reflected light?" or "Can you show me where the light source is coming from?"

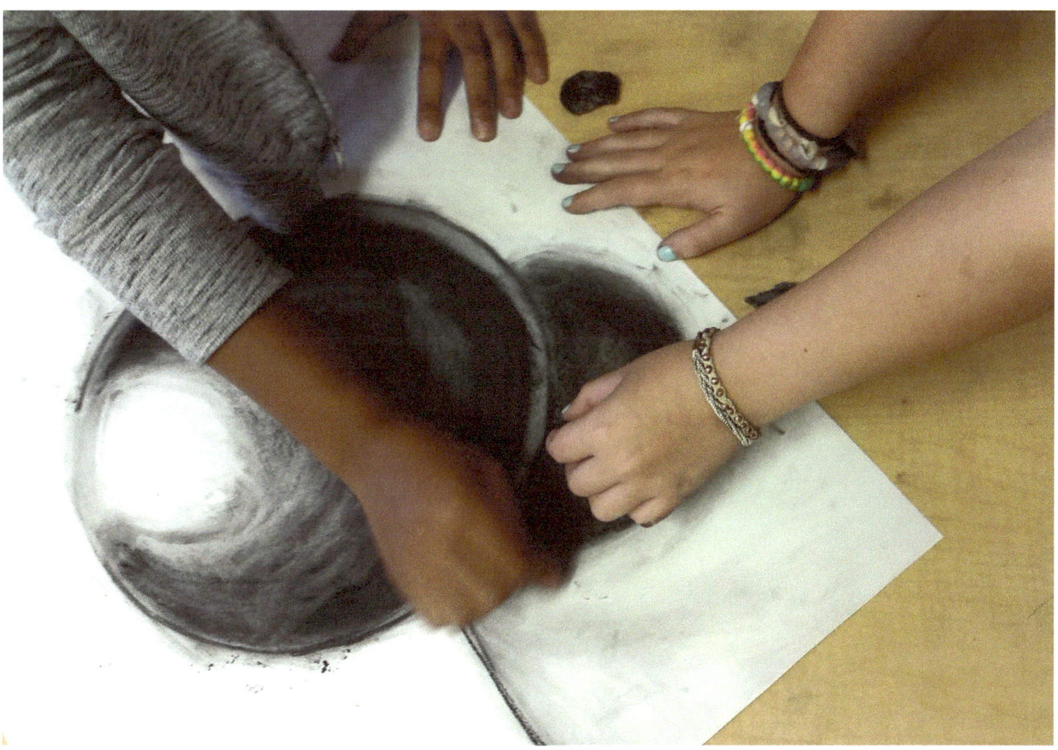

Students work collaboratively to master the process of creating form through value.

MINI-LESSON 2: *Draw Around the Room, Inspired by Diane Jaquith and Cynthia Gaub*

Timeframe: 1 class
Media: Chalk pastel, oil pastel, colored pencil and pen
Learning Goal: Understand the characteristics of drawing media

In Preparation

You will need to create visuals to show students techniques with each of the four materials. One way to do this is to divide a paper into sections for each technique you want to demonstrate, label it, and draw an example. Another option is to make or find video online that shows how to use each media. These resources will provide direction as students experiment with materials at each center. Alternatively, tasks that include techniques can be assigned. Examples of these are shading a sphere with colored pencil or drawing a sunset with chalk pastel.

Whole Group Instruction

Tell the students that they will learn about the characteristics of a variety of media in this lesson by *experimenting,* which is a part of the Artistic Thinking Process and a helpful way to learn. Ask them to look for one they really enjoy using because they will need to select a material to use for a longer drawing in the next class. Explain how you have organized the centers and direct them to try and label each technique in their sketchbook. Let them know how long they will have to work in each center and how the rotation will work. Ask them to bring a pencil, because they will write down their observations at the end of each session.

Guided Practice

Direct students to start working at their first center. As they work, talk to students about what they are working on and give them feedback about how they are using the media. Ask them if they have questions and demonstrate techniques if the need arises. At the end of each session, have students write down their observations of the media they have just tried. Ask them to include what they like about it and what they don't like. At the end of class ask them to take a minute and write down three possible drawing projects they might like. Tell them that they should come in the next day with ideas for the media they want to use and what they might like to spend a few days drawing.

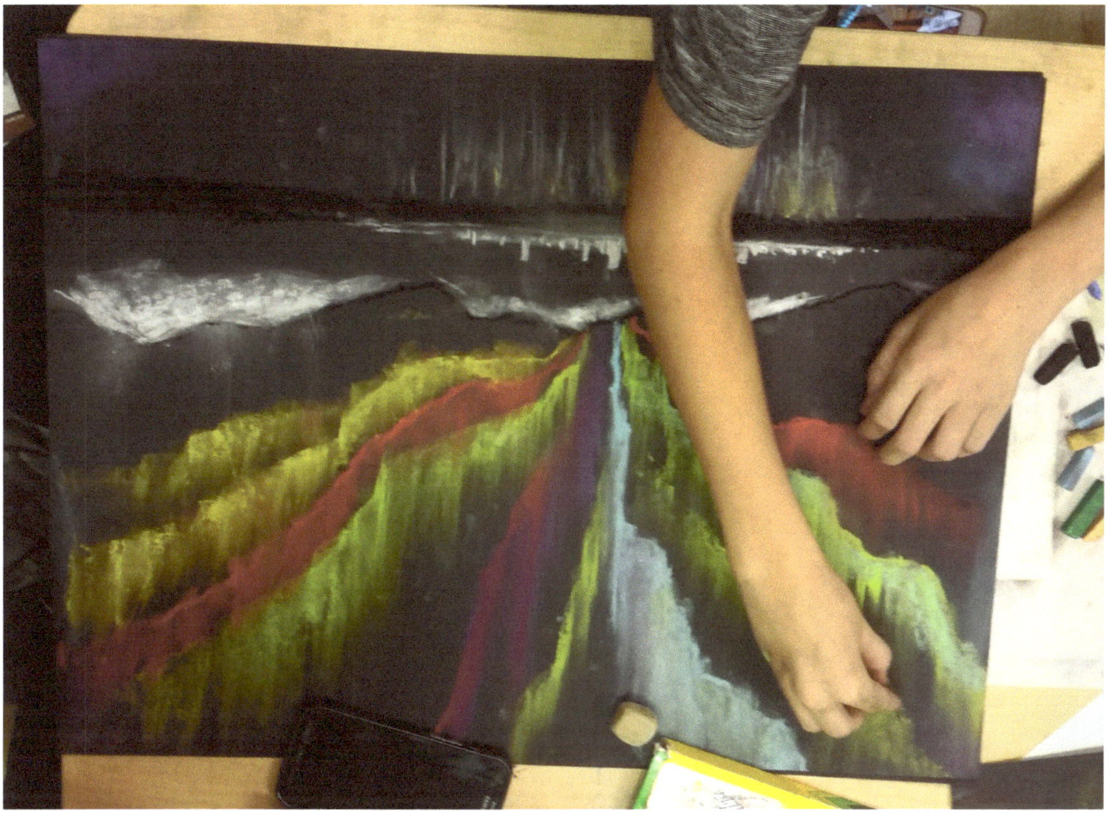

Owen enjoying the expressive qualities of pastel.

INDEPENDENT PRACTICE

Timeframe: 2 to 3 classes
Media: Drawing media of choice
Learning Goal: Apply knowledge of selected medium in a drawing of choice
Design Strategy: Sketch and experiment

Whole Group Instruction

Start by asking students to revisit the drawing ideas that they jotted down at the end of the last class. Ask them to make note of any other ideas that occur to them during the introduction of the project, with the goal of being able to start work when the presentation is done.

Next, present a few example ideas of drawing projects, using examples from artists. Zaria Forman's large-scale chalk pastel seascapes and C. J. Hendry's photorealistic pen drawings of food are two ideas.

Now discuss the design stage of the project. Tell students that once they have an idea they like, they must develop and refine it. One way artists do this is through sketching. Tell your students about the role of sketching

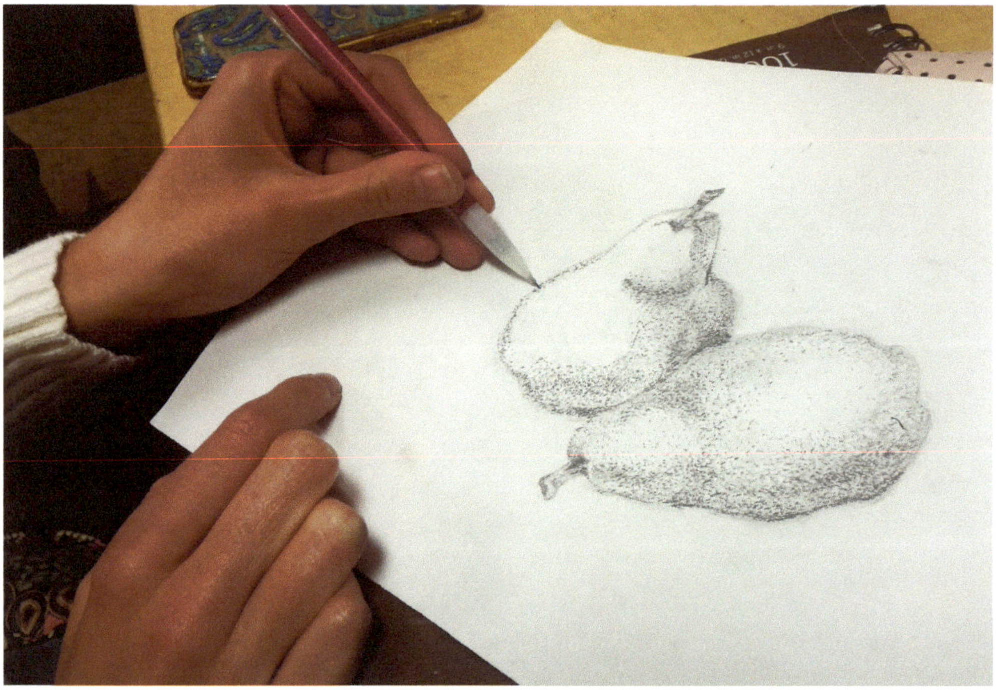

Emma carefully adds value to her pear drawing.

in developing interesting compositions and guide them through making one or two sketches for their drawing project. Make sure to address your requirements for resource images and discuss when you expect students to use reference material. Also mention that sketching is a good way to experiment with how to create any elements of the drawing the artist is unsure of.

Independent Practice

Have students finish working on sketches and begin working on final artwork. As students work, ask them probing questions, such as:

- Can you tell me about your idea?
- Why did you decide to use this material?
- What challenges are you having with this assignment?
- Is there anything you'd like me to demonstrate?

Be ready to provide feedback, one-on-one demonstrations, and other help that students need as they plan and develop work.

Reflection

At the beginning of the second day of work, take some time for in-process reflection. Ask students to take their artwork and form groups of three or four with people that do not sit at their tables. Once in groups, students should spend a few minutes sharing their artwork and describing a challenge or concern they are having so far. Group members can respond with suggestions or advice.

Painting

The goal of this painting Bootcamp is to gain familiarity with available painting media and a strong understanding of color theory. Watercolor and acrylic are the types of media described below, but others can be included or left out to fit the needs of your teaching situation.

MINI-LESSON 1: *Acrylic Paint and Paint Mixing Challenge*

Timeframe: 1 class
Materials: Acrylic paint, magazines, color wheel

Learning Goals

- Understand and apply knowledge of paint procedures and introductory vocabulary.
- Create a range of colors by mixing paint from primary colors.
- Understand and apply acrylic painting techniques.

In Preparation

Create a visual that shows the procedures you would like students to follow when using paint. Reference this while teaching procedures, then make sure it's visible in the room for students to use when they need a reminder.

Whole Group Instruction: Paint Mixing Challenge

Start class by telling students that today they will learn how to use acrylic paint by mixing colors and trying techniques. Next, introduce the procedures you want students to use while using paint. Have students work in groups of three or four to set up a palette with warm and cool primaries, along with white, and get brushes and water. Next, pass out magazines and instruct each group to select one image.

Now give the instruction for the paint-mixing challenge. Students will work in their groups to mix colors to match as many colors as they can to the magazine page they selected, marking directly on the page with the paint they mix to see how close the match is. Point out the color wheel in the room and explain how it can be used to think about colors the groups will need to mix. Mention briefly how to mix tints and shades. Students will explore how this all works as they try to replicate colors with their group. Make sure they know that they will be experimenting, which is a design method in the Artistic Thinking Process that is helpful when learning new information.

Group Work: Mixing

Give groups fifteen minutes to mix paint. During this time, circulate around the room. When challenges arise (and they should), prompt students to problem solve by doing things like trying different combinations of warm and cool or by making shades by adding complementary colors. If needed, demonstrate how to mix specific colors that pose a challenge.

Whole Group Instruction: Painting Techniques

Tell the class that knowing how to mix a color is important, and knowing how to apply it once it's mixed is equally so. Ask students to divide a page in their sketchbooks into sections for each technique you plan to teach. Have students label a square with the name of the technique, then demonstrate it, describing your thinking as you do. Have students try each technique in one of the squares they made in their sketchbooks. Make sure to mention key ideas, like how important drying speed is when blending colors. Examples of techniques that you might include in this activity are dry brushing, layering, wet-on-wet blending, washes, and how to create a gradient. Make sure to leave time at the end of this activity to teach your clean-up procedure.

Reflection

Ask students to take a few minutes at the end of class to reflect on what they've learned by listing at least ten things about using paint. If time allows, have volunteers share what they listed and discuss as a group.

Homework

Tell students that they will be creating a landscape painting in watercolor (they'll learn how to use this in the next class) or acrylic and that they need to bring in a photo reference. Ask them to find an actual photo or a digital copy.

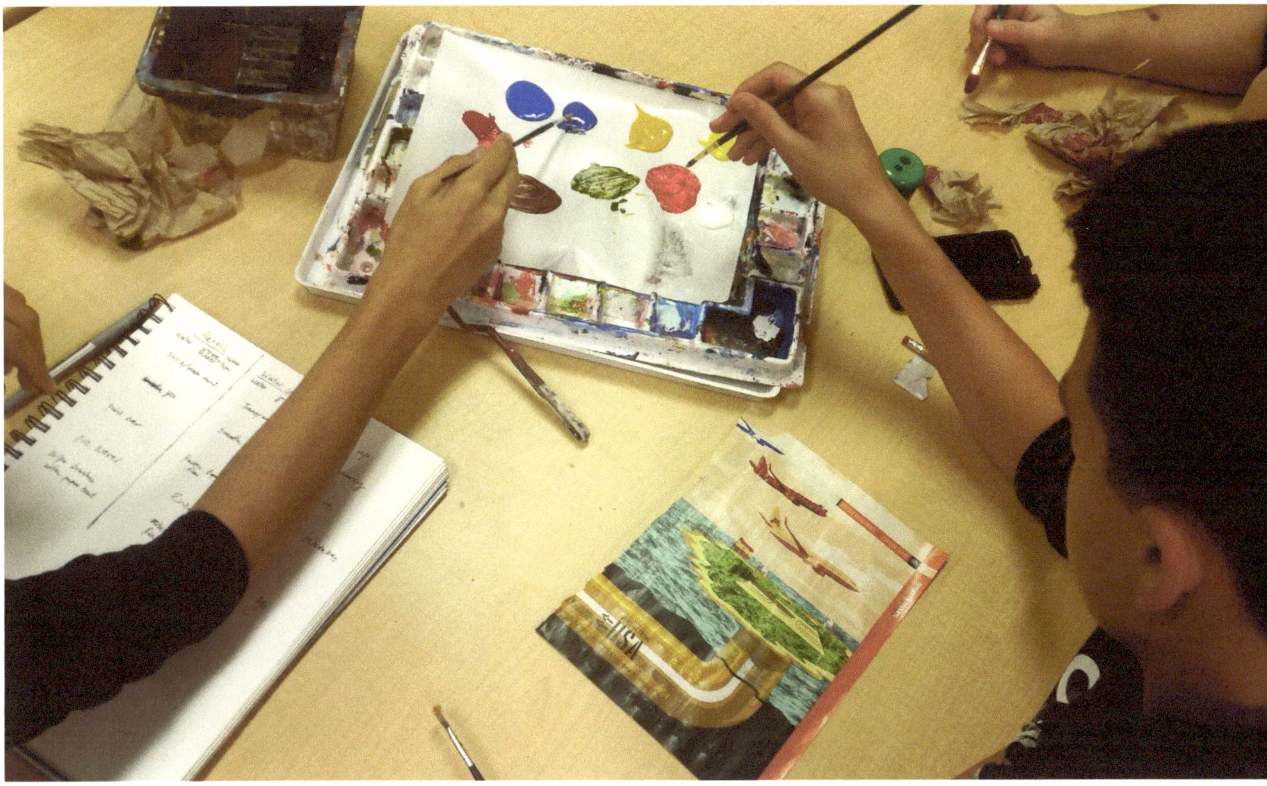

Students participating in the Color Mixing Challenge.

MINI-LESSON 2: *Watercolor*

Timeframe: 1 class
Media: Watercolor paint

Learning Goals

- Understand and apply knowledge of paint procedures and introductory vocabulary.
- Create a range of colors by mixing paint from primary colors.
- Understand and apply watercolor painting techniques.

Whole Group Instruction: Techniques

Tell students that they'll be learning about how to use watercolor paint. Remind them to think about which type of paint they would like to explore further in the painting that they will start in the next class. Show students how to set up palettes for acrylic painting and help them get palettes ready to paint. Next, ask them to divide a page in their sketchbooks into six to eight sections, depending on the number of techniques you plan to teach.

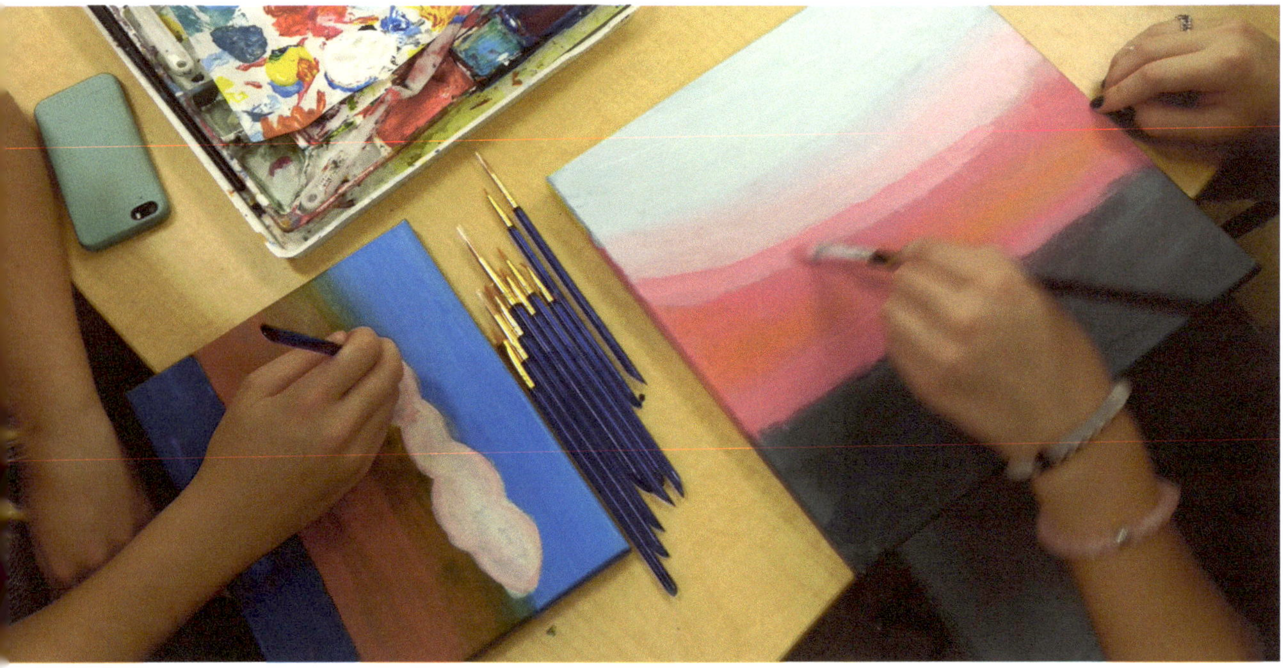

·eate landscape paintings with acrylic.

Next, demonstrate each technique and instruct students to try each in their sketchbook. As you teach, make sure to make comparisons between watercolor and acrylic. Some techniques that you might include in your demonstration are wet-on-wet, gradient blending, layering, resist, dry brushing, washes, and using additives like salt or plastic wrap to make texture.

After students have finished trying techniques, briefly introduce the idea of landscape. Using an example, talk about foreground, middle ground, and background while students sketch an image that has all three parts. Tell the class that a key idea in landscape painting is creating space and explain that painters do this with color and with scale. Have them compare how color and scale are used to create space in one or two examples of landscape painting,

Now play a short video (under ten minutes) of a watercolor landscape being painted. These videos are easy to find—just search "how to paint a watercolor landscape video" and make sure to preview it first, looking for something fast-paced and fun to watch. Instruct students to write in their sketchbooks about what techniques the artist uses in the painting and how the artist uses scale and color to create space. After the video, give students a chance to make sure they've answered the assigned questions, then discuss what they observed about the artist's decision making. Mention that watching how-to videos can be helpful when learning a new skill and is considered research as part of the design stage of the Artistic Thinking Process. Next, discuss the differences in setting up and working on an acrylic painting versus a watercolor, referencing a chart or list that shows the steps you'd like students to follow for each process.

Reflection

Ask students which type of paint they prefer, acrylic or watercolor, and ask them to explain why. If time allows, students can be put into groups by the type of paint they prefer, discuss why it's the best, and present their case to the class in an "acrylic vs. watercolor battle." Remind kids to bring in a landscape photo to use for the next class.

Short Project: Landscape Painting

Landscape painting works well for this short project because of the skills it requires. When students are tasked with mixing colors from only primaries and white, this topic makes sure that they experience mixing a wide range of tints and shades. Also, understanding landscape is a good foundation for understanding the element of space, which we cover in Art 1 in the unit Artists Understand Space. Lastly, landscapes are familiar and non-threatening, which makes them a fairly safe choice for beginning artists who are building skill and confidence.

Timeframe: 3 to 4 classes
Materials: Choice of acrylic or watercolor paint

Learning Goals

- Apply knowledge of acrylic and watercolor paint to select materials and techniques.
- Plan and create a landscape painting.

Inspiration and Design

Most students should know what they are going to paint at this time if you have given them a few days to find an image of a landscape. Of course, some will have forgotten and some will want to paint something they don't have an image of. Also, there will be students who don't know which type of paint they want to use. Start class by addressing both issues.

First, talk about your personal expectations for image use. If students need to use reference material from magazines or online, what guidelines do you expect them to follow? Share this with the class. Next, talk about what the design section of the Artistic Thinking Process will look like for this short project. At this point, students know how to sketch for composition, how to experiment with mixing colors, and they've been introduced to the concept of watching how-to videos as research. Tell students that the point of design is to go from what they currently know to what they need to know in order to make a successful painting. Have them make a list of what they know and what they need to know, including the following:

- What are you painting?
- What type of paint are you using?
- How will you mix the paint colors that you need?
- Are there any parts of your landscape that you are unsure of how to paint?

After students make their lists, ask them to think how they can plan to figure out what they need to know. Share some ideas for tasks that can accomplish this and tell them to pick at least three from the following list:

- Sketch to figure out composition (maybe to improve on the composition of a photo reference).
- Experiment with mixing paint colors or how to paint specific areas
- Sketch a rough draft with paint.
- Watch videos or read through examples of how to paint things you are unsure about.
- Ask for a demonstration.

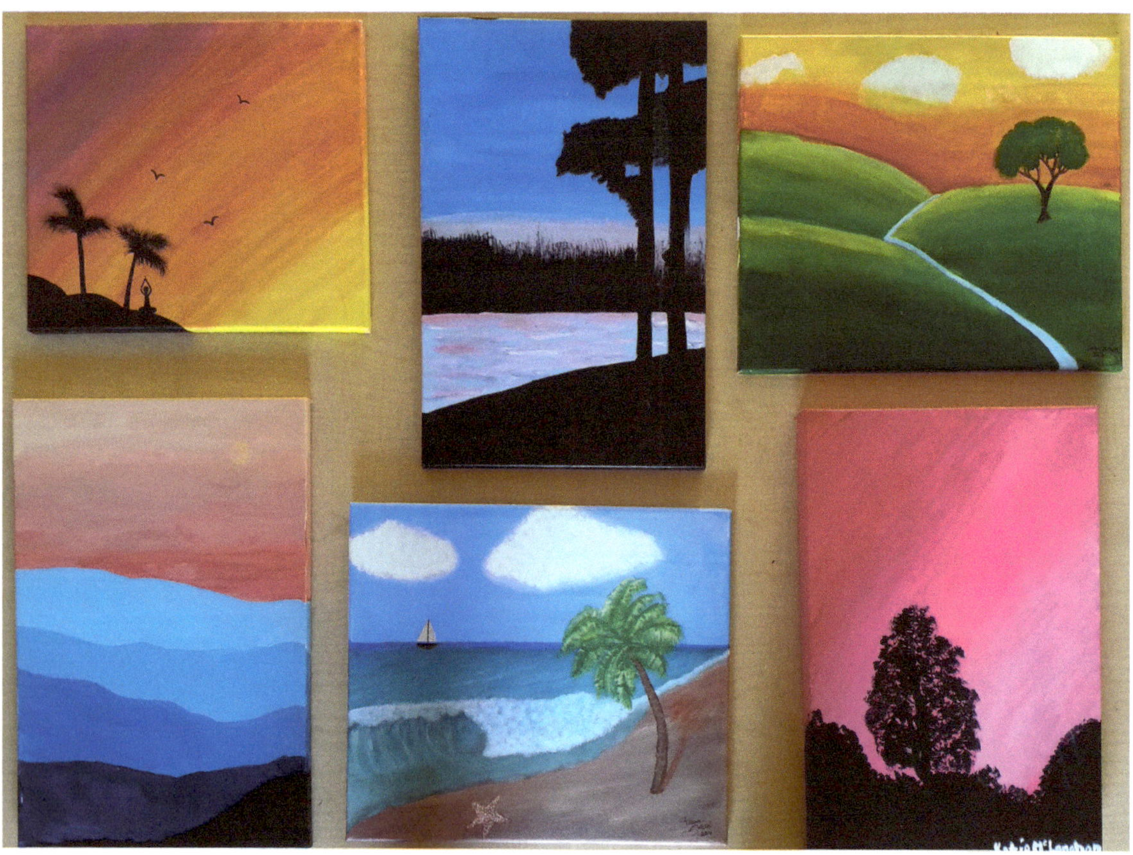

Finished student paintings.

Have students spend class time deciding which tasks they need to work on and completing them. As they work, conference with each student about the tasks they've selected and give them feedback.

Creation

Once students have completed three design activities, they are ready to start working on their final paintings. Have students check in with you before they start to make sure they know what to do. As students work on finishing up design and move on to creation, conference with them, answering questions, giving feedback, and helping with pacing. As students are working on their final paintings some will have questions that they will need to go back to design to answer independently. Point this out—it is a great teachable moment about how artists work.

Reflection

Take a few minutes at the end of this short project to have a "gallery walk." Have the class display their artwork on the tables and walk around and look at all the work. If time allows, ask them to notice one or two paintings that really stand out and call on volunteers to share their observations.

Clay

The focus of the clay Bootcamp is providing students with an overview of how clay works. Relief tiles work well here because they require a wide range of clay technique: slab rolling and carving and working additively with wet clay, then carving and finishing when the clay is leather-hard. Also, this experience with relief work lends itself to understanding printmaking, which comes next. This Bootcamp is the most limited in media choice; everyone uses clay. However, if having foundational experiences with more types of sculpture is important to you, it can be extended to include more media options.

SHORT PROJECT: *Clay Tile*

Timeframe: 3 classes
Media: Clay

Learning Goals

- Students will apply knowledge of clay tools and processes to design and make a relief tile.

Preparation

Create a diagram, slideshow, or video of the process you want students to use to create their tiles. It's also helpful to have a visual that gives information about clay tools and procedures. These types of visual resources help support students as they work with new processes and help them remember what they learned during this experience when they use clay later on in the year.

Introduction

To introduce clay, start by passing a small piece to every student. Talk about the characteristics of clay, the three main types of hand-building, using tools, procedures, and important things to know about when you are working with it. As you talk, encourage students to play with the clay and try some of the things you describe. During this activity make sure to point out where clay materials are stored and where students can find the visual support for the procedures you describe. As you talk and students handle the clay, it will dry out. Mention this and discuss the importance of moisture to make clay pliable and discuss the stage of clay drying.

Inspiration and Design

Start this stage by showing an example of a relief tile and tell students that they'll be designing and creating their own. Ask them to take note of the steps to making a tile using text and images. Next, share your visual support that describes the process you want students to use, stopping to

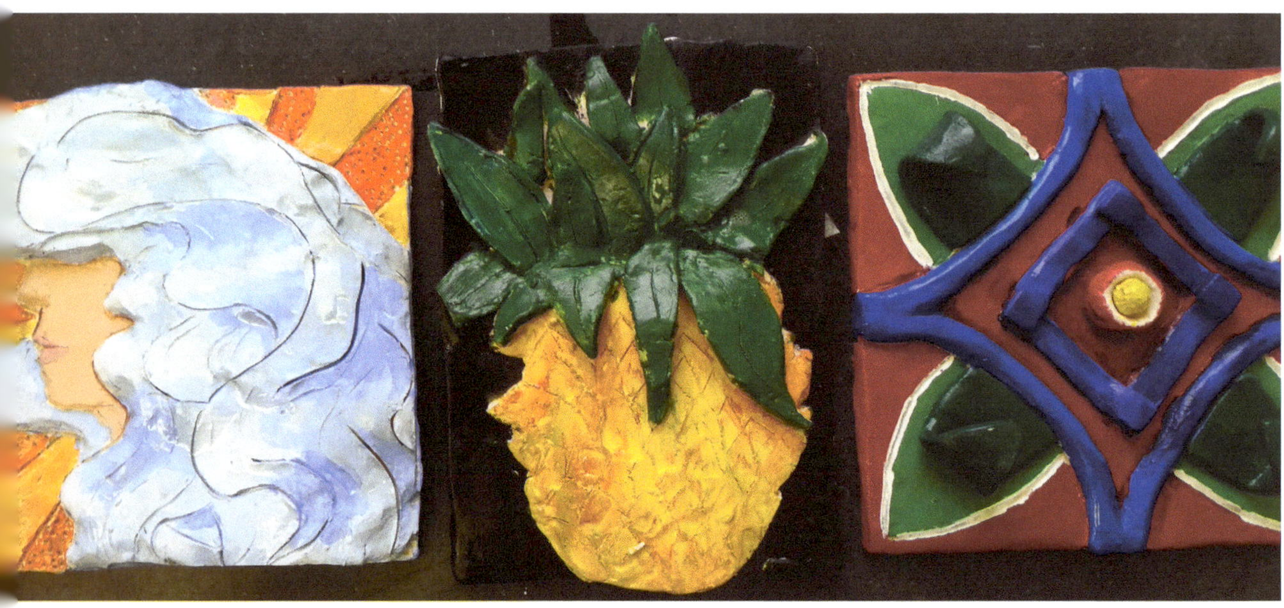

student tile work.

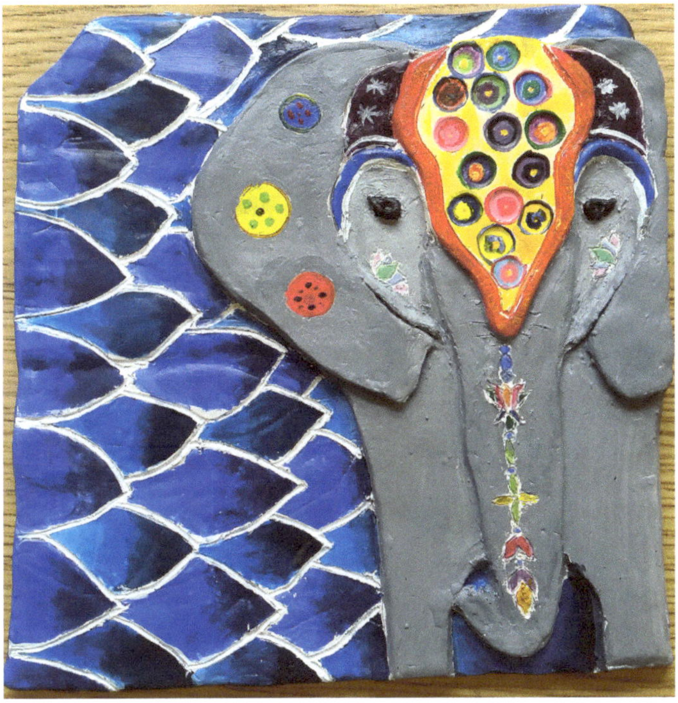
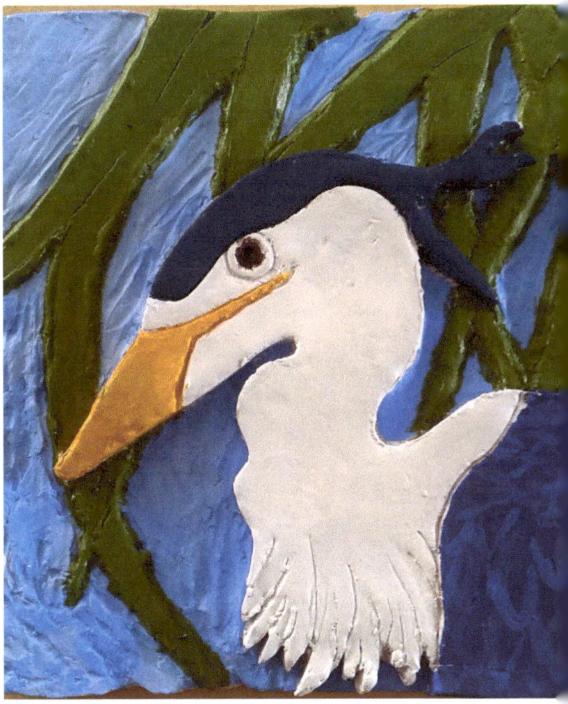

Examples of student tile work.

give students time to take notes. After you've described the process, have students compare notes in small groups, making sure they've all written down similar things.

Next, talk about researching other artists' work as inspiration. Show students how to use Pinterest to research for specific types of work, like "ceramic tile," or even more specific like "ceramic tile fish." Explain that looking at others' work for inspiration can be helpful when developing your own ideas. Add that it is okay to have parts of others' work that inspire your own but that reproducing someone else's work is copying and is not acceptable. Discuss your expectations for originality when taking inspiration from others, allowing students to share their ideas.

Tell students that for planning, they will create a Pinterest board with ten pins. These pins should include examples of tiles that inspire them and reference photos of the subject matter they want to create. For example, if a student plans to make a tile of a wolf, pins might include tiles that show different examples of creating the texture of fur in clay, examples of backgrounds that might work, and a few photo references of wolves.

After students research, they should continue planning by experimenting or sketching. For experimenting, students can use clay that needs to be recycled to practice making textures on. As for sketching, show students an example of a diagram that shows a tile design, including where clay will be removed and where it will be added. As students design their tiles, make sure to look at the Pinterest boards they've made, and talk to each one about how they are using the images that they've researched for inspiration. If you notice students veering toward copying, discuss what you notice with them and help them brainstorm ways to make their work more original.

Creation and Reflection

After students plan, they are ready to start work on their tiles. Circulate around the class as students work, helping problem solve and giving feedback. Clay building should last two classes. On the last day of work, take some time at the end of class to have students list what they learned about working with clay and discuss their observations in small groups. Move on to the next Bootcamp while waiting for the clay to dry and be fired. When it is ready to finish, take a class period to paint with acrylics or glaze.

Printmaking

Printmaking can be a challenging subject to provide an overview of, since individual processes are so different with the materials and techniques they require. To deal with this, we use online resources to teach multiple processes and assess learning. Students watch or read through the process independently, then pass a quiz about the process they want to try. This way, students are exposed to multiple printmaking processes and can focus on learning the one that is most appealing to them. When teaching this Bootcamp, use whatever printmaking processes you like or have the materials for.

SHORT PROJECT: *Learning Multiple Processes*

Processes: Linoleum cut, screen printing, and monoprinting
Timeframe: 3 to 5 classes

Learning Goal

- Students will select, learn, and apply knowledge to create artwork by using the printmaking process of their choice.

Preparation

For each type of printmaking you want to include in this unit you need a resource that explains the process clearly and succinctly. One option is to find videos or written how-to guides online. The benefit of using this type

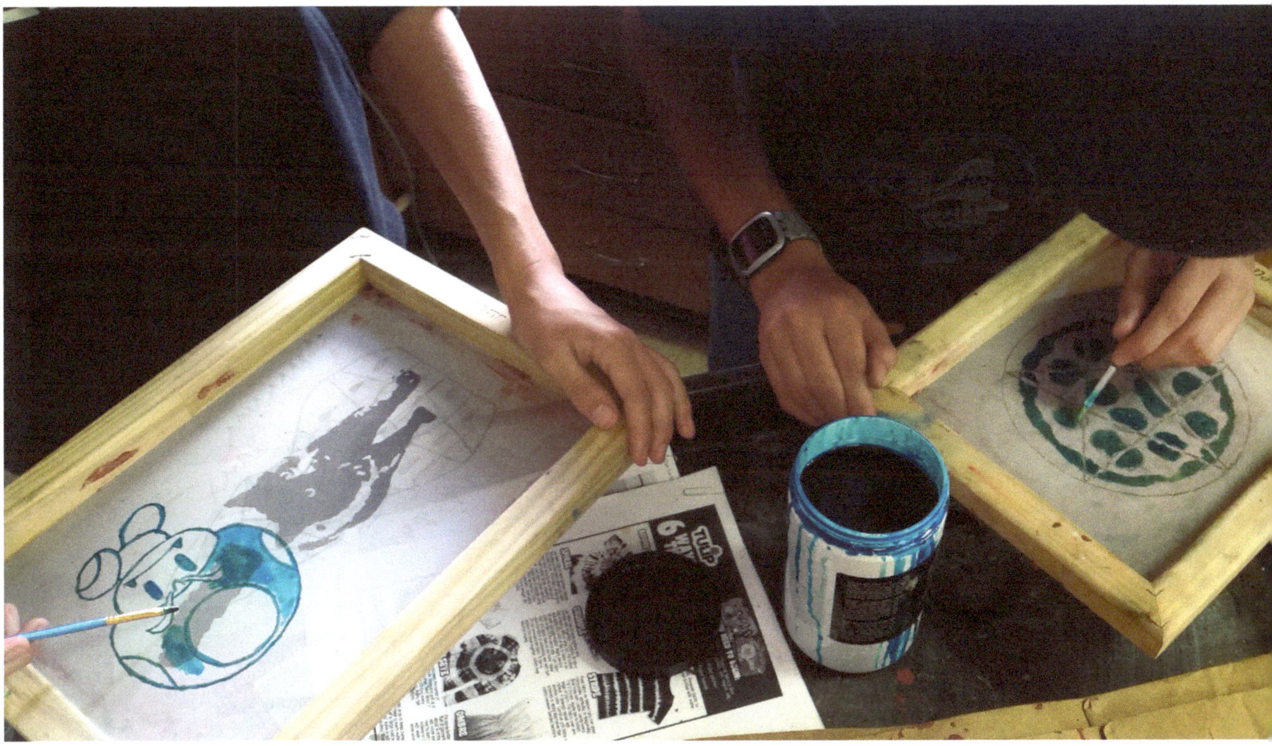

Students apply drawing fluid to screens.

of resource is that it can save time because you don't have to create it. The downside is that sometimes it's hard to locate something that meets your needs. The second option is to create your own content. This can take time, but you are able to include exactly the content you want your students to know, which makes it easier to learn.

Videos and step-by-step instructions both work for creating content. Film or photograph each step and add text or verbal directions explaining the process. The content you create needs to be accessible to students. Post it on a class website where it can be easily accessed.

Next, create quizzes for each process you plan to teach. They should include key information and questions about common mistakes. For example, we ask students to match images of screen printing materials with the name of the product, because mistaking screen filler for drawing fluid is a common and expensive mistake. These quizzes can be pencil and paper, but programs like Google forms work better because they can be set up to show students what the correct answers are in real time. The goal of these quizzes is twofold: to review key concepts, and to correct misconceptions before work starts. They do not have to be graded or assigned a point value. We simply ask our students to retake them until they get all the answers correct.

Introduction

Start the printmaking unit by providing a brief overview of printmaking: that it is used to make copies, that it can be additive or subtractive, that there are many different types. Explain that students will have the option of picking from one of three types, and that they will learn the steps by watching or reading content, then passing a quiz before they start creating. Next, show work examples from each process and explain where materials are located. You want to provide enough information for students to select the process they want to learn about.

Modified Flipped Instruction

During class, students should watch or read the instructions for the process they have selected. Taking notes or drawing diagrams helps students learn and remember the steps. When they feel like they are ready, they can take the quiz for the process they have selected, retaking it as needed until they can answer every question correctly.

Inspiration and Design

At this point in the course, students have experience designing work by sketching, experimenting, and researching. They should be capable of making some decisions about how to design their work in a way that will work best for them. Give them a list of options for design and ask that they pick at least two from the list.

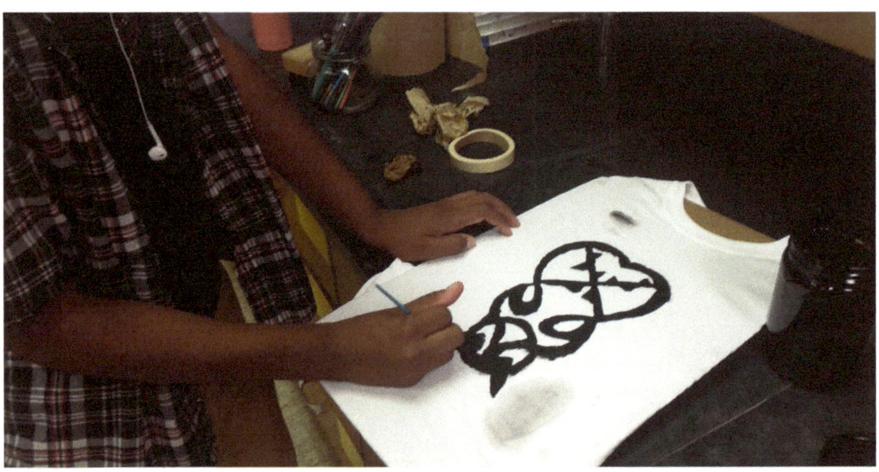

Q working on a T-shirt design.

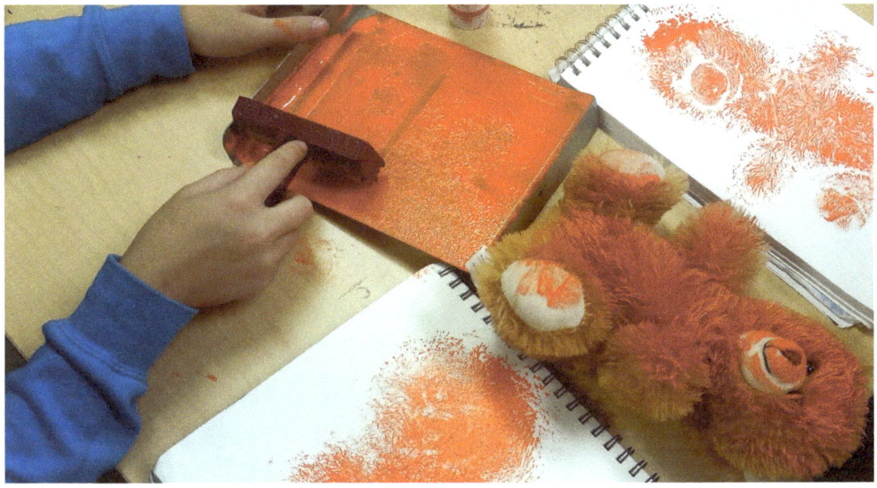

Experimenting with printing surfaces.

Example Design Activities

- Sketch your design.
- Make a Pinterest board of inspirations.
- Research reference images.
- Experiment with technique (for example, try carving with an extra piece of linoleum).
- Ask for a demonstration.

Creation

As students work, circulate around the room, asking questions about where they are in their work process and giving feedback. When students ask a question about a process covered in the resource material they view, prompt them to go back and find the answer on their own to reinforce independent learning.

Reflection

On the last day of work, take a few minutes and ask students to compare the printmaking process they selected to the processes for other media. For example, how is it like drawing, or how is it like making a clay tile?

Bootcamp Wrap Up

Celebrate all the learning that has happened during the Bootcamp by having a Fun Friday or a critique game day. After completing this unit, your students should have a firm foundation of learning from which to introduce a higher level of choice. They now know how to use a range of materials in the context of your classroom procedures. Just as importantly, they have a clear decision-making process to use while making art: the Artistic Thinking Process. Both of these components will help them work successfully as they take on more responsibility for how and why they make their art. As you move on to more complex concepts in the Artistic Behavior units of the next section, help students remember what they've learned here by displaying information that supports independent decision making, like technique charts and illustrated steps of processes.

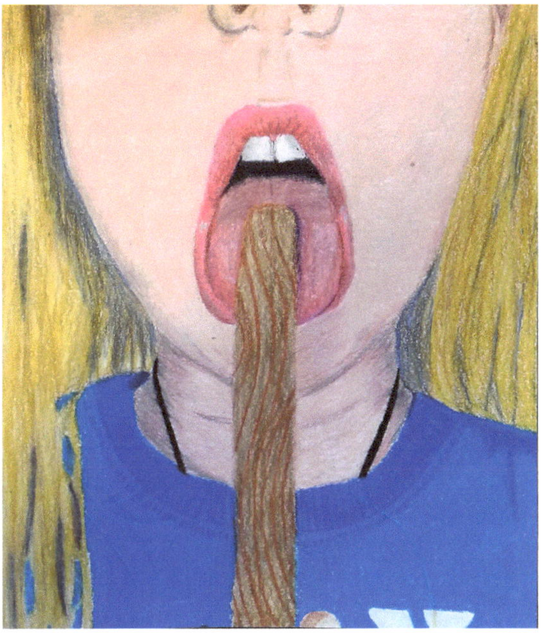

Colored pencil drawing by Anna.

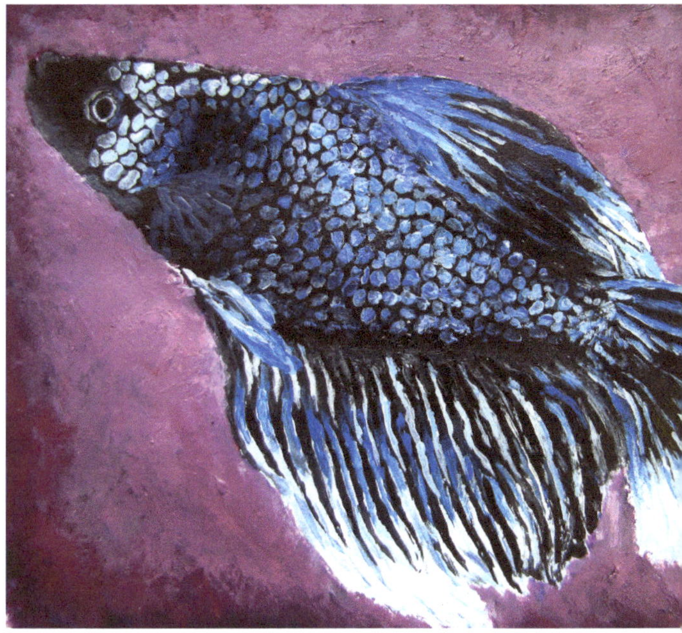

Jessie's fish painting.

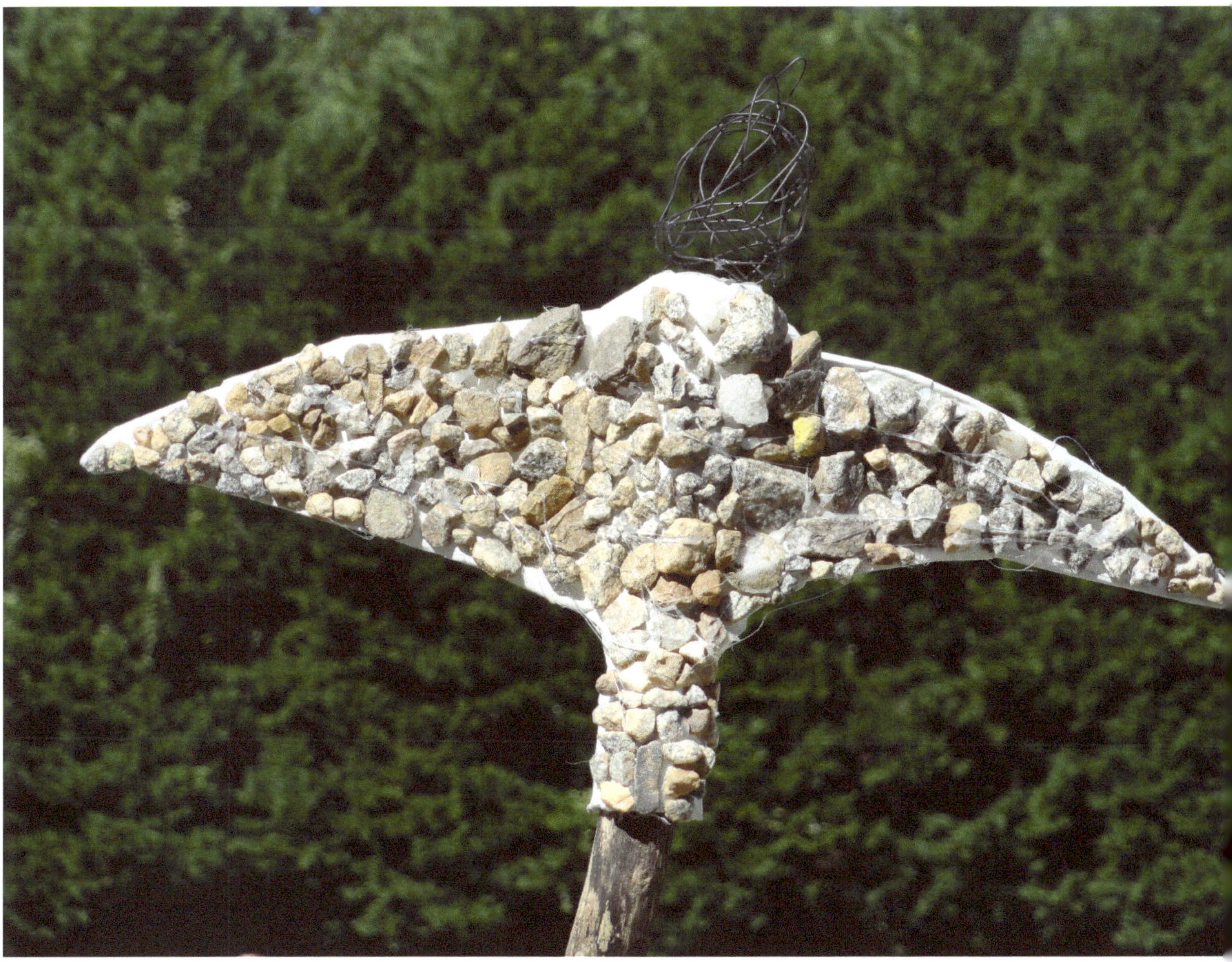

Originally designed to demonstrate the element of line using wire, this project soon took on a life of its own.

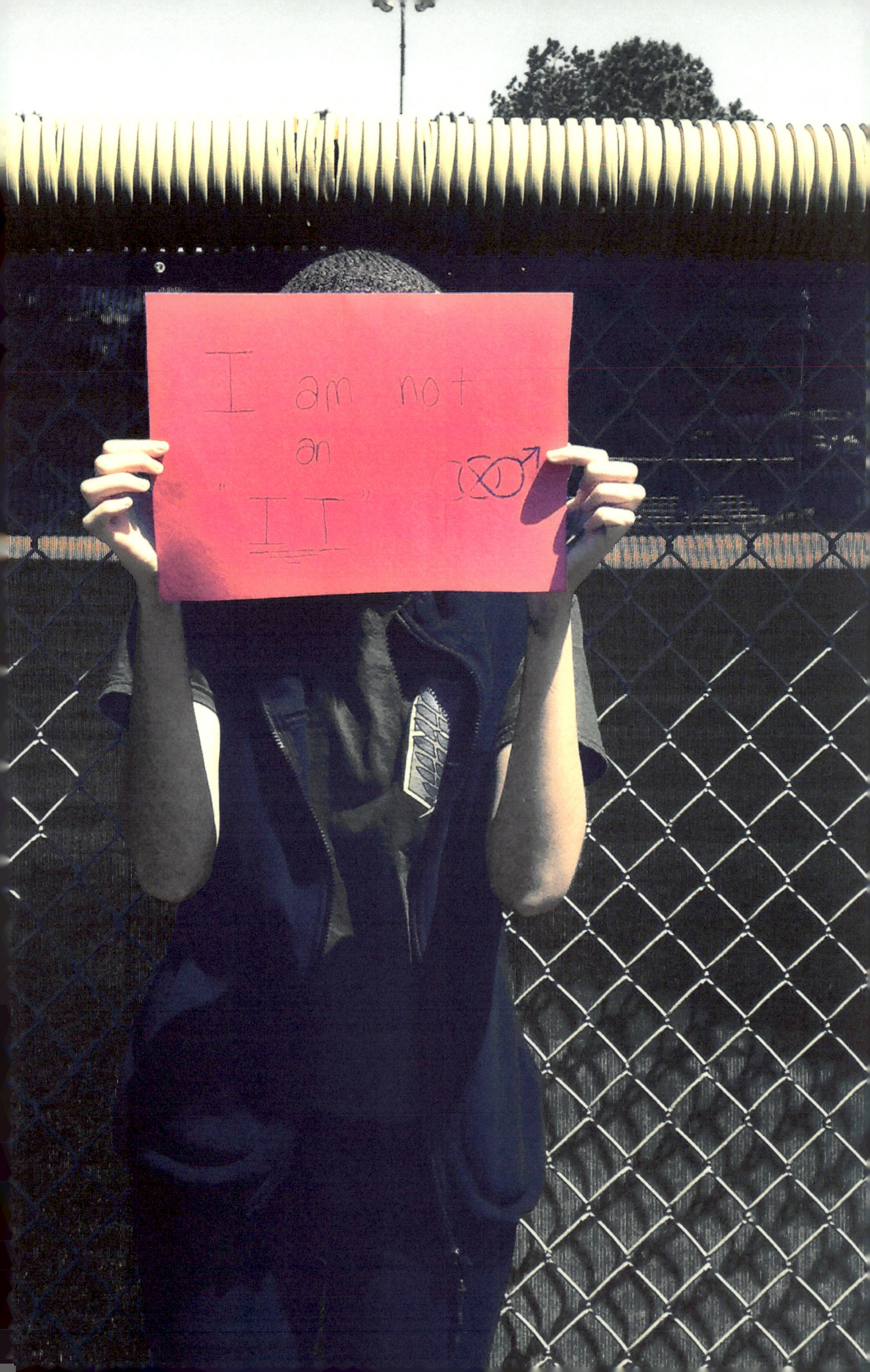
I am not
an
"IT"

8 | Artistic Behavior Unit Plans

When developing a curriculum, unit plans often follow a framework. Sometimes the framework is based on media: for example, developing units around drawing, painting, ceramics, and printing. Another common method is to develop the curriculum around the elements of art: for example, lessons based on line, value, color, and form. The Open Art Room presents an alternate approach, building the curriculum on a foundation of how artists think and work. From this starting point, the student moves through the phases of the design process, learning behaviors that can be applied to current as well as future projects. Previously considered frameworks, such as media and elements of art as well as teaching techniques, are not lost in this new way of developing units; rather, they are built into the unit lessons. This method of unit planning encompasses a richer platform for the student to develop and create art.

The unit plans in this chapter are presented in order from beginner level to advanced, expanding on the level of choice as the chapter unfolds. This ordering is designed to make it easier for teachers to determine which plans would be most successful in their situation. The plans also follow the Artistic Thinking Process as outlined in Chapter Two. Each phase presents specific artists, mini-lessons, demonstrations, brainstorming activities, and reflection ideas.

Each of the unit plans has been tried and tested successfully in an Open Art Room setting. Note, though, that the plans are provided as examples; they may be incorporated or modified to fit the needs of individual teachers. They serve as a template for teachers to use to develop their own Artistic Behavior Unit plans.

Artists Observe

Level: Beginner

National Standards

- B.CX.1.3
- B.V.2.2

Learning Goals

- Understand observational drawing techniques and be able to apply them to depict realistic detail.
- Understand different types of observational art including scientific illustration, still-life compositions, urban sketching, and contemporary methods of observation.

Level of Choice

	Beginner	Intermediate	Advanced
Media	Limited to a few select.		
Process		Students follow directed steps.	
Planning		Students select planning activities from a list.	
Reflection	Students write from teacher-generated prompts.		

Stage 1: Inspiration

Today, capturing an image is as simple as taking out your phone and pressing on the screen. With image-making so conveniently available, many artists rely on digital photography to help create their artworks. We have it good . . . but photography is barely 150 years old. Prior to that, artists had to rely on their own eyes rather than a camera's lens to capture images.

One of the best ways to train the eye and increase one's artistic ability is to draw from observation. Many an artist has set up bottles, fruit, and other items on a table to draw or paint a still life. Models have patiently stood still while artists captured their forms on paper or canvas. Easels have held canvases in place in the sun, rain, and even at night so artists could capture the effects of light reflecting off surfaces.

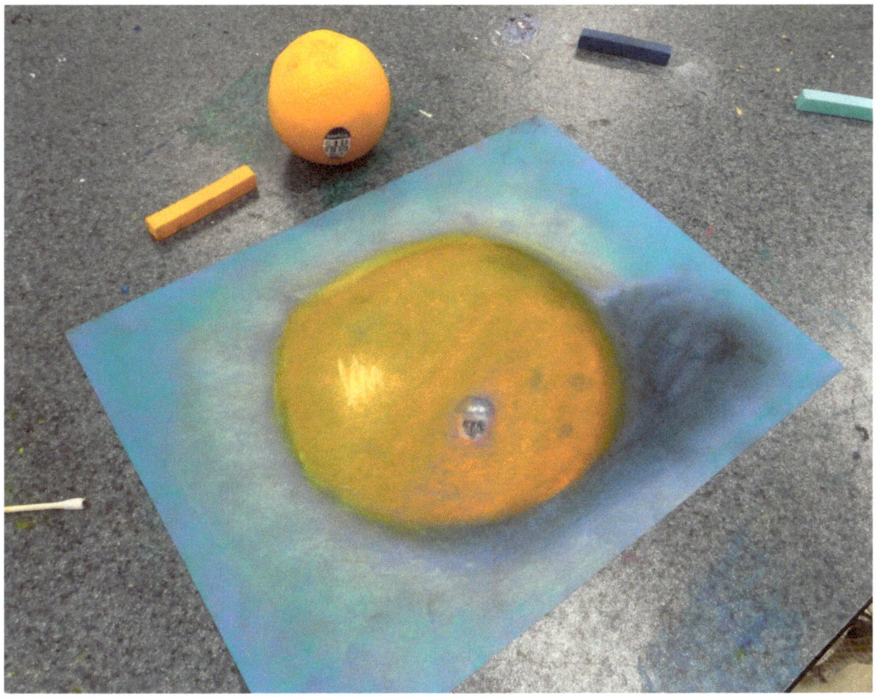

Drawing fruit through direct observation with chalk pastels.

Observational art isn't always created for aesthetic reasons. Naturalists have used artist renderings of animals to identify species. Scientists and engineers have relied on artists' illustrations to demonstrate through images how things work or fit together.

In this unit, students will explore several different methods of creating art from observation. They will be introduced to a limited range of media that will be paired with each method.

In order to introduce the methods and materials, this unit opens with a Bootcamp approach. Each day, for several days, a different concept and medium are introduced so that the students have some understanding of each. Once this is accomplished, a final observational project offers students the opportunity to explore more deeply the method and material of their choosing.

Observational Art Bootcamp

The list of mini-lessons below presents several different methods of observation paired with a suggested medium. Each of these mini-lessons can be covered in one class period. All of these could be covered in a week's time. A second week would then be needed for the final project.

Scientific Illustration

Method. Technical illustrations, such as those found in nature magazines and science journals, can originate from observational studies. While such

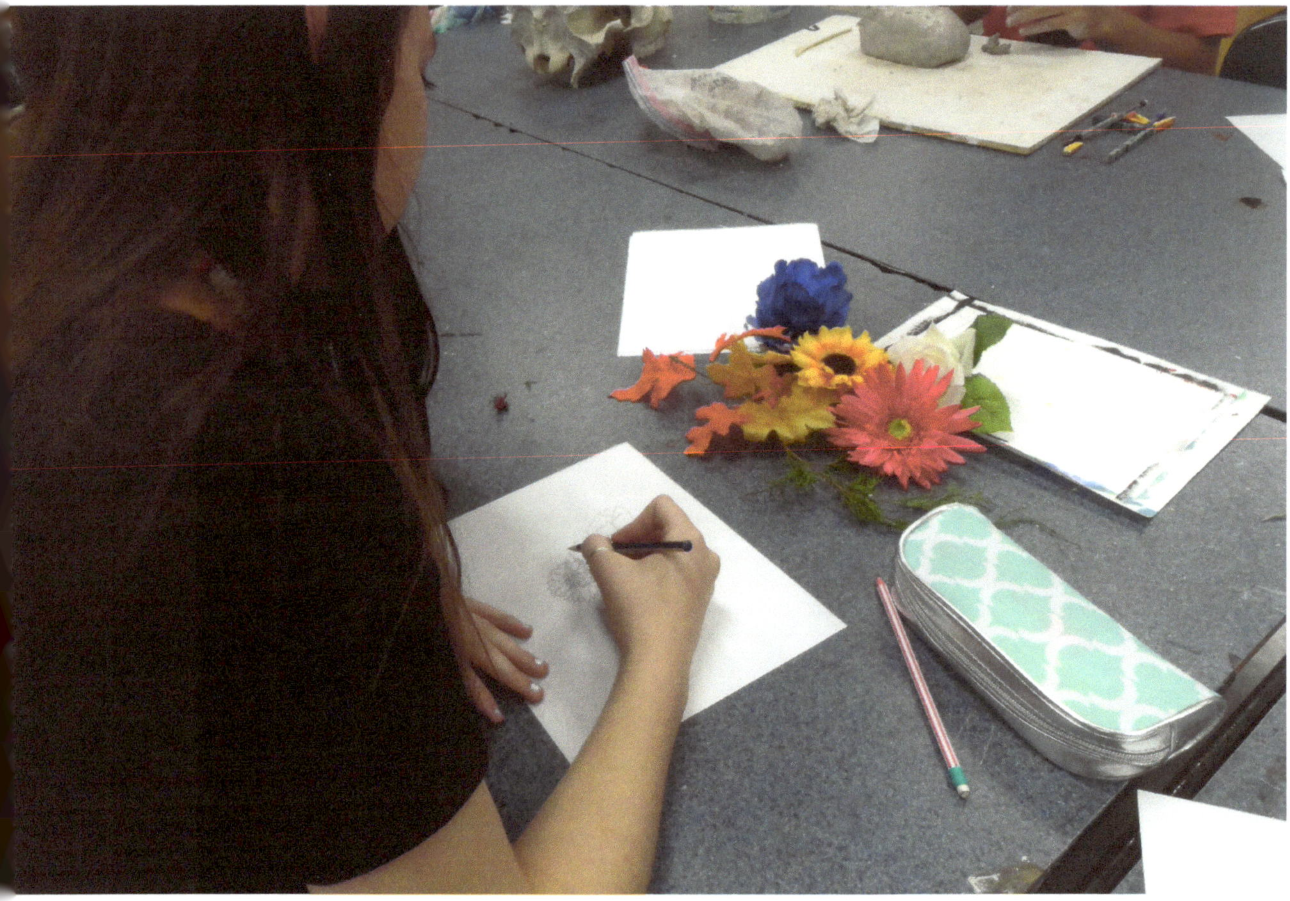

‹etches as part of the unit Artists Observe.

illustrations can be aesthetically pleasing, their primary purpose is the clear presentation of visual information.

One method for providing a variety of different experiences is to set up observational centers that students rotate around during a class period. Each center contains a few objects of similar genre. Groups of students are given a select period of time in which to observe and draw at each center. When the time is up, students rotate to the next center. Here is a sample list of possible types of centers:

- Bones, skulls, and shells
- Bugs and butterflies
- Mechanical objects, such as gears, hardware, and tools
- Branches, leaves, and flowers
- Live animals (such as turtles, frogs, hamsters)

Media. Since the time at each observational center will be short, it is best to keep the drawing tools simple. Pencil or charcoal are good options.

Artist Examples: John James Audubon, Robert Bateman

Urban Sketching

Method. Urban sketching is the contemporary cousin of plein air painting. In its simplest form, it is the art of drawing what one sees in an urban setting such as an outdoor café, park, or train station. These drawings may contain elements of linear perspective but need not adhere to strict standards, instead taking on a loose, sketchy appearance.

In a school setting, urban sketching can be done in the cafeteria, courtyard, hallways, or even the band room while the musicians play. The concept is to draw what you see from life as it is occurring.

Media. Though urban sketching can be completed using a tool as simple as a pencil, mixed media can add depth and richness to the work. Small watercolor sets with a cup of water are portable. Enhancing the line quality with pen and ink once the watercolor dries is also desirable.

Still Life

Method. The still life is the traditional method of drawing from observation using objects as a subject. Many teachers prefer to present their students with preselected objects. These may include items such as bottles, apples, oranges, or shoes. Other teachers include students in the object selection, asking them to bring in personal objects from home for a more contemporary spin. For an even more personal approach, have students create sculptures out of Legos, clay, or aluminum foil. Use these new creations as objects in still lifes.

Media. Oil or chalk pastels work well with still-life drawings. They allow for both color and value, which can be key components of an effective still life. The mini-lesson could begin with a short demo on using pastel to create value for an item such as an apple or orange, followed by an allotment of time for students to work on several objects. Remember that the purpose of this part of the unit is only to provide an overview of working with the still life and with the media, not to create a finished work of art. This will come later if the student selects still life as a final observation project.

Contemporary Art

The concept of observation can go beyond still life and scientific illustration. Some contemporary artists use the principle of observation in unconventional ways, producing artworks with innovative relationships to traditional drawing methods. Here are three such contemporary artists:

Nathalie Miebach uses scientific data from weather events to guide her construction of wondrous sculptures. Though her works look whimsical, they are careful translations of actual information from weather patterns, tide charts, and other such sources.

Deb Sokolow uses anomalous text-based fictions as the basis for her drawings and collages.

Katie Sokoler plays with cutouts to stage humorous photographic vignettes.

Students inspired by artworks such as these might try new ways to incorporate data into their own work. What information does the student find interesting enough to collect? How can this data be translated into a visual piece?

Stage 2: Design

After completing observational Bootcamp activities, students are asked to select one method of observation around which to base a final piece. Their choices of media may comply with the materials used during the Bootcamp, or the teacher may allow them more freedom of choice at this point.

Design Activities

Group Brainstorming, Part One. Divide students into four groups, one for each of the four genres of observational art. Assign one group scientific illustration, the next urban sketching, the third still life, and the fourth group contemporary art. Provide the groups with large paper and markers. Allocate a short period of time, perhaps seven minutes, and have each group brainstorm as many ideas as they can for the observation method they have been assigned. At the end of the seven minutes, have each group rotate to the next genre and complete the same task. Once every group has rotated through all four methods, have the groups present their ideas in a class discussion. The conversation can revolve around how many similar ideas each group wrote, as well as around the most unique ideas.

Group Brainstorming, Part Two. For a follow-up brainstorming session, students can be grouped by the observational method they most want to use in their final project. Group members can then brainstorm more ideas, discuss ideas they each wish to pursue, and gather insight from other students on how best to flesh out their own ideas.

During the design phase, the teacher's role is to support students by acting as a guide and sounding board. Listen to ideas and provide feedback. Instead of giving answers, ask probing questions. Confer with students about the concepts behind their designs and their media possibilities. Suggest planning activities that will help them meet their needs.

Stage 3: Creation

Once students have completed the design phase, they are ready to move on and start producing their final artwork. At this point, students should be able to communicate their intentions to the teacher, including their plans for handling media and composition, as well as their expected turnaround time. Students should also consider how they will manage their time if they finish early or if the scope of the design means they will take longer to complete their projects than the rest of the class.

Stage 4: Reflection

Once students have finished working through the lesson, they should reflect on their learning by writing, blogging, or discussing the following questions:

- How did you incorporate the concept of observation into your piece?
- How did you decide on the subject used for the observational piece?
- How effective was the choice of media in creating this work of art? If it was effective, why? If it was not effective, what other media might have been considered?

Artists Understand Space

Theme: Elements of art

Level: Beginning

National Standards

- VA:Cr1.1.Ia
- VA:Cr1.2.Ia

Learning Goals

- Develop and apply an understanding of how the element of space can be used to create art.
- Use the creative process to develop ideas into artworks that apply new learning.

Level of Choice

	Beginner	Intermediate	Advanced
Media	Limited to a few select.		Students select from all available materials.
Process		Students pick and choose from possible suggestions.	
Planning		Students select planning activities from a list.	
Reflection		Students write or present from teacher-generated prompts.	

Stage 1: Inspiration

Ask students to select a current event that they have an opinion about. Give them a few days' notice, so they can think about it in advance.

Activity 1: Drawing a Cube

Timeframe: 1 or 2 classes

Materials: Graphite or limited drawing tools

Input. Discuss the ways artists make a two-dimensional drawing surface appear three-dimensional. Demonstrate how to draw a cube in one- and two-point perspective. Provide time for guided practice with feedback.

Apply. Ask students to create a composition using cubes and one- or two-point perspective.

Reflect. Ask students how techniques used to make cubes seem three-dimensional could be applied to other types of drawing.

Activity 2: Illusions with Space
Timeframe: 1–2 class periods

Materials: Cell phones

Input. Discuss how artists manipulate the rules of space and perspective to create illusions of realistic or compressed space. Show examples of forced perspective photography and the artwork of Aakash Nihalani, which combines geometric tape murals with figures to create illusions.

Apply. Have students form groups and create a series of forced perspective photographs or an interactive tape mural.

Reflect. Have students share the images they've created and discuss how they collaborated to use space in their artwork.

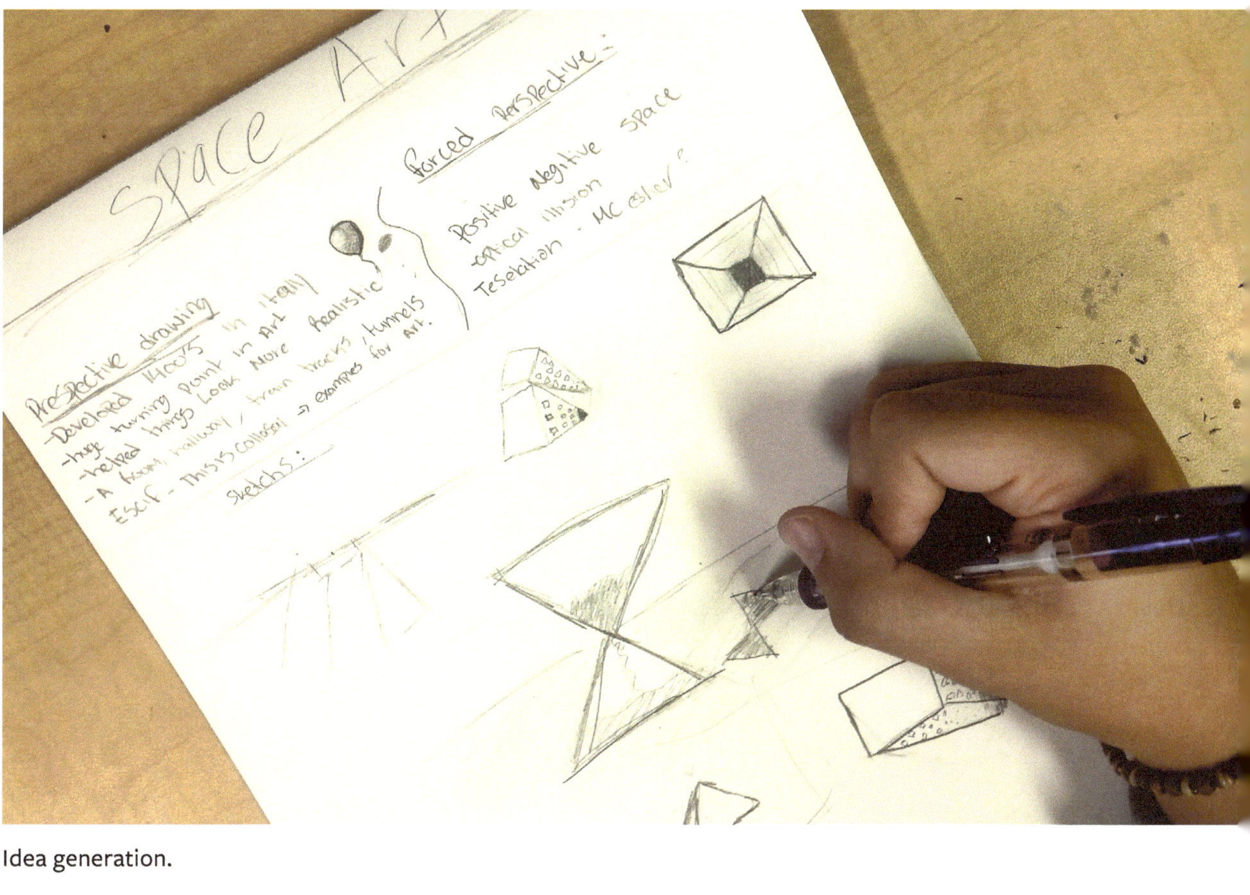

Idea generation.

Activity 3: Positive and Negative Space Stencils

Timeframe: 3 classes

Materials: Poster board, X-Acto knives, Pixlr, computers, spray paint

Input. Discuss how artists use positive and negative space to create graphic images. Show examples of stencil-based graffiti art from artists like C215 (Christian Guemy) or Banksy. In the computer lab, demonstrate how to use programs like Photoshop or the online photoeditor Pixlr to reduce images to two color. Next show students how to trace images onto posterboard and cut them out with X-Acto knives to make stencils.

Apply. Have students work through the process to make stencil art. To reduce time and material use, students can work in groups. Screen printing or block printing are other good options for this lesson.

Reflect. Ask students to share how they worked with positive and negative space to create images.

Final Assignment

Timeframe: 5 classes

Materials: Open

Inspiration. By this point in the unit, students will have developed an understanding of how space can be used to create artwork. To facilitate the selection of ideas for the final project, review the concepts introduced in each activity. Show a limited selection of artwork that represents taking each concept further, like a cityscape for students who are interested in exploring perspective or an optical illusion created with positive and negative space (e.g., the work of Yau Hoong Tang). Have students write down at least three ideas during this discussion.

Stage 2: Design

Students work through the design phase by completing two design activities from the list below. These activities serve as tools that will be used to examine the essential question selected by the student.

Design Activities

- Research artists or styles to help generate ideas.
- Use sketching to work out composition and plan your work.
- Experiment by trying out different ideas, playing with media, and problem solving to find solutions.

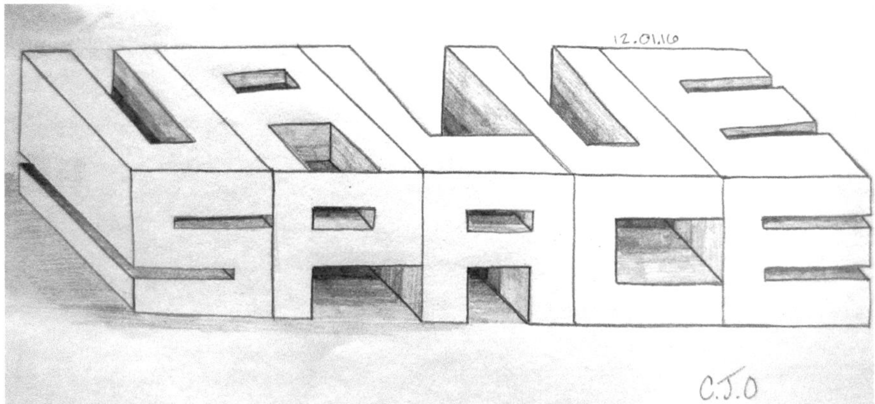

Creating the illusion of space and depth with graphite.

During the design phase, the teacher's role is to support students by acting as a guide and sounding board. Listen to ideas and provide feedback. Ask probing questions instead of giving answers. Conference with students about the concept behind their work and media possibilities. Suggest planning activities that will work well to meet their needs.

Stage 3: Creation

When students have completed the design phase, they are ready to move on to the creation section of the lesson and start production of their final artwork. Continue to conference with students daily, asking probing questions to determine how best to provide support through any issues that arise.

Examples of Probing Questions

- What do you like about the work you have done so far?
- How are you using space in your work?
- Did you think about _______________?

Stage 4: Reflection

Once students have finished working through the lesson, they should reflect on their learning by writing, blogging, or discussing the following questions:

- What did you learn about space and how it can be used to make art during this unit?
- How did you come up with an idea for your final project? What inspired you?
- How do you feel about your final artwork? Is there anything you would add or change?

For critique, have a Fun Friday or a day of critique games. See pages 128–132 for descriptions of these activities.

Modifications

In this lesson the level of student choice is a combination of teacher-directed and modified choice. To make this lesson more teacher-directed, try the following:

- Limit media to fewer choices or one option.
- Preselect planning activities instead of letting students pick.

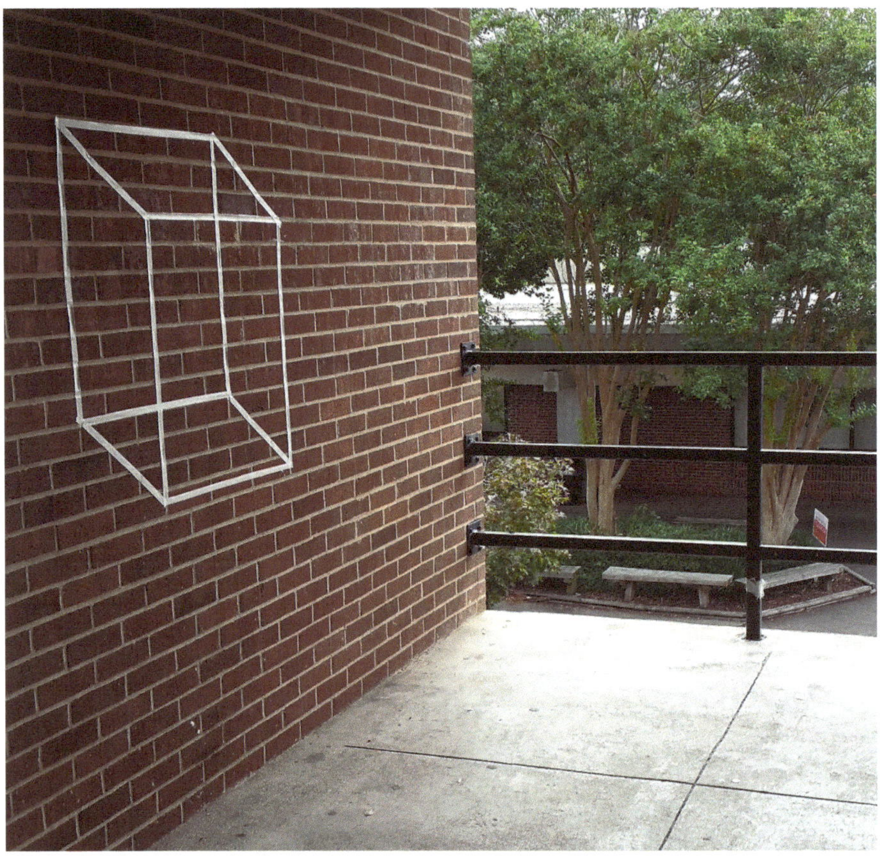

Tape mural.

Artists Apply Proportion

Theme: Observational Drawing
Level: Intermediate
National Standards

- VA:Cr1.1.Ia
- VA:Cr2.3.Ia

Learning Goals

- Apply understanding of how to apply knowledge of proportion to depict the human figure in artwork.
- Use the artistic process to develop ideas, plan, and create artwork.

Level of Choice

	Beginner	Intermediate	Advanced
Media			Students select media.
Process	Students learn specific processes.		
Planning			Students select planning activities.
Reflection	Students write from teacher-generated prompts.		

Stage 1: Inspiration

This phase begins with a series of activities to help students develop an understanding of portraiture and figure drawing.

Activity 1: Proportion

Timeframe: 1–2 class periods

Materials: Graphite or weighted drawing pencils

Input. Demonstrate human proportions while students take notes.

Apply. Put students in groups of three or four and ask them to create a large-scale figure with correct proportions on paper.

Reflect. Ask students how they applied their knowledge of proportions to create their figures.

Activity 2: Figures around Campus

Timeframe: 3 class periods

Materials: Student choice

Input. Discuss the artwork of graffiti artist Daan Botlek, who creates figures that interact with their surroundings. Ask students to apply their knowledge of proportion to create large-scale figures out of paper that interact with the campus.

Apply. Have students form groups and create artwork with paper and other materials they choose.

Reflect. Have students share the images they've created and discuss how they collaborated to use proportion in their artwork.

Activity 3: Facial Proportions

Timeframe: 3 classes

Materials: Graphite or charcoal

Pre-assessment. Prior to instruction, ask students to draw a face. This work establishes a baseline for skill development. Ask students to set a goal for portrait drawing. What do they want to know and be able to do?

Input. Demonstrate drawing the facial features one-by-one, stopping to let students practice. As they work, give feedback and re-teach as needed.

Apply. Ask students to revisit their learning goals. Their task is to complete a drawing that shows work towards mastering it. Have them think about what sort of development activities will help bridge the gap between what they know and what they want to know. Do they need to experiment with technique, sketch, or find additional resource material? Help them make these decisions as they plan and create their artwork.

Final Assignment

Timeframe: 4 classes

Materials: Open

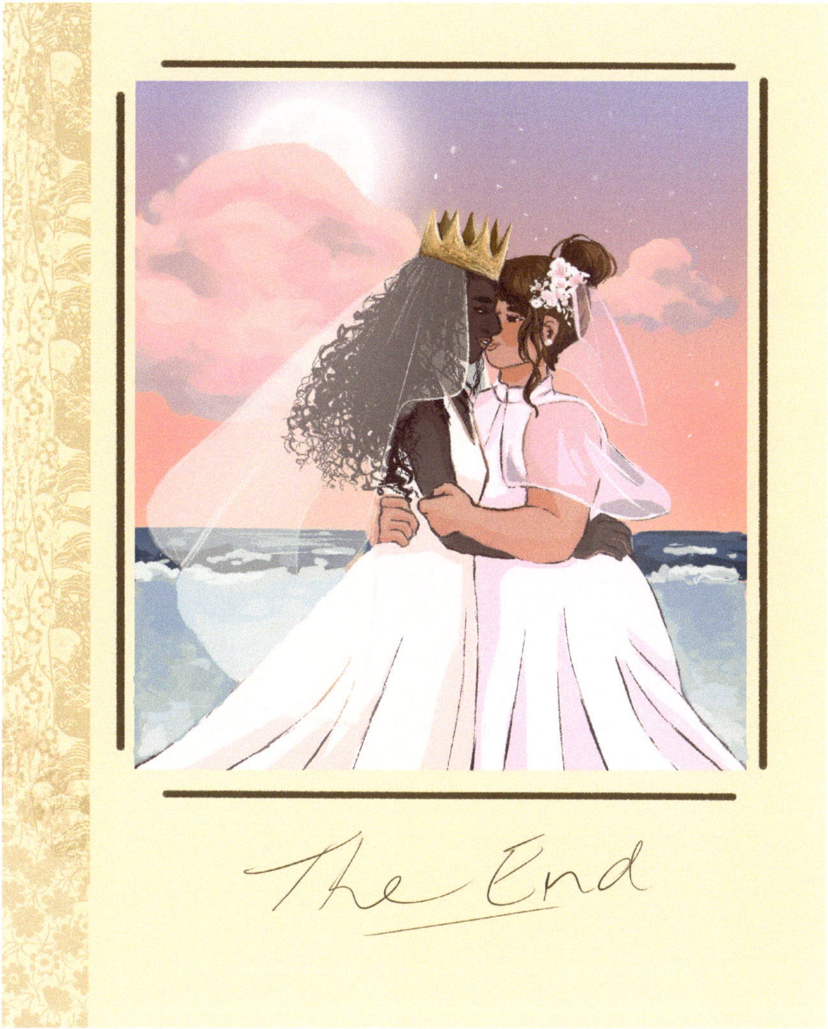

Stevie made this digital image to address the lack of positive depictions of gay relationships in the media.

Input. In the summative assignment for this unit students will apply new learning by creating figurative artwork. This could range from portraiture to work including multiple figures.

Stage 2: Design

Students should select two design activities that best fit the needs of their project.

Design Activities

- Research artists or styles to help generate ideas.
- Use sketching to work out composition and plan your work.
- Experiment by trying out different ideas, playing with media, and problem solving to find solutions.

During the design phase, the teacher's role is to support students by acting as a guide and sounding board. Listen to ideas and provide feedback. Ask probing questions instead of giving answers. Conference with students about the concept behind their work and media possibilities. Suggest planning activities that will work well to meet their needs.

Stage 3: Creation

When students have completed the design phase they are ready to move on to the creation section of the lesson and start production of their final artwork. Continue to conference with students daily, asking probing questions to determine how best to provide support through any issues that arise.

Examples of Probing Questions

- Are you satisfied with the work you have done so far?
- Are there any areas of your project you are struggling with?
- Did you think about ________________?

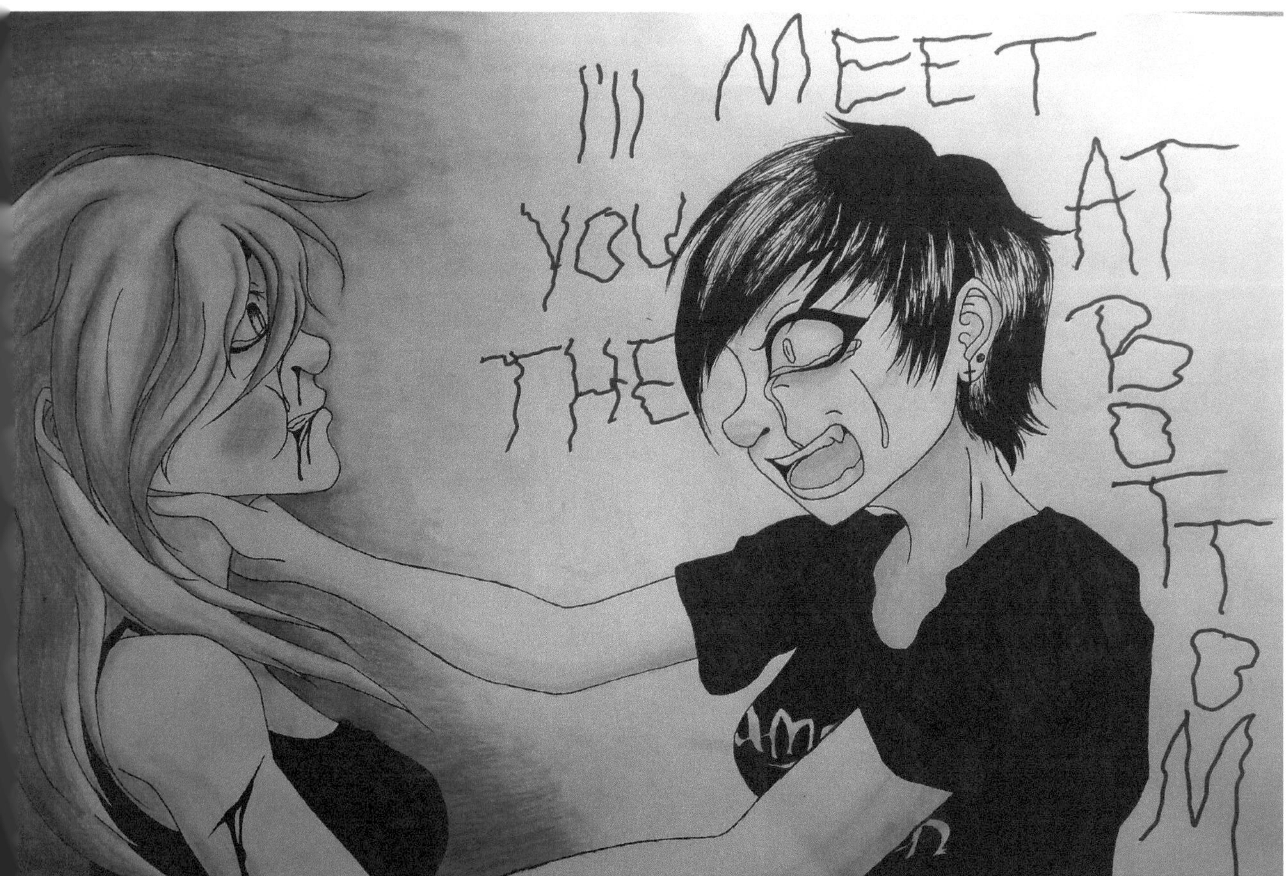

t exploring mental health issues.

Stage 4: Reflection

Once students have finished working through the lesson, they should reflect on their learning by writing, blogging, or discussing the following questions:

- What did you learn about the human figure and proportions during this unit?
- Figurative work is challenging. What areas did you struggle with and how did you resolve challenges that you experienced?
- How do you feel about your final artwork? Is there anything you would add or change?

For critique, have a Fun Friday or a day of critique games. See pages 128–132 for descriptions of these activities.

Modifications

In this lesson, the level of student choice is a combination of teacher-directed and modified choice. To make this lesson more teacher-directed, try the following:

- Limit media to fewer choices or one option.
- Preselect planning activities instead of letting students pick.

The Blind Portrait

Levels: Beginner, Intermediate

National Standards

- VA:Cr2.1.Ia
- VA:Cr3.1.IIa
- VA:Re8.1.IIa

Learning Goals

- Transpose written statements to visual representations.
- Investigate portraiture from a nonrepresentational perspective.

Level of Choice

	Beginner	Intermediate	Advanced
Media			Any 2D or 3D media.
Process		Students follow directed steps.	
Planning		Students select planning activities from a list.	
Reflection	Students write from teacher-generated prompts.		

Stage 1: Inspiration

Capturing a portrait is usually about recreating a physical appearance. However, in this unit students are asked to create a portrait of a fellow classmate without having a photo or physical description or even knowing who the subject of their work is. Their only source of inspiration will come from written responses to a short biographical questionnaire. They must design and produce their work of art without any visual clues at all; this is a blind portrait.

Even when a teacher doesn't assign seats and students are free to move around, few take advantage. Instead, they sit at the same seat at the same table every day. This results in the students not knowing much, if anything, about the other students in the class. However, building relationships with others bolsters cooperation and improves reflections and critiques among students, helping them to develop as artists. The blind portrait is a project designed to help students get to know a little something more about their fellows.

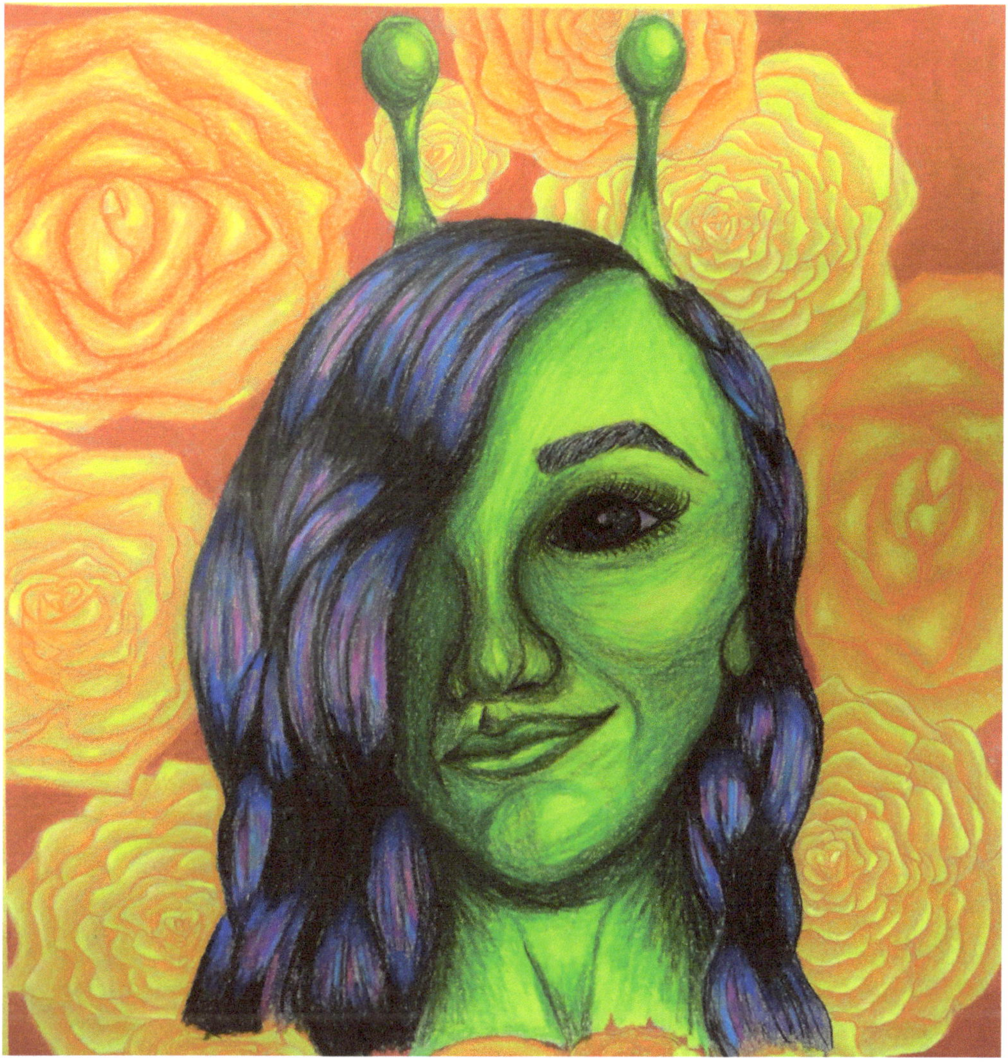

Blind portrait based on student's completed profile.

The objective of the blind portrait is for students to create a work of art that reflects the personality of a classmate without knowing which student is their subject.

The Questionnaire

To kick off the project, have each student provide written responses to the following four questions:

- What are your strengths?
- What are your weaknesses?
- What are your passions?
- What are your dislikes?

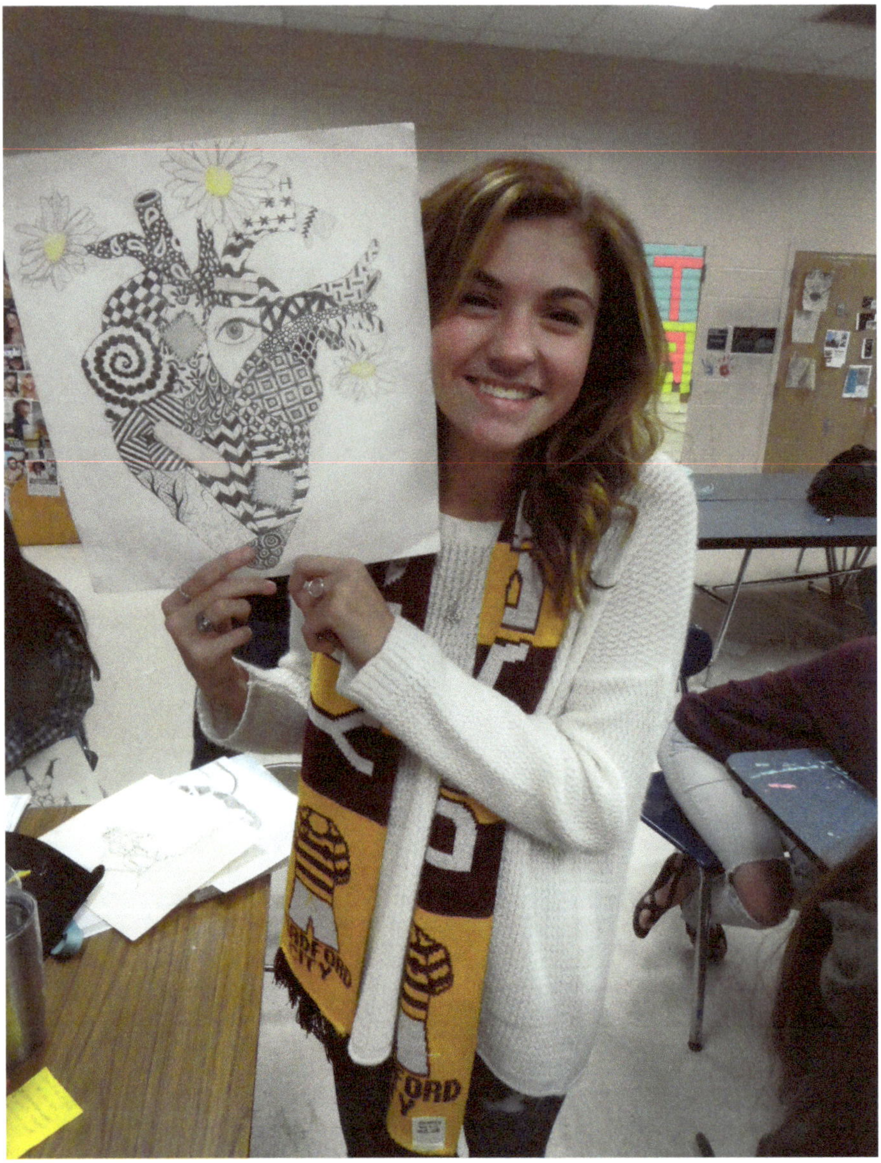

Student excited about receiving her blind portrait.

Notice that no identifying questions such as physical descriptions are asked. The only identification should be a number placed in the top right corner. This number will correlate with the student's name, but only the teacher should have access to this information.

The students should also be given detailed instructions on how to answer the questions. They should avoid nouns whenever possible. As an example, instead of saying, "I like soccer," the student would be encouraged to describe the activity and something about the activity they enjoy. "I like soccer" could be rephrased as "I like fast-paced competitive activities where my speed and endurance are challenged."

Stage 2: Design

Once the questionnaires are completed, they should be randomly distributed to the class, making sure, however, that no student receives a questionnaire from a student at the same table. The students are then told their objective: To read over the biographical information they received, and to use it to create a blind portrait of a fellow student.

Artist Examples

A portrait does not necessarily have to resemble a face or a body. Present to the class works of art that might be considered portraits. Some of these, but not all, may be representational. For example, Michael Richards, *Tar Baby vs. Saint Sebastian*; Vik Muniz, *Pictures of Garbage*; Heather Watkins, *Wallflower*; and Felix Gonzalez-Torres, *Untitled (Portrait of Ross in L.A.)*.

Stage 3: Creation

Knowing that we don't know something is a definite motivating factor to learning. The fact that students don't know whose questionnaire they are using as inspiration will have them buzzing. Though they will want to know whom they are creating a portrait about, possessing that information will skew their results. Again, the objective is to create a portrait based solely on the written responses, not on appearances, preconceived notions, or stereotypes about a person's personality. Implore your students not to seek out their subject. Though some may try to guess, most will respect your request and instead turn to the task of designing a portrait.

Each questionnaire should contain more information than is necessary to create a portrait. They may, in fact, contain too much information. Instead of allowing the students to become overwhelmed, encourage them to focus on the main points in the answers. Similar to how a caricaturist accentuates distinctive visual features, encourage students to characterize the distinctive non-visual features they've recognized from the questionnaire.

The following questions may help students narrow down the information:

- What words or part of the biography struck you?
- How will you incorporate this information into your project?
- What medium will you choose for the final piece?
- What skills or techniques might you need to learn to create the piece?

The media used for this project is open choice. Students should select the medium they believe will be best for visually representing their interpretation of the portrait.

Stage 4: Reflection

In addition to the normal reflection process, which may include writing, blogging, class critique, or discussion, the reflection process for this unit includes the exciting opportunity for revealing the identities of the blind portraits.

Students should present to the class their completed portraits and address the following questions:

- What part of the questionnaire did you focus in on? What words stood out?
- What part of the personality were you attempting to represent?
- What media did you select for this project and how did your media selection tie into the personality of your portraiture?

Once a student has finished presenting a portrait, the teacher can then reveal which student wrote the questionnaire the portrait was based on. If the class agrees, the portraits may be presented as gifts to each student.

Modifications

The level of student choice in this lesson is beginner to intermediate. This level was determined based on the more modified use of blind portrait as a theme. The level of choice in this unit revolves more around the freedom to select materials. A beginner level unit might offer fewer choices in media; the intermediate level would offer more options.

Artists Solve Problems

Level: Intermediate, Advanced

National Standards

- B.V.2.1
- B.CX.1.5
- I.V.2.1

Learning Goals

- Investigate various problem-solving methods.
- Apply self-imposed limitations to create works of art.

Level of Choice

	Beginner	Intermediate	Advanced
Media			Any 2D or 3D media.
Process			Students select limitations.
Planning		Students select planning activities from a list.	
Reflection	Students write from teacher-generated prompts.		

Stage 1: Inspiration

Artists have problems. Yes, there is the occasional ear being lopped off or the need to leave town after stabbing a man over a tennis bet, but not all artists' problems are self-inflicted. Sometimes artists face problems they seem to have no control over. There comes a point at which the artist must decide whether to concede defeat because an obstacle seems too daunting, or press on and find a solution.

Not all artists who face such issues succeed, but when they do, the results tend to be remarkable. Consider Michelangelo's *David*. The block of marble, with its imperfections, that Michelangelo eventually used presented such an issue that several artists tried to carve it and failed. Michelangelo believed he could solve the problem. He was awarded the commission and created the marvelous statue that stands in Florence today.

Just as they did five hundred years ago, today's artists still face problems. Artist Phil Hansen, well known for his TED Talk *Embrace the Shake*, tells the story of how he developed a tremor in his hand that converted his pointillist dots into streaks. This posed a problem since he was no longer able to create art as he had once done. It wasn't until a doctor told him to embrace the shake and learn to solve his artistic problem through this limitation that Phil Hansen was able to transform his art into the extraordinary work it is today.

This unit asks students to look at how artists consciously confront, overcome, and incorporate limitations to create a work of art.

Artist Examples

- Kacie Kinzer, *Tweenbots*
- Phil Hansen, *Embrace the Shake*. TED Talk, 2013
- Oliver Herring, TASK Party
- Performa, *Tantamounter 24/7*
- The Fun Theory

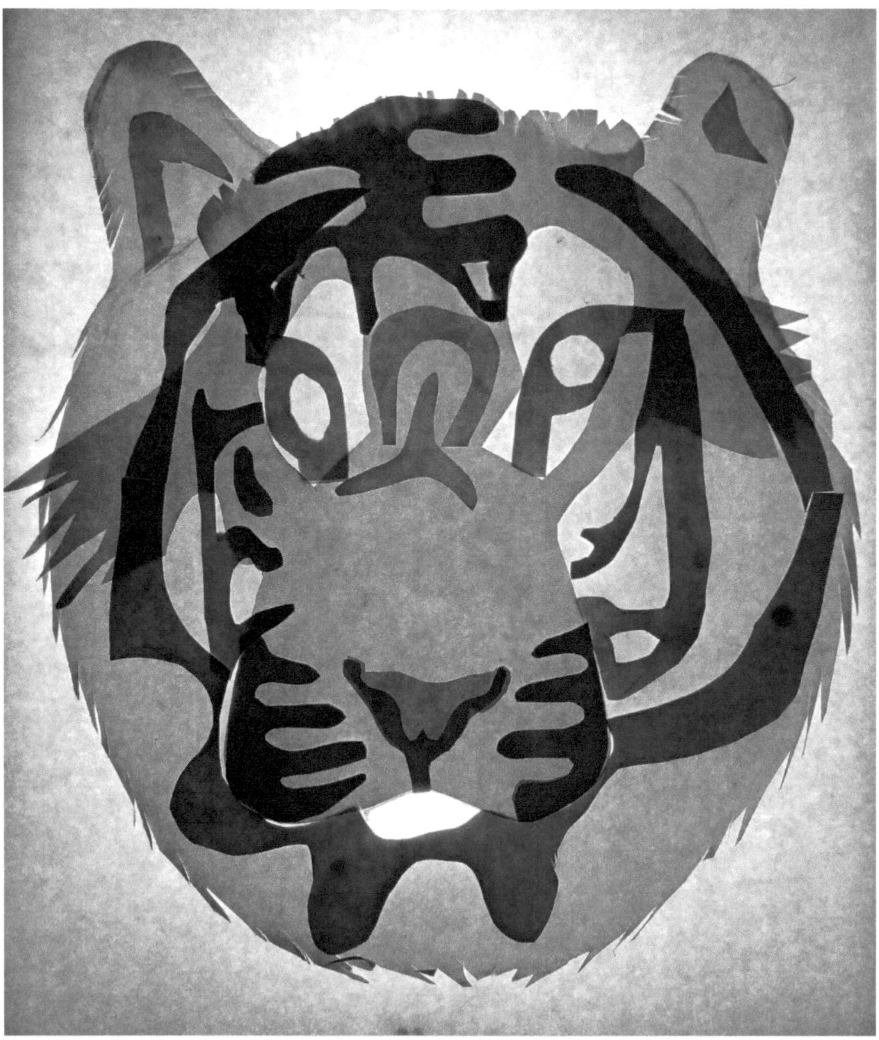

How can art be created using only white paper? Value created by layers and displayed on a light table.

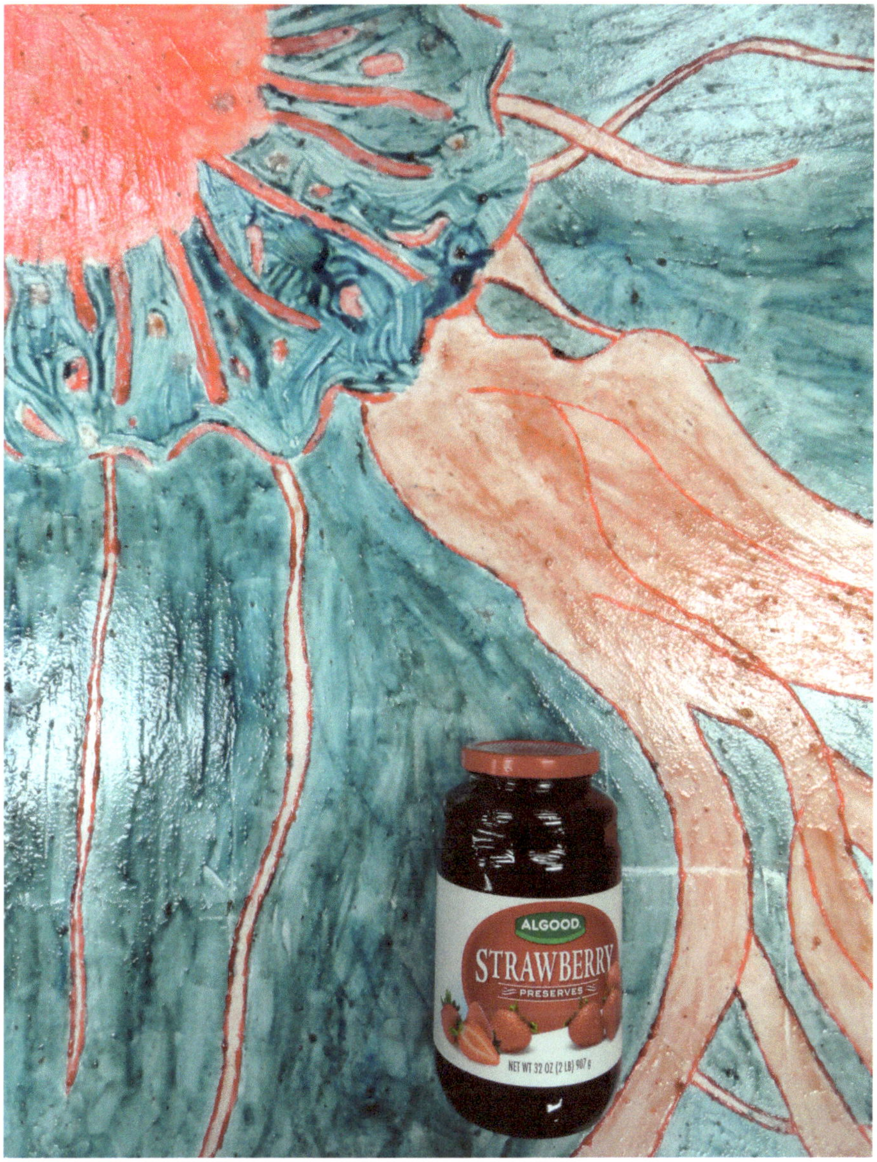

What if the student was limited to only jelly to paint a jellyfish?

Stage 2: Design

Students may be introduced to the concept of creating within limitations through one or more of the following design activities. Several of these can be group projects.

Design Activities

- TASK Party: Created by Oliver Herring, a TASK Party asks students to select a written task from a box and then complete the task as they see fit using any available materials. Once the task has been completed, students then write their own task to replace the one they just completed, This process is repeated until time runs out.

- Tantamounter: The idea, originally titled *Tantamounter 24/7*, was first implemented by the art group Performa. Participants were encouraged to provide the group with an object. The object was taken behind closed doors and a little while later, the object was returned along with a piece of art that was tantamount to the original object. As a design challenge, students can be given an object and one class period in which to produce a work of art that should resemble the original object.
- Clothespin Inspired: Designed by art teachers at St. Thomas More Catholic High School in Lafayette, LA, this challenge provides students with an ordinary item and asks that they use it as inspiration to create an extraordinary work of art. The ordinary item should be something simple and inexpensive, such as a clothespin or a cotton swab. This object, which students only receive one of, should be used as the inspiration but does not necessarily need to be physically incorporated into the work.
- Illustration Friday: Each week, the website Illustration Friday (http:www.illustrationfriday.com) posts a single word and asks artists from all over the world to create a work of art using the given word as inspiration. Teachers can ask students to take part in Illustration Friday, which can be given as a sketchbook assignment.
- Brainstorm: Students create lists of three different types of limitations:
  Physical—A limitation having to do with the body.
  Material—A limitation having to do with the medium.
  Conceptual—A limitation that comes from an idea.

Individually or in teams, students write down twenty examples of each, and then share their top five limitation ideas with the class.

Stage 3: Creation

After students have been inspired by several of the artists and completed a few of the design challenges presented, they should have a considerable understanding of how artists can work within limitations. At this point they should be able to try imposing their own limitations for creating an original artwork.

The brainstorming activity is particularly helpful in getting students to solidify their ideas. The teacher can help by reviewing the different limitations a student has listed and helping the student identify which type of limitation—physical, material, or conceptual—best suits that student. Students can also work in small groups, discussing possible ideas and explaining to one another how they might produce a work of art within a given limitation. These types of conversations are generally very productive.

It may be necessary to direct some students towards more realistic limitations, especially when considering materials. Many times, students will want to use a medium that is not available in the classroom and therefore will need to be provided by the student. Students should select media that are readily available and affordable.

Stage 4: Reflection

Once students have finished working through the lesson, they should reflect on their learning by writing, blogging, or discussing the following questions:

- What limitation did you place on yourself in order to make this artwork?
- What challenges or obstacles did you encounter while working within this limitation?
- How did you overcome the obstacles that you encountered while creating this artwork?
- Did you gain or develop new skills by working within this limitation?

Modifications

The level of student choice in this lesson is mainly advanced. To make this lesson more teacher-directed, try the following:

- Limit media by offering only a few predetermined options. Examples might include using only found objects, only newspaper, or only candy.
- The conceptual aspect of the final project may also be modified. Examples might include offering a predetermined theme or topic.

Artists Answer Essential Questions

Level: Intermediate, Advanced

National Standards

- VA:Cr1.2.Ia
- VA:Re.7.2.IIa

Learning Goal

- Investigate critical thinking by developing and responding to self-generated questions through visual representations.

Level of Choice

	Beginner	Intermediate	Advanced
Media			Any 2D or 3D media.
Process		Students follow some directed step.	
Planning		Some group brain-storming activities may be helpful.	
Reflection			Students should reflect on their own original questions and their ability to respond to these questions through visual means.

Stage 1: Inspiration

Artists often develop essential questions when creating a work of art. Sometimes these questions come before the art is created and are used as a way to formulate ideas. Other times, these questions are formulated after a work has been created, which in turn, generates another work. To the viewer, these essential questions may appear as themes the artist is following, but more often they are guiding concepts and the theme is determined after the work has been completed.

When students begin generating essential questions, it's best for them to explore ideas and concepts that they already feel passionate about. If the student takes no interest in a question, the visual solution that will come later will be lackluster at best. However, when students explore subjects of great personal concern, both their questions and, later, their products will have much better chances of success.

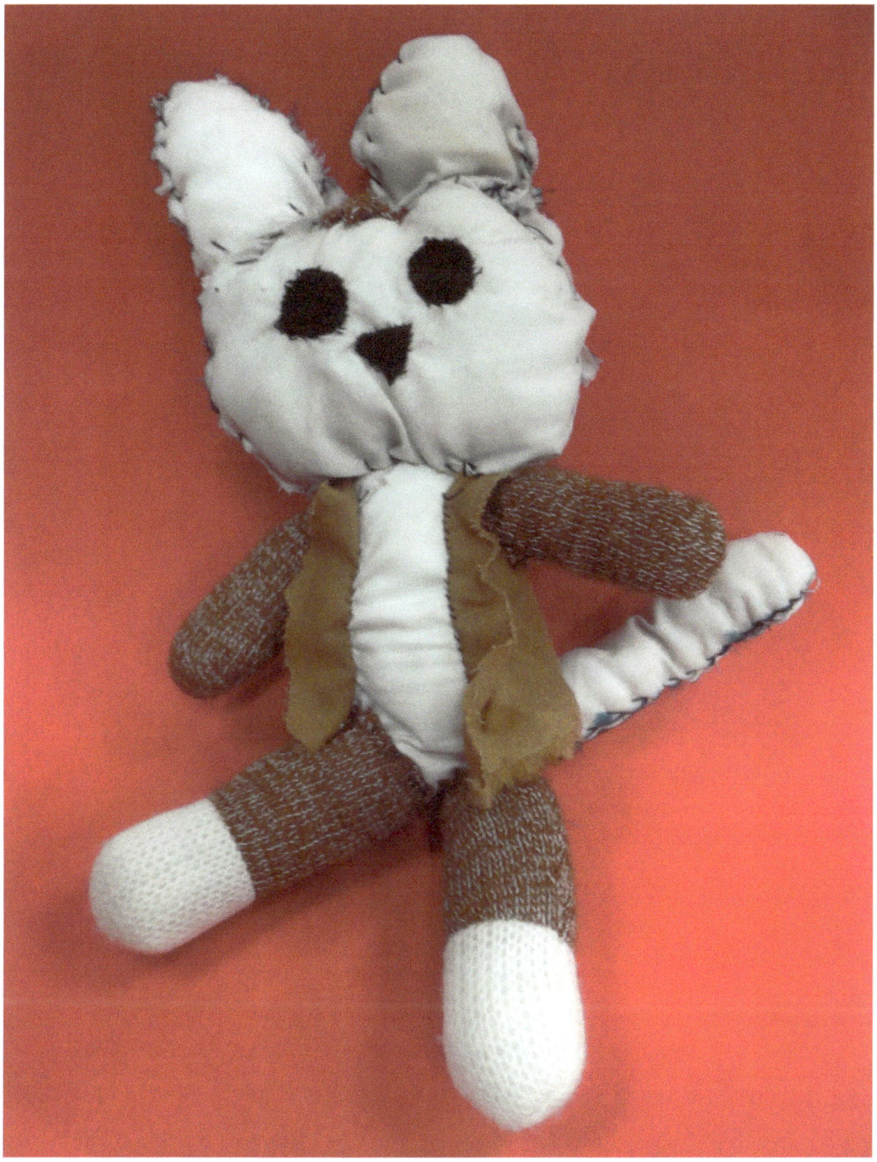

This student learned how to sew to answer the question, How does our perspective of things change when knowledge is brought into the mix?

To introduce this lesson, students should address open-ended questions that explore adjectives. Adjectives, which tend to be subjective, allow for many different responses and therefore many different solutions.

Sample Questions

- What makes something cute?
- What makes something creepy?
- What makes something awkward?
- What gives something value?

Each of these questions can be broken down into progressively more specific questions:

- Why is cute considered a good thing?
- What does creepy feel like?
- Is something awkward only when we consider it awkward?
- What makes something lose its value?

Artist Examples

Present artist examples that demonstrate how artists might respond to the sample questions:

- What makes something cute or creepy? Look at work by Patricia Piccinini, Ross Bonfanti, or *The Maker*, an animated video by Zealous Creative.
- What is life? Look at the work of artist Theo Jansen.
- How can you make something old, new? Eleanor Antin is a good artist here.

Stage 2: Design

The following is a design activity to help students generate ideas for a summative project. This is one method and it can be incorporated with other ideation activities, such as group brainstorming and research.

Essential Questions Planning

Have students begin by writing three words they wish to explore. Be sure to select words that elicit interesting responses instead of easy clichés, such as temporary, societal standards, or fake.

Then, students will write five questions for *each* word.

Sample Questions:

Temporary: Can temporary art have the same value as traditional, "permanent" art?

For Societal Standards: How do societal standards affect individuals?

Fake: Can an imitation be so lifelike that it becomes real?

Finally, students should create four thumbnail sketches based on their most interesting questions.

During the design phase, the teacher's role is to support students by acting as a guide and sounding board. Listen to ideas and provide feedback. Rather than giving answers, ask probing questions. Confer with students about the concepts behind their work and their media possibilities. Suggest planning activities that will work well to meet their needs.

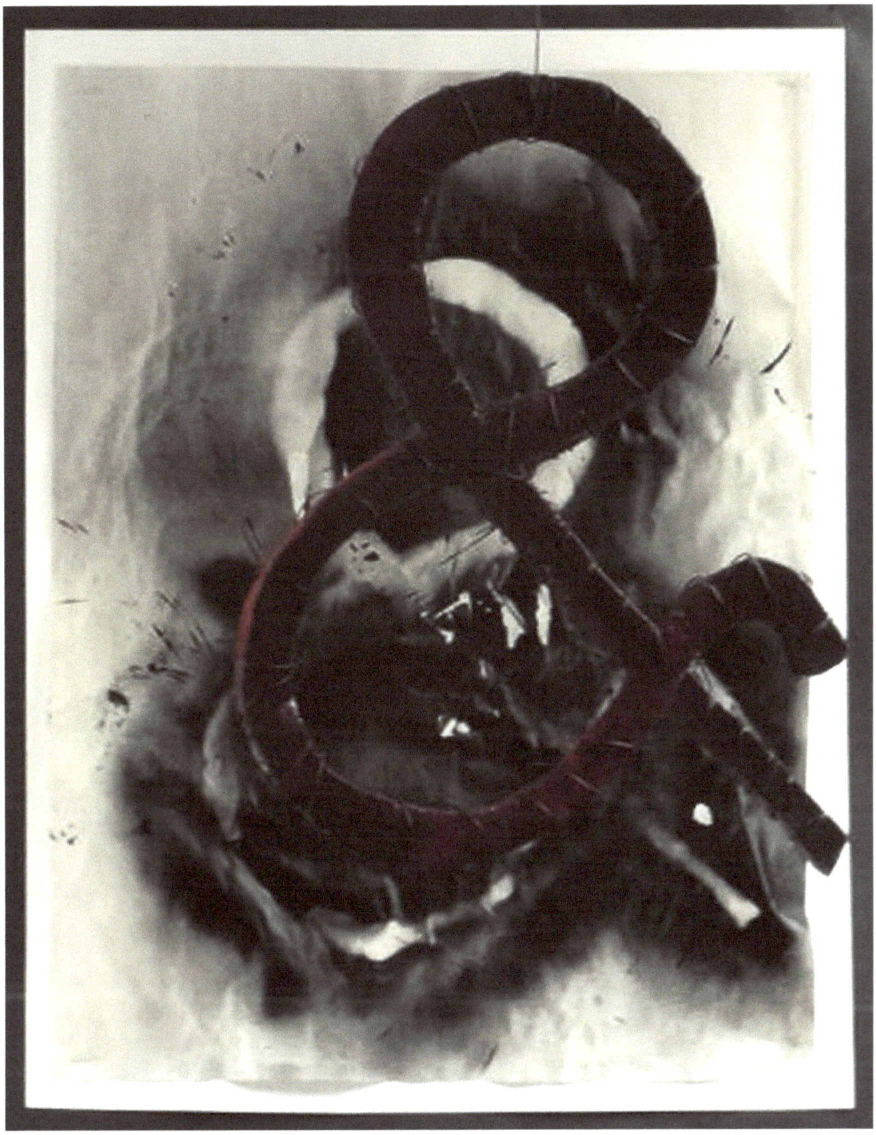

An answer to the question, And then what?

Stage 3: Creation

Once students have completed the design phase by developing an essential question and designing a visual representation as a solution, they will be ready for the creation phase. Since this is an advanced unit in regards to media, the scope of their projects will vary greatly. Solutions for earlier or late finishers should be established. Skills and techniques will most likely be explored on the back end. Students may also be interested in exploring nontraditional materials with this unit. These topics may lead to individual, group, or whole class discussions.

Stage 4: Reflection

When reflecting on this unit, emphasis should be placed on the essential question posed and the visual response created. Students should be able to discuss the following:

- What was your essential question?
- How did you arrive at this question?
- What other questions did you consider?
- How does your work's content and use of media respond to this question?
- How successful is your final piece?

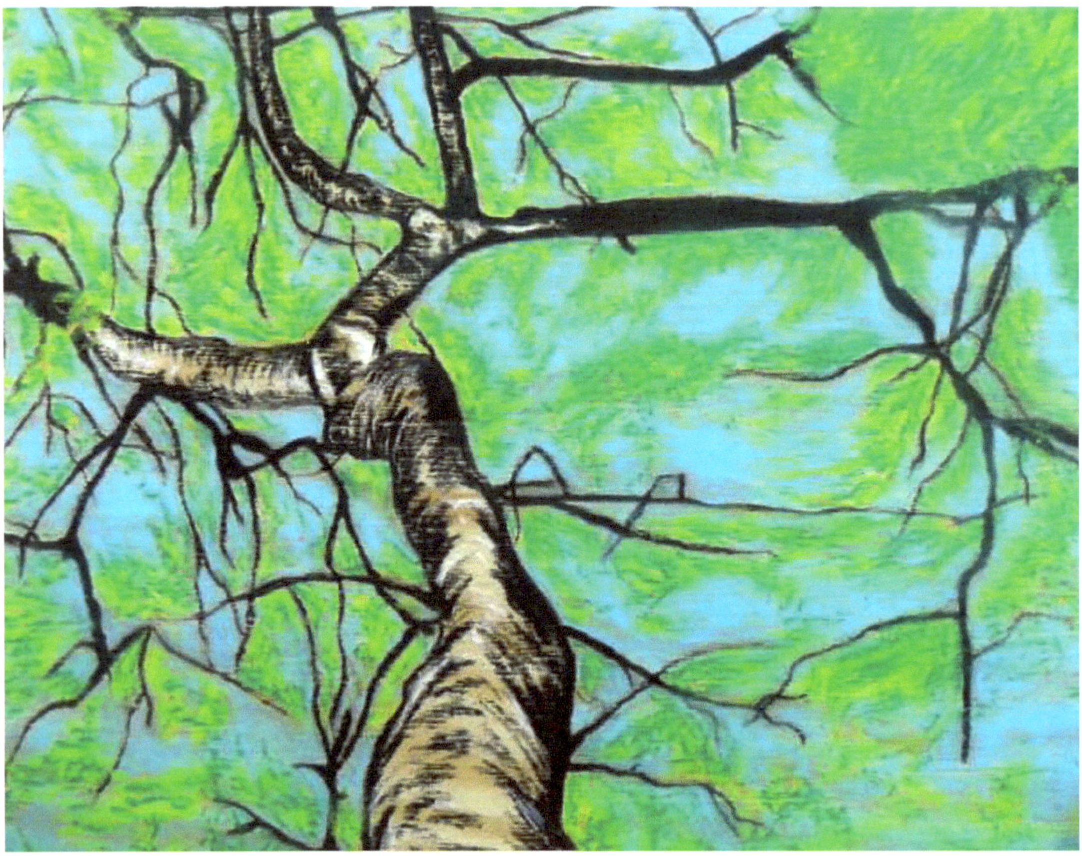

Learning how to use chalk pastel on wood panel.

Artists Are Self-Learners

Level: Intermediate, Advanced

National Standards

- VA:Cr1.2.IIa
- VA:Cr2.1.IIa

Learning Goals

- Research new techniques and apply the newly acquired knowledge to the work.

Level of Choice

	Beginner	Intermediate	Advanced
Media			Full choice in media.
Process		Students follow some directed steps.	
Planning		Students select planning activities from a list.	
Reflection	Students write from teacher-generated prompts.		

Stage 1: Inspiration

The inspiration for this project begins with the students following a short (less than one day) teacher-directed project. There are many tutorials on YouTube that can be redone and presented to the class. The activity itself isn't as important as the fact that it is teacher-directed, preferably step-by-step.

At the end of the lesson, have a class discussion on what occurred during the lesson, what the role of the student was, and what the role of the teacher was. The results should be as follows:

- The teacher picked the project idea.
- The teacher found the tutorial.
- The teacher determined the materials.

Continue the conversation with the following questions:

- Should picking project ideas, finding the tutorial, and deciding on materials be the role of the art teacher?
- If these are the role of the teacher, then what should the role of the student be?
- If these are not the role of the teacher, then what is the role of the student?

The conversation should conclude with the students understanding that if they are to assume the roles of artists, they should step up to:

- Decide what inspires them.
- Seek out "how-to" information when needed.
- Determine the media.

Stage 2. Design

The design phase of this unit includes a series of activities that assist the students in acquiring the knowledge that will be necessary to complete their final project. Tasks will include discovering what types of materials are available in the class, gaining an understanding about the function and purpose of different tools, and learning how to search for and follow online

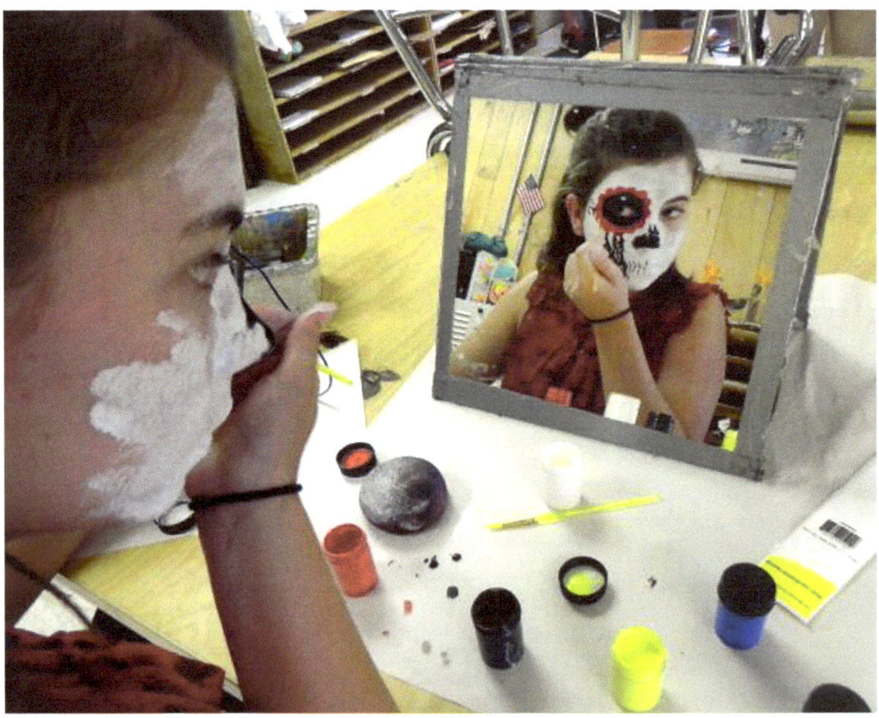

Self-learners explore a full range of media and techniques.

tutorial instructions. All these activities will later be applied to a summative project.

Design Activities

Material Scavenger Hunt. Depending on when the teacher presents this unit, the students may or may not know what materials are available to them in the art room. Even if students are familiar with much of the media, there may still be some materials they have never explored. A material scavenger hunt is ideal for providing students with an understanding of what materials are available, as well as an understanding of how particular materials may be used.

To begin the material scavenger hunt, provide students with a list of questions about art supplies that are available in your art room or supply closet. These may include different types of papers, paints, sculpture materials, etc. This not only helps students identify materials but also gives them insights into the specific functions a material may have.

Students can document their findings in a sketchbook, on a worksheet, or by posting their findings along with photographs of select items on a blog.

Scavenger Hunt Sample Quests:

- Find four types of paper and explain their differences.
- Find four non-paper materials that could be used to create art on.
- Find four types of paint and explain their differences.
- Find five non-paint materials that could be used to create a color artwork.
- Find five non-paint materials that could be used to create a black and white artwork.
- Find five different materials that could be used to create a 3D work.
- Find five different types of adhesives.
- Find two items that you have no idea what they do and find out what they are used for.
- Find five items of any other material not listed that you could use to make art.

Identify a New Interest. For this section of the design process, students will seek out and complete a tutorial for learning a new skill or technique. The objective of the unit should not be to simply follow along and complete a tutorial. The goal is for the student to incorporate the knowledge gained into a final project. Before students search for a tutorial, it is beneficial for them to consider what their interests and passions are. Students who have an interest in the tutorial they study are more likely to incorporate their gained knowledge later.

The teacher should conduct small group or whole class discussions about interests and passions. Ask students to try pairing their interests with possible techniques. For example, a student who is interested in urban sketching might find a linear perspective tutorial helpful to learn how to better draw buildings.

Identifying a new interest might also be presented in categories. These categories can be discussed as a class, with the teacher providing visual examples of each.

Possible sources of inspiration include:

- Artists and artwork: including images, methods, and techniques
- Physical things in the world: e.g., a beautiful sky or seeing things differently
- Non-physical things: e.g., feelings, social issues, dreams

Complete a Tutorial. For this section of the unit, students will seek out a tutorial that demonstrates a new technique or skill, or shows how to use a medium the student is unfamiliar with. The lesson learned should be on something that the student does not have previous knowledge of, or that increases a skill they already know.

For those with Internet access, the web provides easy access to an unlimited number of tutorials. Tutorials are available online both in step-by-step written formats and as videos, such as those found on YouTube. For classes without Internet, the teacher may need to provide books or handouts. The school media center may also be a resource for locating tutorials.

Tutorial lessons should be short enough to complete in a day or two. Once the students complete the tutorials, the teacher may choose to have a day of presentations when students can demonstrate what they have learned.

Stage 3: Creation

Once students have completed all three design activities, they will begin their summative piece.

Students will need time to formulate ideas for incorporating the lessons learned from the scavenger hunt and the tutorials into a summative work of art. The teacher may need to provide additional individual or group activities to assist students as they consider their final project. Such activities may include brainstorming, research, sketches, and thumbnail designs.

Once a design has been worked out by the student, the final piece should be completed. The scope of each individual project will vary. Considerations for earlier finishers or those who need extra time should be planned.

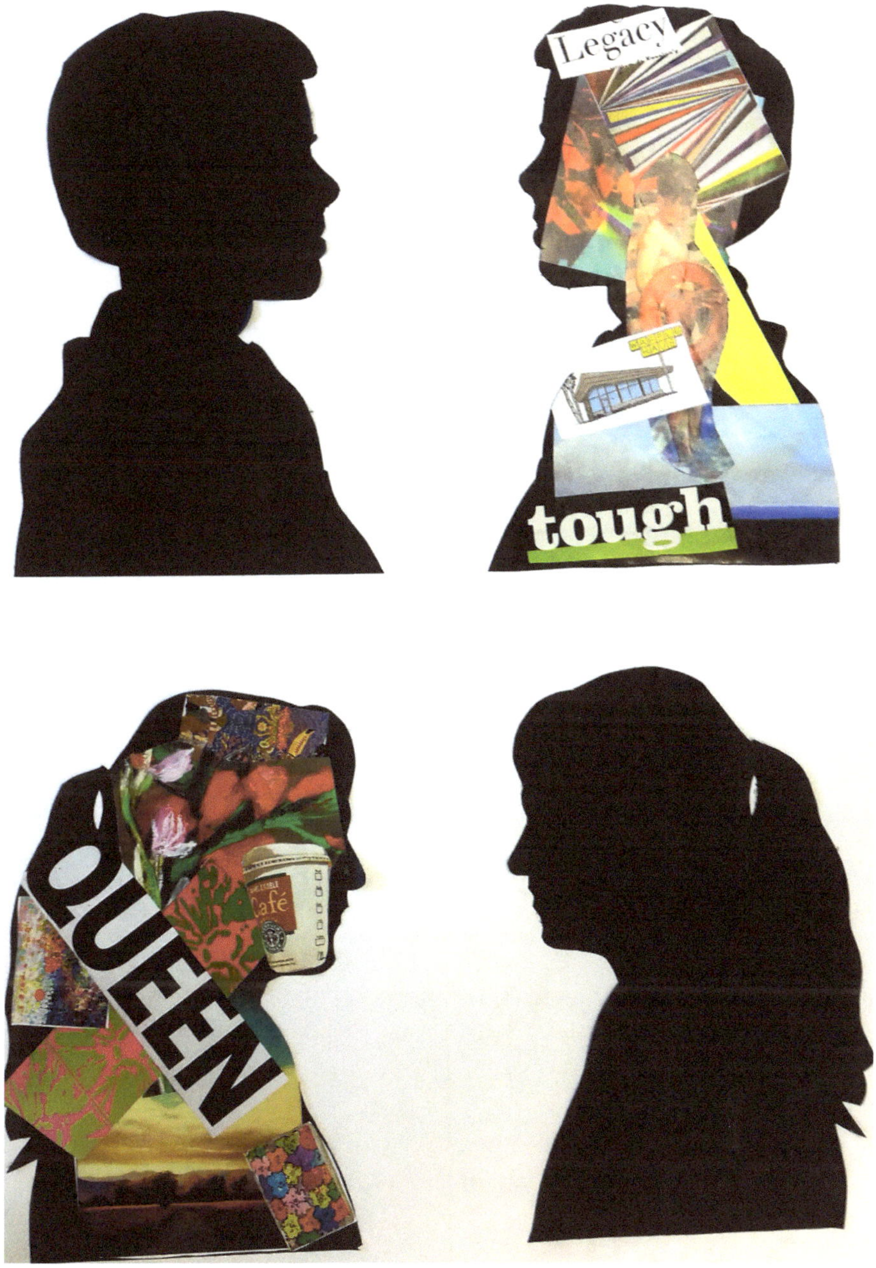

A portrait of stereotypes in silhouette.

Stage 4: Reflection

In this section, the learning gained through both the design phase and completion of the summative piece is reflected upon and analyzed.

Have students reflect on learning by writing, blogging, or discussing the following questions:

- What media did you learn something new about?
- What new knowledge did you gain from your selected tutorial?

- How did you incorporate this new-found knowledge, both media and tutorial, into your summative work?
- How did you incorporate your personal interests into your summative work?

Modifications

The level of student choice in this unit is mainly intermediate to advanced. This lesson can be modified to serve as a beginning-level lesson by considering the following:

Media. The teacher can limit the range of media to modify this to a beginner unit. The questions asked during the scavenger hunt can be limited, with the students only exploring a circumscribed area, e.g., the hunt can be limited to only color materials such as markers, colored pencils, and oil and chalk pastels.

Tutorials. The tutorials can be limited to match the modified scavenger hunt list. Students would only seek out tutorials for certain materials. In most cases, students should be able to seek out these tutorials independently; however, the teacher may prefer to provide a list of tutorials that match the limited media list. Using the same example as above, tutorials could be limited to only color materials such as markers, colored pencils, or oil and chalk pastels.

Artists Communicate

Theme: Identity
Level: Intermediate, Advanced
National Standards

- VA:Cr1.1.Ia
- VA:Cr1.2.Ia

Learning Goals

- Apply knowledge of planning activities and personal working style to research concepts and work through ideas as the start of the creative process.
- Investigate the human experience through the lens of identity to create personal, expressive works of art.

Level of Choice

	Beginner	Intermediate	Advanced
Media			Any 2D or 3D media.
Process			Students' choice.
Planning		Students select planning activities from a list.	
Reflection	Students write from teacher-generated prompts.		

Learning to express abstract concepts visually is a challenge for student artists. This unit addresses this challenge by approaching the complex subject of identity from multiple points of view. This gives students experience with navigating big ideas by breaking them down to a more manageable, personalized approach. The theme of identity can be highly personal or interpreted through the lens of another person or even as part of the human condition. This works well because artists who want to can make work that is deeply introspective, while others who are less comfortable looking inward can focus on identity in a more generic sense. Broad themes such as this one work to support divergent thinking and allow for seamless scaffolding based on interpretation.

Stage 1: Inspiration

Start with a discussion of identity that includes defining terms, examples of related work, and guiding questions. Identity refers to "the qualities or beliefs that make a person or group different from others." Have students think about the following questions and write answers in their sketchbooks:

- What are some things that influence how society sees us?
- What life experiences shape or influence identity?
- Can identity be altered or changed?

Explain that identity is really complex, and that for this assignment, students will have to pick an aspect of identity to focus on. Have them create a chart in their sketchbooks to fill out as you share some examples of how artists address the subject of identity in their work.

Artist Examples

Select artist examples that approach the theme in a range of ways. For example:

- Identity in terms of relationships. Frida Kahlo, *Self Portrait with Cropped Hair*, 1940 (Image A)
- Identity from the perspective of common human experience. *Memento Mori*. Philippe de Champaigne, *Vanitas*, 1671 (Image B)
- Cultural identity. *Made in China*. Joe Black, 2011 (Image C)

The section "ideas for your own work" is just to get the ball rolling. Make sure students know they aren't committed to what they write here.

Artist and title of work	How does the work address the subject of identity?	Ideas for your own artwork

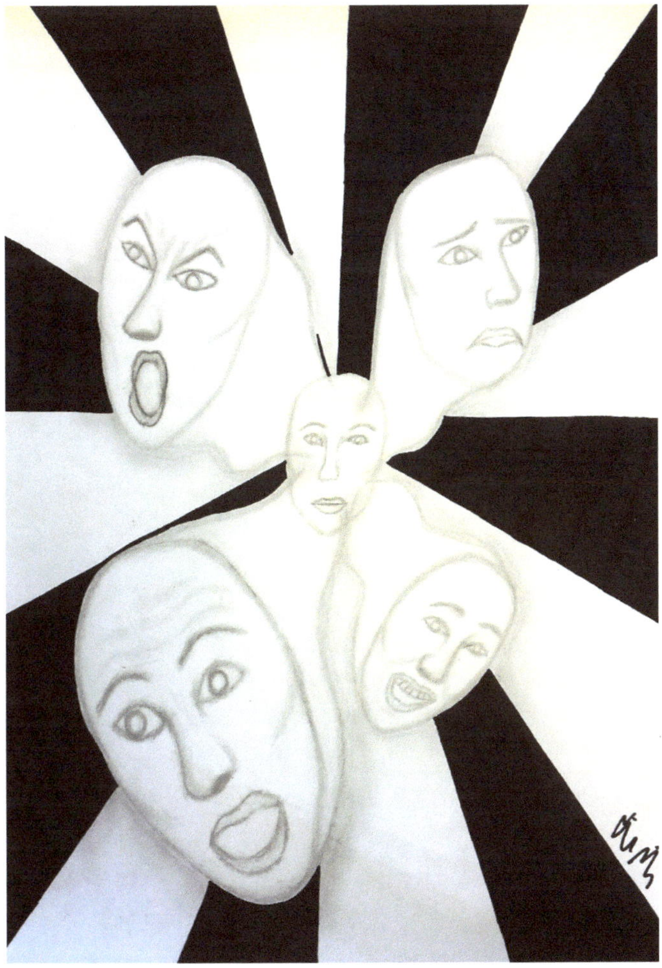

Drawing exploring mental health issues.

After you share and discuss how identity is addressed in artwork, give students some time to fill out their charts, then ask them to share one idea that they had for an artwork. After everyone has shared, give students some time to work independently on developing a concept for their artwork. If students are stuck, go over their responses to the three questions you asked in the beginning of class and what they wrote on their charts.

Stage 2: Design

Once students have an idea, have them work through the design phase by completing three design activities from the list below. These activities serve as tools that will be used to examine the essential question selected by the student.

Design Activities

- Brainstorm: Create a list of ideas about how to communicate your idea without worrying about feasibility. List everything that pops into your head.

- Find and print resource images: search online or in magazines for the images you want to create in your artwork. Combine parts of a variety of images to create original work.
- Sketch: Use sketching to work out composition and plan your work.
- Experiment: Try out different ideas, play with media, problem solve to find solutions.
- Rough draft: Make a practice version of what you plan to create.

During the design phase, the teacher's role is to support students by acting as a guide and sounding board. Listen to ideas and provide feedback. Ask probing questions instead of giving answers. Conference with students about the concept behind their work and media possibilities. Suggest planning activities that will work well to meet their needs.

Stage 3: Creation

When students have completed the design phase, they are ready to move on to the creation section of the lesson and start production of their final artwork. Continue to conference with students daily, asking probing questions to determine how best to provide support through any issues that arise.

Examples of Probing Questions

- What do you like about the work you have done so far?
- How are you communicating your idea about identity?
- Are there any symbols that could capture that idea visually?

Stage 4: Reflection

The student has finished working through the lesson. In this section the learning that has occurred is reflected on and analyzed.

Have students reflect on learning by writing, blogging, or discussing the following questions:

- What does your artwork communicate? Summarize how you chose to interpret the theme of identity.
- How did you use the planning activities you selected to work through your ideas?
- How did you use media and images to capture your ideas about identity? How effective is the work you produced?

For critique, have a Fun Friday or a day of critique games. See pages 128–132 for descriptions of these activities.

Modifications

In this lesson the level of student choice is modified to full choice. To make this lesson more teacher-directed, try the following:

- Limit media to a few choices.
- Preselect planning activities instead of letting students pick.

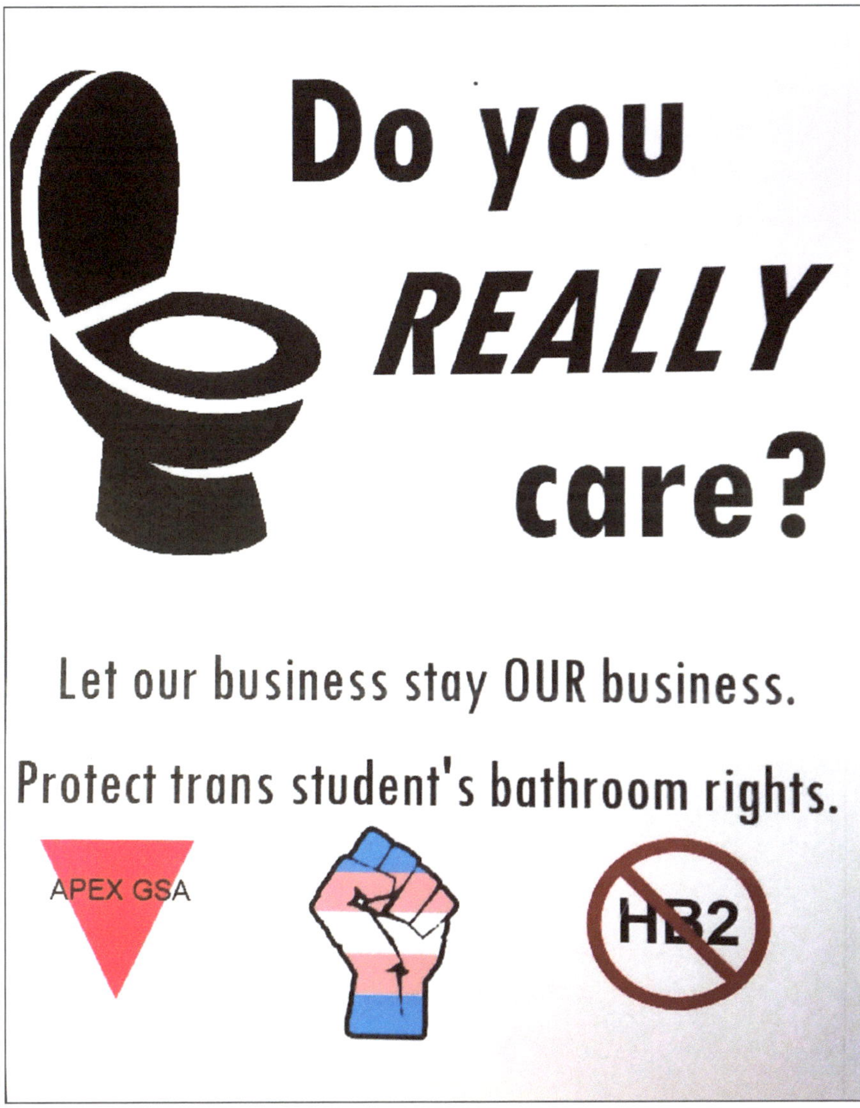

Poster made by a trans student that was copied and hung up around the school.

Artists Take a Stand

This unit gets at the deep value the arts have in our society: to address issues that the artist believes in. Many students have opinions on issues, but to bridge the gap between opinions and artistic response, we need to teach strategies for making complex ideas visual. This lesson also works to expose students to diverse points of view, which is as important for their development as artists as it is for teaching tolerance.

Theme: Current Events
Level: Advanced
National Standards

- VA:Cr2.1.IIIa

Learning Goals

- Apply knowledge of planning activities and personal working style to research concepts and work through ideas as the start of the creative process.
- Select and investigate a current event or social issue students care about, then plan and create artwork in response.

Level of Choice

	Beginner	Intermediate	Advanced
Media			Any 2D or 3D media.
Process			Students select processes independently.
Planning			Students select planning methods.
Reflection	Students present from teacher-generated prompts.		

Introduction

Introduce the unit by explaining that students will make artwork about a current social issue of their choosing. Go on to tell them that the following few classes will teach them some skills that will help them do this successfully, and that they should start thinking about what topic they might like to make art about. Next, set some ground rules about respecting others during this unit. This is what I say:

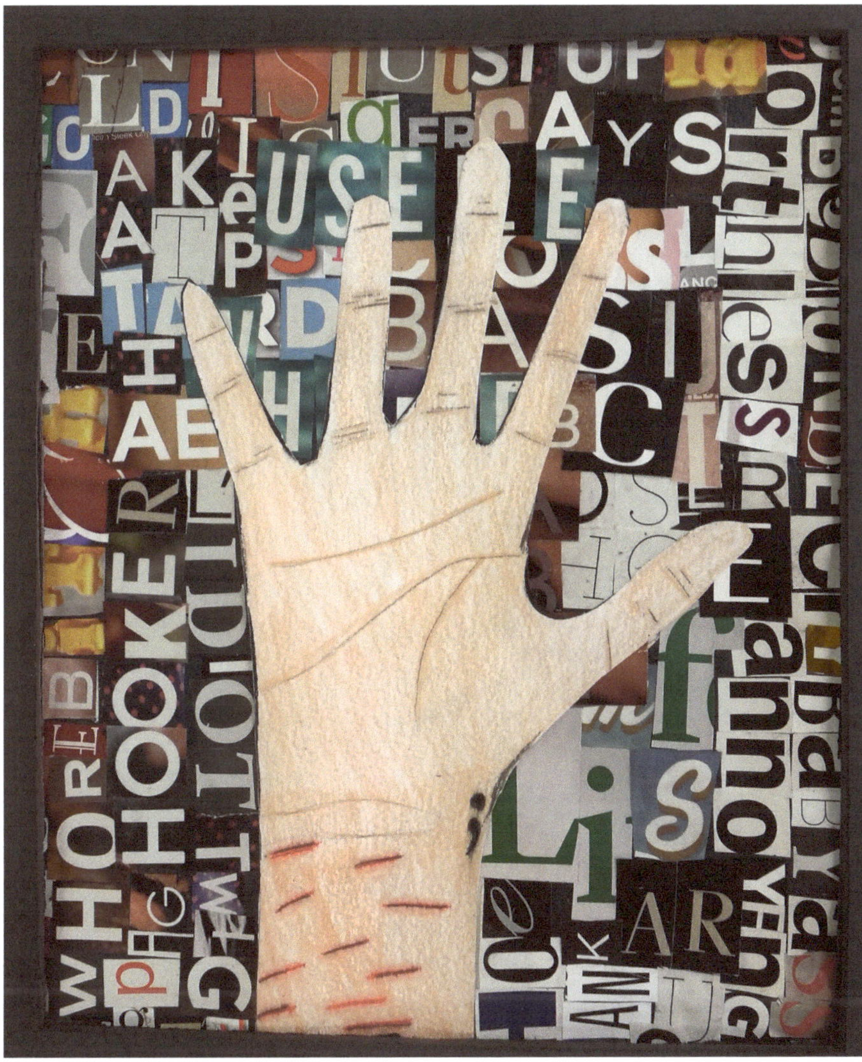

Work by Anna dealing with self harm.

"Everyone in this classroom deserves respect. I will respect your ideas and I expect you to do the same to others. I want you to make art about your opinions, but it is my responsibility to make sure everyone in this class respects the right of others to feel safe and included. If I worry that your artwork might make someone else uncomfortable or that it's inappropriate for school, I will work with you to come up with a plan to make something that we are both okay with. Also, it's okay to disagree but it is not acceptable to insult, make fun of others, or use offensive stereotypes."

Exercise 1: Newspaper Meme

Timeframe: 30 minutes

Media: Newspapers and other collage materials.

Learning Goals: Understand and apply strategies for adding meaning to images with text.

Tell students that adding text to an image can add to its meaning, as with memes. Ask students to use their cell phones to find an example of a school-appropriate meme. Have them discuss, in groups, how the meme uses text. Is it sarcastic or funny? Does it make the viewer think? Let students share and discuss in groups. Next, pass out newspapers and have each student select one image and cut it out. After this is complete, students should work in groups to develop text to go with each image. Give them fifteen minutes to do this, then have each group pick their best image to share with the whole class.

Exercise 2: Symbol Challenge
Timeframe: 1 class
Materials: Sketchbooks and drawing materials
Goal: Students will examine how to communicate meaning through images.

In Advance: Select a few phrases for groups to illustrate. Pick topics that are interesting but not too loaded for this activity. Examples of words that work well are: breakup, stress, sleepless, and curfew. Write the words you select on slips of paper for groups to draw from.

Start class by introducing symbolism by discussing Norman Rockwell's *The Problem We All Live With*. Explain the context of the painting and lead a discussion about how Rockwell uses symbolism to make his feelings about this moment in history clear. Address how juxtaposition is used in the paint to point out the contrast between Ruby Bridge's actions and that of the protesters.

Next, explain the symbol challenge. Tell students that they will work in groups to depict a complex idea visually. Place students in groups, then have each group draw one of the slips of paper prepared for the lesson. Lead the groups through planning. First, have them examine what their word means by listing at least twenty things that they associate with their word. Next, have them work together to create an illustration. Leave time at the end of class for each group to share their work and explain their thinking.

Summative Artwork: Create artwork about the current event or social issue of your choice.
Timeframe: 1 Week
Media: Full Choice

Stage 1: Inspiration

Share and discuss with students examples of how artists address current events or social issues in their art. Select a limited number of artworks that represent a range of approaches. For each artwork, have students answer the following questions:

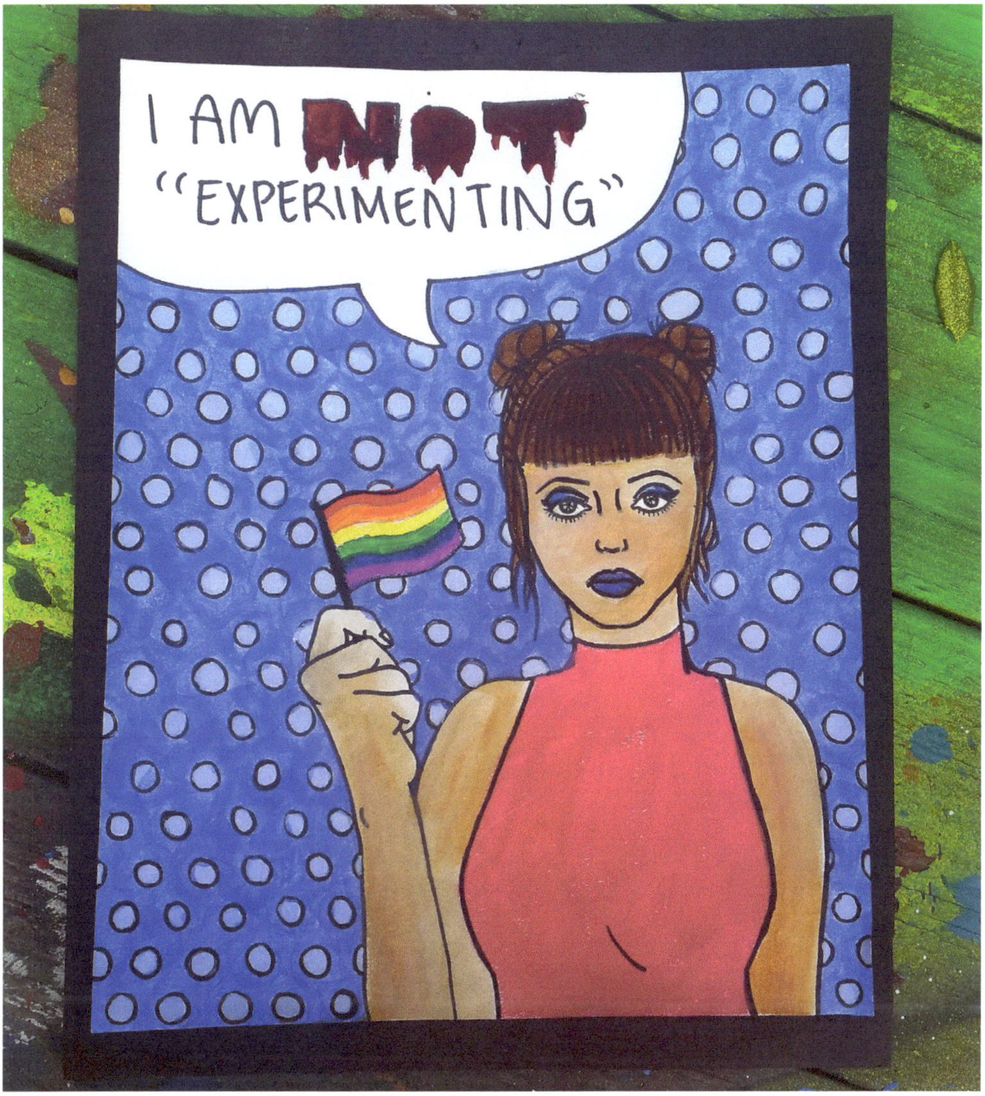

This piece was created as part of a series dedicated to confronting stereotypes.

- What issue is the artist discussing? What is the artist's opinion on it?
- What strategies (symbolism, juxtaposition, use of text) does the artist use to communicate about his or her point of view?
- Did the media or placement of the work add meaning to the art? How?

Suggestions for artwork to feature:

- Tatyana Falalizadeh, *Stop Telling Women to Smile*
- The Amplifier Foundation, *We The People Campaign*
- Ai Weiwei, *Remembering*

After this introduction, ask students select an issue to focus on for this project. Remind them of the expectations for mutual respect you discussed at the start of the unit. Next, have them list the issue they would like to focus on and write a paragraph explaining it and what their position is. Have them summarize their position in a sentence or a few words. The goal is to boil down the issue to the core of what they want to express. Some examples:

- On gun rights: "Guns protect us" or, conversely, "Access to guns makes everyone less safe."
- On immigration: "Welcoming refugees is patriotic."
- On rape: "Rape not your fault, no matter how you are dressed."

Expect that students will have different points of view. Some you will disagree with. If any ideas are inappropriate or offensive, view them as a starting point for a conversation. Ask the student to explain why this is important to her and help brainstorm other options. For example, if a student wants to make an image of the Confederate flag, she may be trying to express Southern pride. Help her come up with more appropriate images to use in her work.

Stage 2: Design

Students work through the design phase by completing three design activities from the list below. These activities serve as tools that will be used to examine the essential question selected by the student.

Design Activities

- Brainstorm: Create a list of ideas without worrying about feasibility. List everything that pops into your head.
- Find and print resource images: Search online or in magazines for the images you want to create in your artwork. Combine parts of a variety of images to create original work.
- Sketch: Use sketching to work out composition and plan your work.
- Experiment: Try out different ideas, play with media, problem solve to find solutions.
- Research: Find resources to learn more about the issue selected.

During the design phase, the teacher's role is to support students by acting as a guide and sounding board. Listen to ideas and provide feedback. Ask probing questions instead of giving answers. Conference with students about the concept behind their work and media possibilities. Suggest planning activities that will work well to meet their needs.

Stage 3: Creation

When students have completed the design phase, they are ready to move on to the creation section of the lesson and start production of their final artwork. Continue to conference with students daily, asking probing questions to determine how best to provide support through any issues that arise.

Examples of Probing Questions

- What do you want to say about your issue?
- Why did you select this image?

Stage 4: Reflection

The student has finished working through the lesson. In this section the learning that has occurred is reflected on and analyzed.

Have students reflect on learning by presenting their artworks to the class. Their presentations should include the following:

- Explain the issue that you chose to focus on for this project. Why did you select it?
- How did you use materials or content to communicate about your issue? How did you use symbolism, juxtaposition, or text to convey your intended meaning?

For critique, have a Fun Friday or a day of critique games. See pages 128–132 for descriptions of these activities.

Modifications

In this lesson, the level of student choice is mainly full choice. To make this lesson more teacher-directed, try the following:

- Limit media to a few choices.
- Preselect planning activities instead of letting students pick.

Resources

Books

Bedrick, Anna. *Choice Without Chaos*. Anna Bedrick, 2012. E-book.

Douglas, Katherine M., and Diane B. Jaquith. *Engaging Learners through Artmaking: Choice-based Art Education in the Classroom*. New York, NY: Teachers College, 2009. Print.

Jaquith, Diane B. *The Learner-Directed Classroom: Developing Creative Thinking Skills through Art*. New York, NY: Teachers College, 2012. Print.

Pearson, P. David and Margaret C. Gallagher. *The Gradual Release of Responsibility Model*. University of Illinois at Urbana-Champaign Library, 1983.

Articles

Hathaway, Nan E. "Smoke and Mirrors: Art Teacher as Magician." Alexandria, VA: NAEA, *Art Education Journal*, May 1st, 2013.

Hathaway, Nan E. "Boost Creativity and Innovation." San Diego, CA: *Arts & Activities*, November 2013.

Hathaway, Nan E. and Diane B. Jaquith. "Where's the Revolution?" Arlington, VA: *Phi Delta Kappan*, March 1st, 2014.

Jaquith, Diane B. "When Is Creativity?" Alexandria, VA: NAEA, *Art Education Journal*, January 2nd, 2011.

Jaquith, Diane B. "The Continuum of Choice: Finding the Right Fit for Teaching and Learning." San Diego, CA: *Arts & Activities*, November 2015.

Purtee, Melissa. "Examining Originality." Worcester, MA: *SchoolArts Magazine*, December 2016.

Sands, Ian. "What to Expect When You Change to Choice." Worcester, MA: *SchoolArts Magazine*, September 2016.

Sands, Ian. "Authentic Growth in the Open Classroom." Worcester, MA: *SchoolArts Magazine*, January 2017.

Sweeny, Robert. "Assessment and Next Generation Standards: An Interview with Olivia Gude." Alexandria, VA: NAEA, *Art Education Journal*, January 2014. https://arteducators.org.

Toole, Julie. "Talking with Your Administrator About Choice-Based Art." San Diego, CA: *Arts & Activities*, September 2014.

Zalmstra, Dale. "Assessing in a Choice-Based Classroom." San Diego, CA: *Arts & Activities*, January 2015.

Websites

Art21, https://art21.org. 2017.

National Core Art Standards, http://www.nationalartsstandards.org. 2017.

Forums

Assessment and Accountability in TAB, www.facebook.com. 2017.

Midwest TAB Teachers, www.facebook.com. 2017.

TAB High School, www.facebook.com. 2017.

TAB Room Design, www.facebook.com. 2017.

TAB for Urban and Low-Income Populations, www.facebook.com. 2017.

Index